# Georgia

JOHN T. EDGE

Photography by Robb Helfrick

COMPASS AMERICAN GUIDES
An Imprint of Fodor's Travel Publications

# Georgia
## Second Edition

Compass American Guides, Inc., 5332 College Ave., Suite 201, Oakland, CA 94618, USA
ISBN: 0-676-90137-9

Editors: Kit Duane, Lesley Bonnet, Cheryl Koehler
Managing Editor: Kit Duane
Creative Director: Christopher Burt

Designers: Christopher Burt, Julia Dillon
Production Editor: Julia Dillon
Map Design: Mark Stroud, Moon Cartography
Cover design: Siobhan O'Hare

10 9 8 7 6 5 4 3 2 1
Production House: Twin Age Ltd., Hong Kong; Manufactured in China

PUBLISHER'S ACKNOWLEDGMENTS

Abby Aldrich Rockefeller Folk Art Center p. 19; Atlanta History Center pp. 37, 127; Augusta-Richmond County Museum p. 164; The Columbus Museum pp. 23, 199; Kelly Duane p. 118, 160, 179; Dr. John Duncan, photo by Richard Sommers p. 16; Georgia Dept. of Archives & History pp. 17, 20, 44, 46, 83, 105, 110, 165, 208; Georgia Dept. of Natural Resources p. 55; Georgia Museum of Art, Univ. of Georgia, gift of Mrs. Will Moss p. 99; Mr. & Mrs. Harvey Granger Jr. p. 285; Greenville County Museum of Art p. 18; The Henry Francis du Pont Winterthur Museum p. 252; Herndon House p. 132; Muriel Gassett James files, Sacramento, California p. 141; Library of Congress pp. 21, 24, 25, 28, 32, 34, 35, 38, 39, 41, 47, 60, 109, 111, 242, 254; Mariner's Museum p. 257; Metropolitan Museum of Art, New York, New York, Gift of Edgar William and Berenice Chrysler Garbisch, 1963 (63.201.3), photograph © 1984 The Metropolitan Museum of Art p. 29; The Morris Museum p. 161; National Park Service p. 15; New Britain Museum of American Art, © T.H. Benton and R.P. Benton Testamentary Trusts/Licensed by VAGA, New York, New York p. 51; New York Historical Society p. 276; Kenneth Rogers p. 45; Richard Sommers p. 275; Mr. & Mrs. Richard and Kay Tarr p. 297; Underwood Archives, San Francisco p. 198; Univ. of Georgia Press p. 223.

Thanks also to Ellen Klages for proofreading and to Lesley Bonnet for indexing, and thanks to Michael Brubaker of the Atlanta History Center and to Nelson Ross for their expert reading.

*Photographer **Robb Helfrick** would like to dedicate his work in this book to his parents, Bill and Peg.*

*For Blair and Jess, on the road and off.*

## AUTHOR'S ACKNOWLEDGMENTS

The author would like to thank the faculty and staff of the Center for the Study of Southern Culture at the University of Mississippi, the staff of the Washington Memorial Library in Macon, the good folks at the University of Georgia Library in Athens, and the Georgia Department of Archives in Atlanta.

Individuals who gave advice, provided shelter, and shared their tales of Georgia past and present include: Nelson Ross of Atlanta, Bert Way of Hawkinsville, John and Mary Anne Edge of Macon, Charlie and Laura Hammond of Savannah, Greg Coleson of Atlanta, Richard Fausset at Flagpole in Athens, Christianne Lauterbach at Knife and Fork in Atlanta, Judy Long and the folks at Hill Street Press in Athens, Kevin Gantz of Ball Ground, and Spyros Dermatas at Nu Way in Macon. Thanks to sometime Georgian Jay Hale for pointing the way to the Power Line, to David Nelson of Living Blues for telling me about Andrew's Oyster Bar, and to the Yacht Club for the beers. The offices of tourism in the towns of Athens, Atlanta, Macon, Columbus, Augusta, and Americus were especially helpful.

Without the determined efforts of Kit Duane, my editor at Compass, this book would be but a shell. She is a marvel of patience and editorial talent. Thanks to Lesley Bonnet, copy and map editor extraordinaire, who did yeoman's duty. To Chris Burt of Compass, thanks for the wonderful design. And for Blair Hobbs, my bride, thanks for the support and for all the welcomes home.

# C O N T E N T S

## Maps

## Literary Extracts and Topical Essays

# CHAPTER DIVISIONS

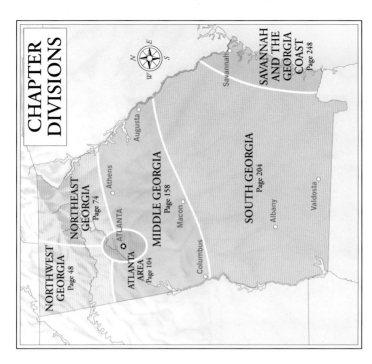

NORTHWEST GEORGIA
Page 48

NORTHEAST GEORGIA
Page 74

ATLANTA AREA
Page 104

MIDDLE GEORGIA
Page 158

SOUTH GEORGIA
Page 204

SAVANNAH AND THE GEORGIA COAST
Page 248

Augusta

Athens

ATLANTA

Columbus

Macon

Savannah

Albany

Valdosta

# MAP INDEX

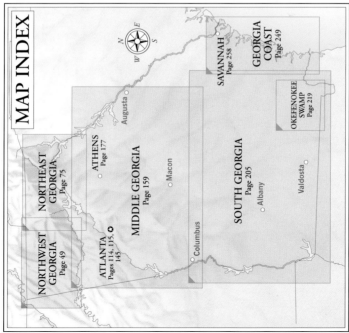

NORTHWEST GEORGIA
Page 49

NORTHEAST GEORGIA
Page 75

ATLANTA
Pages 114, 115, 145

ATHENS
Page 177

MIDDLE GEORGIA
Page 159

SOUTH GEORGIA
Page 205

SAVANNAH
Page 258

GEORGIA COAST
Page 249

OKEFENOKEE SWAMP
Page 219

Augusta

Columbus

Macon

Savannah

Albany

Valdosta

# GEORGIA

**Elevation**
in feet
4,784
2,600
2,200
1,800
1,400
1,000
Sea Level

8 Miles
4
12 Kilometers
8
4

United States
GEORGIA

**TENNESSEE**

**NORTH CAROLINA**

**SOUTH CAROLINA**

**ATLANTA**

**COLUMBIA**

Union
Newberry
Greenwood
Lake Greenwood
McCormick
Abbeville
Calhoun Falls
Aiken
Augusta
Edgefield
Clarks Hill Lake
Barnwell
Denmark
Allendale
Garnett
Newington
Sylvania
Statesboro
Waynesboro
Sardis
Millen
Swainsboro
Wrightsville
Dublin
Louisville
Wadley
Vidette
Wrens
Warrenton
Thomson
Washington
Lincolnton
Lexington
Elberton
Royston
Commerce
Athens
Toccoa
Cornelia
Clarkesville
Tallulah Falls
Dillard
Clayton
Highlands
Cashiers
Walhalla
Westminster
Clemson
Anderson
Hartwell
Hartwell Lake
Greenville
Spartanburg
Union

Brasstown Bald
4,784
(highest point in Georgia)

Hiawassee
Blairsville
Murphy
Cisco
Blue Ridge
Ellijay
Cleveland
Dahlonega
Gainesville
Buford
Jefferson
Winder
Monroe
Social Circle
Madison
Greensboro
Eatonton
Sparta
Milledgeville
Sandersville
Toomsboro
Jeffersonville
Macon
Warner Robins
Gray
Monticello
Berner
Jackson
Forsyth
Roberta
Fort Valley
Butler
Geneva
Columbus
Opelika
Phenix City
Auburn
Roanoke
West Point
La Grange
Hamilton
Manchester
Woodbury
Talbotton
Thomaston
Barnesville
Griffin
Alvaton
Greenville
Luthersville
Franklin
Newnan
Carrollton
Bremen
Villa Rica
Rockmart
Cedartown
Tallapoosa
Bowdon
Fairburn
College Park
Riverdale
Jonesboro
McDonough
Stewart
Fayetteville
Stone Mountain
Lithonia
Covington
Social Circle
Lawrenceville
Norcross
Chamblee
Duluth
Cumming
Dawsonville
Woodstock
Canton
Acworth
Marietta
Smyrna
Mableton
Roswell
Springer Mtn
3,782
Lake Sidney Lanier

Fort Oglethorpe
Chattanooga
Summerville
LaFayette
Dalton
Chatsworth
Calhoun
Cartersville
Rome

Lake Oconee
Lake Sinclair
Lake Hartwell
Lake Keowee
Lake Murray
Reedy River
Savannah River
Ogeechee River
Oconee River
Flint River
West Point Lake
Weiss Lake
N. Fork Edisto River
S. Fork Edisto River

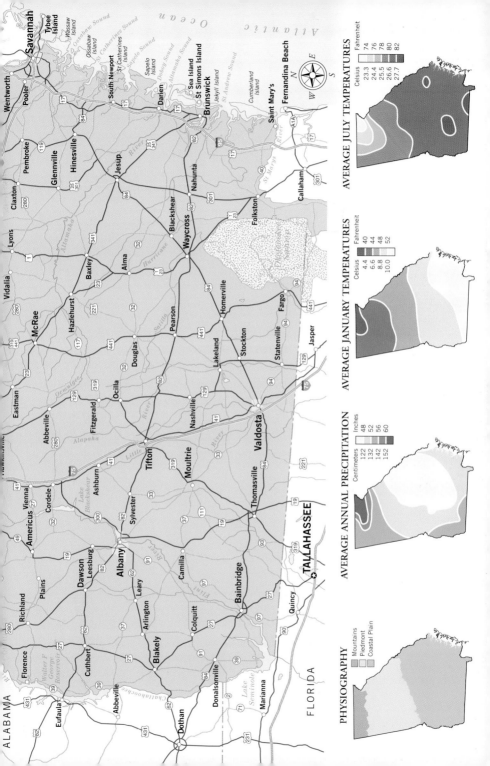

# O V E R V I E W

## GEORGIA

With the Appalacian Mountains in the north, a fertile agricultural plain across its center, and lush sea islands hugging the coast, Georgia's landscape is diverse and inviting. In addition to two great cities—bustling, modern Atlanta and sedate, charming Savannah—Georgia also has regal plantation homes, meandering back roads, small cities with historic downtowns, and the magical Okefenokee Swamp.

### NORTHWEST GEORGIA  *pages 48-73*

Beautiful and remote, the mountains of the northwest contain many interesting pockets of culture. Come here to visit New Echota, last home of the Cherokee people before they were expelled to Oklahoma, and Chickamauga National Battlefield, where the Confederacy held off the Federals in a bloody battle. Visit Paradise Gardens, home of famed visionary artist Howard Finster.

### NORTHEAST GEORGIA  *pages 74-103*

Known for Blue Ridge Mountain scenery and Appalachian culture, this is an area with many small resorts. Come for a country music and crafts festival, or to rent a cabin and hike through the woods. Rent a canoe or try your hand at cane-pole fishing. Rushing rivers and towering trees provide a soothing backdrop to all adventures.

**ATLANTA** *pages 104-157*

Founded in 1835 and staked as a railway terminus in 1837, Atlanta was of great importance to the Confederate war effort and became the target of the Union's General Sherman, who burned the city on his march to Savannah. Today it is a sprawling metropolis with huge hotels, a dynamic nightlife and music scene, and sophisticated restaurants. Although the city can be difficult for the outsider to navigate, those with a car and good directions can visit lovely intown neighborhoods such as Virginia-Highland and Inman Park.

**MIDDLE GEORGIA** *pages 158-203*

Athens, home to the beautiful University of Georgia campus, has a charming downtown, a vital music scene, and innovative restaurants. Augusta, Macon, and Milledgeville are all easily accessible and exude charm. This is a beautiful region of small historic cities, undulating farmland, and a gracious way of life. Come here to eat barbecue at roadside cafes, to browse in antique stores, and to soak up the comfortable ambiance of a courthouse square on a warm winter afternoon.

**SOUTH GEORGIA** *pages 204-247*

From the piney woods near Augusta, to wet, mysterious Okefenokee Swamp with its canoe trails and alligators, southern Georgia is a delight. Pecan and peach orchards line the roadways, and traffic goes slow. Take in Plains, hometown of former President Jimmy Carter and capital of the peanut-growing region. If you're lucky, he'll be teaching Sunday school at the local church. Visit country resorts, float down a lazy river, and drink in the sunshine.

## SAVANNAH
*pages 250-275*

Founded in 1733 as a British colony that would offer a new start to England's economic unfortunates, Savannah retains the city plan designed by James Oglethorpe, the city's idealistic founder. Twenty-one lovely green spaces—or squares—each with benches, walkways, and abundant greenery, are surrounded by fine old homes, many dating from the early 1800s. Savannah is one of America's most beautiful and cities.

## THE GEORGIA COAST
*pages 248-301*

Long ago the province of Muscogee Indians, and later unsuccessfully colonized by Spanish missionaries, the Sea Islands were planted with rice, sugar, and long-staple cotton on vast plantations owned by an aristocratic planter society. So many slaves were imported into this region that by the time of the Civil War the area was 80 percent African, and the people of some of the more remote islands developed a unique culture still in evidence today. This is a lush region, with tropical vegetation, white sand beaches, and luxurious resorts.

# INTRODUCTION

I SPENT THE BETTER PART OF MY YOUTH on a five-speed Schwinn bicycle, burning up the blacktop road that ran between my home, a modest Federal-style farmhouse built in 1814, and Old Clinton Barbecue, a wonderful roadhouse shrouded in what seemed a perpetual wreath of sweet smoke. Behind the counter stood Mrs. Coulter, mother of the proprietor, keeper of the flame. Always kind, and nearly as sweet as the tea she mixed up by the gallon, she dished out barbecue, coleslaw, and Brunswick stew to the boys of Jones County, dispensing a good measure of motherly love at no charge. I can still taste the smoked pork napped with pepper-laced vinegar; I can still hear shoes shuffling on the sawdust-covered floor.

The community I grew up in was called Clinton, Georgia, and by the time I remember noticing, it appeared a humble collection of regal older homes, a few new redbrick faux colonials, and more than a few tumbledown tarpaper shacks. There was a time, my parents always told me, when Clinton was the third largest town in Georgia. But when the railway diverted to Gray, three miles up the road, Clinton receded from view. By the time I came into the world, the past had a stranglehold on Clinton that the present couldn't loosen.

I spent early fall mornings traipsing through the woods, sometimes with my father, other times with friends. We were digging for Confederate relics. They must be buried close by, I reasoned, for my house had once been the home of Confederate brigadier general Alfred Iverson Jr. Surely there were bayonets and muskets, minié-balls and buttons to be exhumed from the red clay. Instead we found treasures of another sort—rusted tin cans, busted bottles, and shattered plates—the detritus of the more recent past.

I was born in 1962. I was old enough to watch and listen as the Civil Rights Movement swirled around me. I recall sitting in a federal courtroom, rapt, watching my father work to put away white men accused of murdering a black Georgian. I came of age in Clinton. The Civil War and the Civil Rights Movement held equal sway. In my pantheon Alfred Iverson Jr. and Martin Luther King Jr. were compatriots, not combatants.

Though I would leave for college in Athens, later moving to Atlanta and beyond, it was in Clinton that I learned the lessons that would define my life. And though I don't make it back to Old Clinton Barbecue as often as I once did, I can't think of another place I would rather be come dinnertime.

# HISTORY & CULTURE

GEORGIA WAS CONCEIVED AS A SOCIAL EXPERIMENT to lessen crowding in England's debtor prisons, realized as a military buffer between colonial Spain and England, tortured like much of the American South by more than two centuries of slavery, and finally heralded as the jewel in the crown of the Sunbelt economy. Thus Georgia's history is not easily encapsulated. Nor is the physical landscape of this, the largest state east of the Mississippi River. Whether your destination be the Blue Ridge Mountains of northern Georgia, the stooped irregularity of the red clay Piedmont, the piney woods of the sandy lowlands, or the wetlands and inlets of the seashore, Georgia's landscape is as diverse as its people.

## ■ IN THE BEGINNING

The first inhabitants of Georgia, nomadic tribes of big game hunters, made their way to the southeast of present-day America some 12,000 years ago. Save a scattering of spearheads and the skeletal remains of a few of these Paleo-Indian peoples, there is little that remains of their presence.

About 3,000 years ago, a new Native American culture emerged. Its people built hundreds of earthen mounds over the next several thousand years, some as burial mounds, others as ceremonial stages of a sort. Kolomoki Mounds is one of the more famous examples still existent in Georgia. It was also during this era that the bow and arrow came into use, farming became commonplace, and the use of pottery became widespread.

As agriculture became more important, the settlements in which people

*This Mississippian-era figurine, once a bottle top, was
found at an Indian burial site at Ocmulgee.
(National Park Service)*

*(opposite) Autumn color at Banks Lake National Wildlife Refuge in southern Georgia.*

*This 1837 engraving,* Village Indien, *was done after an illustration by Theodore de Bry in the 1590s. (courtesy Dr. John and V. Duncan)*

lived grew increasingly large and complex. Soon, moats and wooden palisades protected villages. Not long thereafter, most people were living in wood-framed, thatched houses. In time, chiefdoms were established whereby a single powerful ruler might govern a network of many villages.

Since most of these tribal groups lived in the bottomlands along the Mississippi River, this period—from around a thousand years ago until the arrival of Europeans—has come to be known as the Mississippian era. It was during this era that Native American culture in the region reached its zenith.

In 1540, when Spanish explorer Hernando de Soto arrived in Georgia, he found large permanent farming villages built around enormous earthen temple mounds. De Soto's expedition and the European settlement that followed destroyed much of the original population of Georgia. Skirmishes fought between these two groups killed people on both sides, but it was European diseases—in particular measles and smallpox—that wiped out the majority of the native people. Remnants of native tribes eventually drew together in the hinterlands, and from these survivors came the formidable Creek and Cherokee nations, the histories of which are intertwined with that of the colony and state of Georgia.

## ■ UTOPIAN EXPERIMENT

Created by royal decree in 1732 and entrusted to the care of British parliamentarian James Edward Oglethorpe, the colony of Georgia was, at its outset, an experiment in utopian idealism. The poor and downtrodden (including those so down on their luck that they were indeed in debtors' prison) were recruited. And in the interest of avoiding temptation, all manner of suspicious persons were prohibited, including attorneys and Catholics. Because Georgia's founders were idealists, slavery was forbidden; because they were entrepreneurial, they embarked on silk production, decreeing that two mulberry trees per acre must be planted on all land grants, as food for silkworms.

Touted by Oglethorpe and the 20 other trustees as a "lush Edenic paradise," Georgia attracted the interest of more than the poor and bankrupt it was originally intended for. Among the 114 colonists on the first ship to sail for Georgia were two merchants, five carpenters, two wig makers, five farmers, a gardener, an upholsterer, a vintner, a baker, a miller, a surgeon, a writer, and not a single convict. Perhaps it was the unflagging boosterism (a recurrent theme in Georgia history) that compelled Britain's yeoman farmers and skilled laborers to come running. But come they did, enticed by a slew of perquisites including free passage and 50 acres of land as well as a year's worth of support. One historian has gone so far as to posit that "the first Georgians were

*Parliamentarian James Edward Oglethorpe is credited with the founding of Georgia. (Georgia Department of Archives & History)*

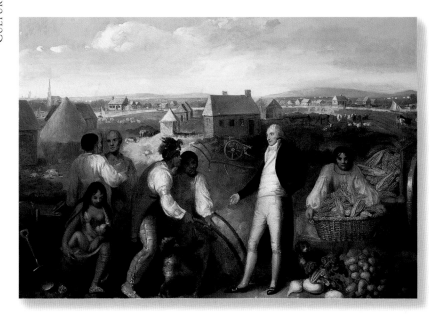

*This painting, circa 1810, shows Benjamin Hawkins at a trading post with members of the Creek nation. (Greenville County Museum of Art, Greenville, SC)*

perhaps the most selectively chosen group of colonists to come to British North America." Yet the grand colonial experiment was not to last long as it was first conceived. Attempts made to raise silkworms sputtered. Ditto for European varietal grapes, oranges, and olives. Indeed, for its first 50 years, Georgia, the last of the 13 British colonies, floundered. In 1740, just seven years after Oglethorpe established the city of Savannah on the Yamacraw Bluff overlooking the Savannah River, traveler Henry Garret was so disturbed by what he saw of colonial Georgia that he observed: "I got into a very bad corner of the world, where poverty and oppression abound to such a degree that it has become proverbial this way to say as poor as a Georgian."

## ■ SLAVERY AND PROSPERITY

Just up the coast in South Carolina, planters prospered growing indigo and rice—with slave labor, of course. While Georgia farmers struggled, South Carolina planters lived a life of comparative ease, a distinction that did not escape the notice of some of the colony's more prominent business people. "The poor people of

Georgia may well as think of becoming Negroes themselves—as of hoping to be ever able to live without them," argued colonist Thomas Stephens. Slavery, land-holding Georgians of wealth and influence argued, was the answer to these economic ills. By 1750, pro-slavery advocates had won out. And by 1760, thousands of Africans had been brought into Georgia. By 1773, the state could claim 15,000 slaves and 18,000 whites. Sea Island cotton flourished along the coast, and rice plantations spread up the Savannah River and down the coast. By the eve of the Revolutionary War, Georgia looked less and less like a radical utopian experiment than its antithesis, an agrarian outpost reliant upon slave labor.

Most slaves sold into Georgia bondage were of West African origin. Among them the Wolof and Mandinka peoples were prominent, though a wide variety of regions and peoples were represented, for the native region of Georgia slaves described a wide arc along the African coast, stretching from present-day Senegal through Ghana and on into Nigeria. Slaves from the Sierra Leone area were especially valuable to low-country planters, who valued their knowledge of rice cultivation.

*The instruments shown in this painting*—The Old Plantation, *artist unknown, circa 1800—are similar to those used by the Yoruba in West Africa.*
*(Abby Aldrich Rockefeller Folk Art Center, Williamsburg, VA)*

HISTORY & CULTURE

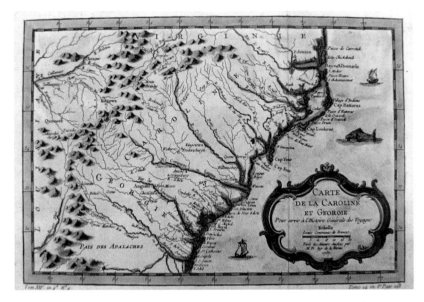

*This French map from 1767 shows Georgia extending west from the Atlantic coast between the Savannah River to the north and the Altamaha River to the south. (Margaret Davis Cate Collection, Fort Frederica National Monument, Georgia Department of Archives & History)*

## ■ SHRINKING GEORGIA

As conceived, the colony of Georgia was bounded by the Altamaha River on the north and the Savannah River on the south. At the headwaters of each river a line was drawn westward to the Pacific. Had these borders been maintained, the largest city in Georgia today would be not Atlanta but Los Angeles.

Instead, in accordance with the Treaty of Paris, signed in 1763 at the conclusion of the French and Indian War, Britain gave up all claims to lands west of the Mississippi River, while in 1802, modern-day Alabama and Mississippi were ceded to the U.S. government. By the close of the 18th century, Georgia's borders were fixed much as they remain today.

## ■ REVOLUTIONARY WAR

Despite what the Daughters of the American Revolution may tell you, Georgia remained at the periphery of the fighting for most of the Revolutionary War, if for no other reason than that Georgia was a geographically peripheral colony, at the tail end of a region close to revolt, distanced by time and territory from the patriotic fervor of the New England colonies. Closer to home, in the Carolinas, after 100-plus years of limited self rule, some citizens may well have been chafing under the yoke of British tariffs and taxation, yet most Georgians remained content.

Exports were booming. Georgia's rich farmlands were yielding bumper crops. In short, after years of privation, many Georgians were too busy making a living (or, in some cases, making a fortune) to pay heed to the protests coming from colonies to the north. Georgia was the sole colony to comply with the Stamp Act, and when it came time to send delegates to the first Continental Congress, Georgia mustered no official delegation. Indeed, on the eve of hostilities, both Tory and Whig factions claimed the loyalty of equal numbers of Georgians.

Still, Georgia joined the other 12 colonies in declaring independence from Britain in 1776. Just two years later the British attacked and gained control of Savannah, and by the close of 1779 much of colonial Georgia was under British control. Fighting, mostly restricted to small skirmishes and guerrilla warfare, was relegated to the backwoods, far from towns of import like Savannah. Nevertheless, according to historian E. Merton Coulter in his *Georgia, A Short History:*

*The* war had been unusually destructive in Georgia as it developed through the bitterest partisan struggle into a war of extermination of life and property. Half the property in the state had been destroyed, the institution of slavery was upset, and the people were torn asunder through hatreds and suspicions….Robbers and murderers after the close of the war continued to infest the highways to such an extent as to endanger the life of the government….

*General Casimir Pulaski died in the attempt to recapture Savannah.*
*(Library of Congress)*

# SHE'S A TOUGH GAL, NANCY HART

Cross-eyed, pockmarked, and masculine in bearing, Nancy Morgan Hart was no storybook heroine, yet to this day she remains the most lionized and mythologized of Georgia Patriots. Though the tale of her exploits may well be apocryphal, that possibility has done nothing to dampen the fervor with which her story is told.

Legend has it that Nancy's cabin in the north Georgia woods near what is now Elberton, was a refuge for Georgia Patriots intent upon escaping British troops. One afternoon, six redcoats, aware of her reputation, decided to pay her a little visit. Seeing no Patriots about, they demanded supper. Obligingly, Hart prepared a feast of venison, turkey, and hoecake, and she provided a jug of whiskey. Soon the Tories were in their cups, unaware that Hart was slipping their rifles out the cabin through a chink in the wall. When they finally realized what she was doing, she hefted a rifle and demanded that they "surrender their Tory asses to a Whig woman." Owing to Nancy's crossed eyes, the Tories were at a loss as to where her gaze fell, and when one Tory made a grab for his rifle, he guessed wrong and paid for the mistake with his life. A second guessed wrong; a second fell. By the time her husband Benjamin Hart arrived home, Nancy had the remaining four at bay and was making plans to hang them. And hang them she did.

In 1912, the veracity of this legend was strengthened when a gang of railroad workers unearthed six skeletons less than a mile from the site of the Hart cabin.

*This 1855 etching shows Nancy Hart attacking the Tories.*

# ■ EXPANSION INTO INDIAN LANDS

During the late 18th and early 19th centuries, the population of Georgia swelled, moving northward and westward as Revolutionary War veterans bought up acreage in exchange for service, and land lottery winners laid claim to nearly three-quarters of present-day Georgia at a rate of around seven cents an acre.

Much of this newly settled land had previously been part of the Cherokee and Creek nations. By hook, crook, and "treaty," Georgia wrested lands away from these indigenous peoples. Land speculation was pursued at a feverish pace until the Yazoo Land Fraud—an aborted at-

*This hand-tinted lithograph was made after Henry Inman's oil portrait of Creek chief William McIntosh. (The Columbus Museum, Columbus)*

tempt by four land companies to bribe Georgia legislators to sanction the sale of 35 million acres of land for the paltry sum of $500,000—was exposed in 1795.

As Georgia farmers moved west, the tribal lands of the Creeks and Cherokees were encroached on again and again. Andrew Jackson's defeat of the Creeks in the War of 1812, coupled with the discovery of gold near the Cherokee capital of New Echota in 1829, signaled the beginning of the end.

In 1827, hard on the heels of a fraudulent treaty signed by Chief McIntosh, most of the Creeks were removed to Oklahoma. The Cherokee followed, though their removal was not completed until 1838, when U.S. general Winfield Scott and his men rounded up the last 15,000 Cherokee and marched them west to Oklahoma, on a journey now remembered as the Trail of Tears. Forced to travel on foot more than 1,000 miles in the dead of winter, nearly one in three Cherokee died on the five-month march, considered one of the more shameful acts in American history. Missionary Daniel Buttrick, a firsthand observer of the removal, wrote in 1838 that, "from their first arrest, the Cherokees were obliged to live very much like brute animals, like hogs. Driving them is only a most expensive and painful way of putting the poor people to death." One Georgia soldier in Scott's company was so disturbed by what he witnessed that, writing many years later, he observed: "I fought through the Civil War, and have seen men shot to pieces and slaughtered by the thousands, but the Cherokee removal was the cruelest work I have ever seen."

Though Georgians of the day rationalized the removal of the Cherokee as being in the best interest of a savage people, the Cherokee culture, even when measured by European standards, was far from uncivilized. Aware that their homeland was under siege, the Cherokee adopted Western modes of government and conduct. Under the leadership of Sequoya, the Cherokee devised a constitution modeled in part after that of the United States, and they set fixed borders for what was to be a sovereign country. With New Echota, Georgia, as the capital, the Cherokee nation stretched across four states.

Concurrently, the Cherokee developed what was called a syllabry, a set of written symbols, each representing a different syllable in the Cherokee language. Today, the press used in printing the bilingual *Cherokee Phoenix* newspaper offers visitors to New Echota a glimpse of the accomplishments of these native Georgians.

*Sequoya—Cherokee warrior, silversmith, and painter—invented the Cherokee syllabry in 1821. He created a system of 86 symbols, adapting letters from English, Hebrew, and Greek. (Library of Congress)*

*Because it increased the speed with which cotton fibers could be separated from the seeds, the cotton gin made short-fiber cotton commercially viable. (Library of Congress)*

## ■ KING COTTON

The years between Independence and the Civil War were ones of progress and prosperity for Georgia. Cotton may well have emerged as king, but its ascendance was the result of neither rich soil nor agricultural acumen. Instead, the introduction of two "engines" would transform Georgia from an isolated state at the new nation's periphery into the South's leading economic force.

In the fall of 1792, fresh from Yale College, Eli Whitney, a New Englander by birth, accepted a job as the tutor at Catherine Greene's Mulberry Plantation just outside Savannah. Whitney may have earned his keep as a tutor, but it was his tinkering with a mechanical means of separating cotton lint from seeds that was to win him fame.

Intrigued by neighboring planters' tales of the difficulty and expense involved in combing the precious white cotton fibers from the seeds, Whitney set about finding a solution. By the spring of 1793, he had completed a model for what he called a cotton engine or "gin," as we now know it. It was a simple affair consisting of a cylinder studded with wire teeth; when turned by hand, it pulled the fiber

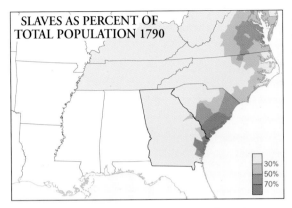

SLAVES AS PERCENT OF
TOTAL POPULATION 1790

30%
50%
70%

*Increased cotton production between the Revolutionary and Civil Wars was directly related to the growth of slavery during that period.*

from the seed. At the suggestion of Mrs. Greene he further refined the gin when he added a row of brushes that rotated in the opposite direction, pulling the cotton from the teeth. The gin, even in its most rudimentary form, could do the work of ten men.

Whitney's invention revolutionized cotton production in the South. Previously, most cotton farming had been restricted to the coastal areas where the long-staple Sea Island cotton flourished. The short-fiber variety of cotton, though it grew well in the interior and produced more cotton per acre, had been little cultivated because it was difficult to seed. With Whitney's invention, the short-staple cotton became commercially viable, thousands of acres of land were planted with it, and planters sought many more slaves to work the newly planted acres.

Georgia came late to the institution of slavery. At the time of the American Revolution, New York had five times as many slaves as Georgia. And yet Georgia wasted little time in catching up and finally surpassing almost everyone else. By 1790, the slave population was almost 60,000, by 1840 more than 280,000, and by the eve of the Civil War, Georgia was second only to Virginia in number of bondsmen, and 40 percent of its population was enslaved.

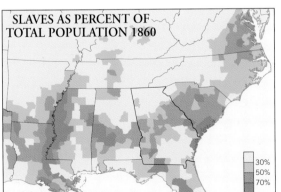

SLAVES AS PERCENT OF
TOTAL POPULATION 1860

30%
50%
70%

In 1790 only 1,000 bales of cotton were grown in Georgia, but by 1840 the figure was 400,000 bales, and by

*Between 1820 and 1860 farmland in western Georgia, Alabama, Mississippi, and Louisiana, was increasingly planted in cotton.*

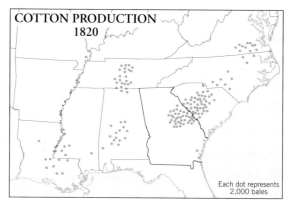

COTTON PRODUCTION
1820

Each dot represents
2,000 bales

1860 it exceeded 700,000. And as cotton acreage skyrocketed, so did the dependence on slave labor. The cotton gin may well have been a labor-saving device, but it did nothing but fuel the seemingly insatiable desire for enslaved black laborers. It should come as no surprise to learn that, though in the days just before the cotton gin, the price for a good field hand had hovered around $300, by 1850 the price was over $1,000, and by 1860 the average was nearly $1,800. In 1844, a Scottish visitor to Georgia observed, "Nothing was attended to but the rearing of cotton and slaves. The more cotton the more slaves and the more slaves the more cotton!"

## ■ COTTON AND THE RAILROAD

The second engine of import employed in Georgia pulled railroad cars rather than cotton fibers. In December of 1833 the Georgia legislature chartered two railroads to connect the cotton market towns of the day, one from Augusta to Athens and another from Savannah to Macon. Rail lines proved to be a highly efficient means of transporting cotton, and Georgians set about building them at a remarkable rate. By 1836, the legislature had passed a law calling for a state-owned railroad connecting Georgia's

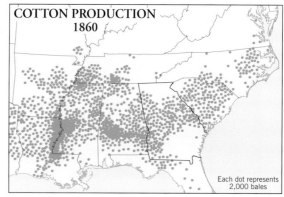

COTTON PRODUCTION
1860

Each dot represents
2,000 bales

existing rail lines and thus affording Georgia farmers better access to U.S. markets, as well as to ports serving trade with England and its textile mills. The new railroad, the Western and Atlantic, would run from the Chattahoochee River in Dekalb County north to the Tennessee border. Surveyors drove a stake in the ground at the southernmost point of the new line and named this spot Terminus. Soon, with construction in high gear, Terminus was booming. By the 1850s, sporting the more cosmopolitan moniker of Atlanta, the city was one of the South's most important rail centers. And the cotton kept coming.

## ■ PLANTERS AND FARMERS

Thanks to novels like *Gone With the Wind,* antebellum Georgia is often perceived as being a genteel land of moonlight, magnolias, and mint juleps. In this world white Georgians raised cotton on plantations run by devoted, amusing slaves. Flirtatious girls in gorgeous pastel gowns went to balls on neighboring estates, and young men galloped about on fine horses.

In reality, by 1860 less than one percent of Georgians belonged to the planter class (roughly defined as men owning more than 20 slaves). Though grand plantations worked by hundreds of slaves furnished a very small oligarchy with a sumptuous lifestyle, reality was more picaresque than picturesque. Often times, slave

*Rail lines facilitated the export of cotton to markets around the world. (Library of Congress)*

*An idealized version of a plantation, done by an unknown artist in 1825. (Metropolitan Museum of Art, Gift of Edgar William and Bernice Chrysler Garbisch, 1963; photograph © The Metropolitan Museum of Art)*

and master worked the fields side by side, up one row and down another, from first light to first dark.

If most white Georgians were small farmers, owning few or no slaves, they considered themselves respectable family people, churchgoing frontiersmen. The lowest class of whites—called by blacks and whites alike white trash—lived on the fringes of society.

## ■ THE "LATE UNPLEASANTNESS"

Ask a native why Georgia seceded from the Union and you are not likely to get a straight answer. For years, Georgia schoolchildren were taught that the primary issue was that of states' rights. Few Georgians, black or white, replied with the single word answer uppermost in most outlanders' minds: slavery.

Today, most Georgians will concede that the South seceded from the Union in order to protect the institution of slavery from a rising tide of abolitionist sentiment in the North. And leading historians concur that much of the impetus

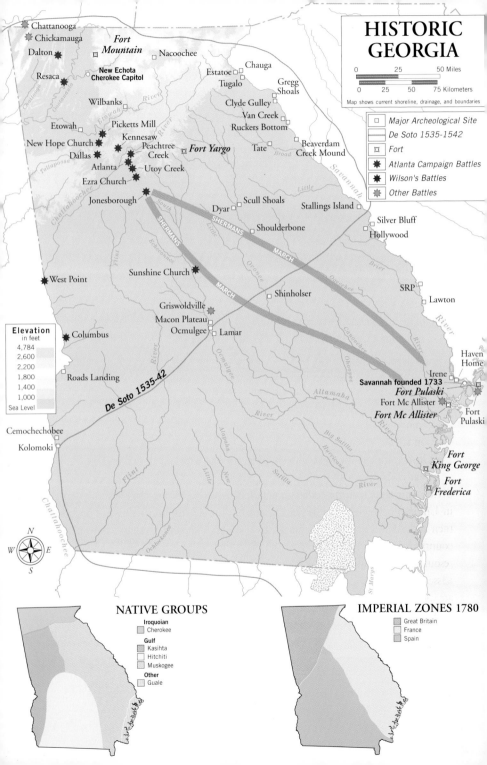

# HISTORIC GEORGIA

0        25              50 Miles

0    25      50      75 Kilometers

Map shows current shoreline, drainage, and boundaries

☐ Major Archeological Site
━━ De Soto 1535-1542
⌂ Fort
✳ Atlanta Campaign Battles
✴ Wilson's Battles
✷ Other Battles

Chattanooga
Chickamauga
Dalton
*Fort Mountain*
Nacoochee
Resaca
New Echota Cherokee Capitol
Estatoe
Tugalo
Chauga
Gregg Shoals
Wilbanks
Clyde Gulley
Van Creek
Ruckers Bottom
Etowah
Picketts Mill
New Hope Church
Kennesaw
Tate
Beaverdam Creek Mound
Dallas
Peachtree Creek
*Fort Yargo*
Atlanta
Ezra Church
Utoy Creek
Jonesborough
Dyar
Scull Shoals
Stallings Island
Silver Bluff
Hollywood
West Point
Sunshine Church
Shoulderbone
Shinholser
SRP
Lawton
Columbus
Griswoldville
Macon Plateau
Ocmulgee
Lamar

**Elevation**
in feet
4,784
2,600
2,200
1,800
1,400
1,000
Sea Level

Roads Landing

De Soto 1535-42

Cemochechobee
Kolomoki

Savannah founded 1733
Irene
Haven Home
*Fort Pulaski*
Fort Mc Allister
*Fort Mc Allister*
Fort Pulaski

*Fort King George*

*Fort Frederica*

N
W    E
S

SHERMANS MARCH
SHERMANS MARCH

## NATIVE GROUPS

**Iroquoian**
☐ Cherokee
**Gulf**
☐ Kasihta
☐ Hitchiti
☐ Muskogee
**Other**
☐ Guale

## IMPERIAL ZONES 1780

☐ Great Britain
☐ France
☐ Spain

for Georgia's exit was the need to defend the state's greatest repository of economic capital and its primary means of agricultural production—in short, slave labor.

Georgia seceded from the Union on January 21, 1861, the fifth state to do so. Contrary to popular belief, Georgia did not secede and then immediately join the Confederate States of America. Instead, for two months Georgia considered itself a sovereign nation, even going so far as to name ambassadors to Britain, France, and Belgium.

But when the other Southern states convened in Montgomery, Alabama, for the purpose of forming a new nation, the Confederate States of America, delegates from Georgia were in attendance. Alexander Stephens was elected vice president, while another Georgian, Thomas Cobb of Athens, crafted the new nation's constitution. The constitution, modeled in part on that of the United States, assuaged the fears of slaveholding Southerners by expressly prohibiting the Confederate Congress from passing any law to abolish slavery.

The first few years of the war were relatively quiet ones in Georgia. Though tens of thousands of Georgians volunteered and served in the Confederate Army, little fighting took place this far south. Meanwhile, Georgians were at work in munitions plants and textile mills churning out firearms, clothing, and other essentials for the boys in gray. Soon the cities of Macon, Augusta, Columbus, and Savannah were among the Confederacy's primary manufacturing centers. And thanks to its location at the center of Georgia's umbilical network of rail lines, Atlanta was the most important transportation center in the Confederacy.

By early 1864, Atlanta had become the prime target in General Grant's plan to divide and thus decimate the Confederate States of America. With Atlanta in Union hands, Confederate supply lines would be severed. Backed by 99,000 men and charged with orders from Grant to "get into the interior of the enemy's country as far as you can, inflicting all the damage that you can against their war resources," Gen. William Sherman marched southward from Chattanooga, Tennessee. Just 30 or so miles south, Gen. Joseph Johnston and his 62,000 Confederate soldiers dug into defensive trenches.

All spring long, the armies of Sherman and Johnston did battle. At Dalton, Resaca, and New Hope Church, Johnston's men fought and lost, retreating again and again, only to dig a new set of trenches and fight another day. When on June 27, Sherman attacked Johnston's troops head-on at Kennesaw Mountain, the Confederates dealt Sherman a nasty blow, killing more than 3,000 of his troops. But the victory was short lived. Soon the Confederates were retreating and digging in yet again, this time to defend Atlanta.

In an attempt to turn the tide, Confederate president Jefferson Davis replaced General Johnston with General John Hood—to no avail. Sherman pressed on, and for 40 days his artillery bombarded the city of Atlanta. "War, fearful and bloody, was each hour coming nearer," wrote one Atlantan. "Terrific cannonading on every side, continual firing of muskets, men screaming to each other, wagons rumbling by or pouring into the yard." By September 1, most Atlantans had evacuated; the next day, Mayor James M. Calhoun surrendered a largely abandoned city. In less than two weeks, Sherman gave orders that Atlanta be burned.

A Union soldier wrote of what he witnessed:

On the night of November 15th, the torch was applied to the railroad shops, foundries, and every one of the many buildings that has been used in fitting out the armies of the enemy in this vast "workshop of the Confederacy," as Atlanta was called. The flames spread rapidly and, when morning came, it is doubtful whether there were a score of buildings remaining in the city, except on the very outskirts.

*This photograph of Sherman (in foreground, leaning on breach of cannon) was taken in Atlanta in the fall of 1864. (Library of Congress)*

The next day, Sherman began his "March to the Sea." Southward and eastward out of Atlanta, through Macon, Madison, and Milledgeville and on into Savannah, Sherman cut a swath of destruction unprecedented in the annals of American warfare, leaving wreck and ruin in his wake. For years thereafter the landscape was cluttered with his handiwork: "Sherman's sentinels" (blackened, lone chimneys) and "Sherman's neckties" (rails twisted around trees).

When Sherman's men entered Savannah on December 21, 1864, the general telegraphed President Lincoln with the good news:

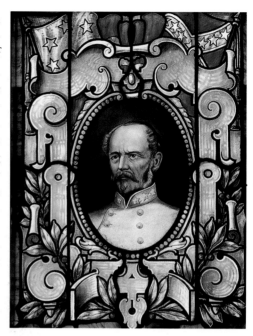

*General Johnston is the subject of this stained glass window in Rhodes Hall, Atlanta.*

> *I* beg to present to you as a Christmas gift, the city of Savannah, with 150 guns and plenty of ammunition, also about 25,000 bales of cotton.

By the spring of 1865, the Southern armies were hapless, the Southern fight for independence hopeless. Of the 120,000 Georgians who had marched off to war, more than one in five did not return. On April 26, 1865, General Johnston formally surrendered the state of Georgia to Sherman, and soon thereafter, on May 10, Union forces captured a fleeing President Jefferson Davis near Irwinville in South Georgia.

## ■ RECONSTRUCTION AND REDEMPTION

With the defeat of the Confederacy and effective release of all slaves from captivity, $400 million vanished overnight from the coffers of white Georgia. This loss of slave capital, coupled with the physical destruction of nearly all important rail lines and manufacturing facilities, left Georgia in a postbellum economic lurch.

Many black Georgians, emboldened and empowered by their newfound freedom, left the old plantations, striking out for points north. Others remained, forging an uneasy alliance with their former masters, working the same fields, tending the same cash crop.

Meanwhile, Northern profiteers, intent upon taking advantage of the economic and social turmoil of the day, descended upon Georgia. Derided as carpetbaggers by white Southerners because they often carried baggage made from old carpets, these men were, in effect, land speculators who sought to buy up Georgia's decimated acreage at a pittance and resell at a monstrous profit.

While economic change came swiftly, it would be two years before real governmental change came, and only then at the threat of force. When Georgia and nine other former Confederate states refused to ratify the Fourteenth Amendment guaranteeing all citizens "equal protection of the laws," Congress acted. Early in 1867, the 10 states were placed under military stewardship. Georgia was governed by a U.S. Army general, and his decisions were enforced by federal troops. Soon the occupying troops set about registering black voters and making plans for the adoption of a new state constitution.

Concurrently, the federally mandated Freedmen's Bureau was at work in the state, providing support and education to struggling black Georgians. Among the bureau's most important tasks was helping freed slaves negotiate labor contracts with white landowners, a development that eventually gave rise to the sharecropping system.

*President Ulysses S. Grant is here depicted as a wealthy tyrant atop the huge carpetbag crushing the "Solid South." (Library of Congress)*

From 1867 through 1870, Georgia flirted with a true overhaul of its governmental system. In 1868, 32 black Republicans were elected to Georgia's General Assembly, but 28 of the 32 were soon expelled on the grounds that the state constitution did not grant blacks the right to hold office. The four who remained were judged to be mulattos and thus worthy of service.

By the time the federal troops finally withdrew in 1870, a new force in Georgia politics was ascendant: the Ku Klux Klan, a fraternal order of sorts dedicated to the preservation of Protestant, Anglo-Saxon rule. For the next century, these white-hooded hooligans would exercise extralegal control over the affairs of Georgians both black and white.

*A farmer plows a deeply eroded field in Heard County. (photo by Jack Delano, Library of Congress)*

## ■ BLEAKEST OF YEARS

As the century came to a close, the entire nation sank into an economic depression, with the South suffering the worst fate. Interest rates skyrocketed. Cotton prices plummeted. Once-fertile land, spent from years of one-crop farming, washed away in ruddy torrents, leaving deep red gorges cut into the landscape, a testament to years of abuse and neglect.

While planters scrambled to reassemble their fiefdoms, Georgia's smaller farmers eked out the barest of livings, raising cotton for cash and corn for feed. Black Georgians, rather than work for their former masters in a gang-style arrangement as they had done in the days of slavery, took to sharecropping. Their white neighbors worked beside them, subsisting on the same meager and monotonous diet of cornbread, molasses, and fatback.

With cash in short supply, Georgians depended on the sharecropping system as their de facto banking system. It worked this way: Farmers secured loans from planters and other large landholders under the guise of a crop lien, leveraging not the value of the land they were to be working but the crop they would bring in come fall. Planters provided what was called "the furnish"—seeds, tools, and other essentials necessary for survival. At "settlement time," the planter would weigh and price the cropper's harvest, deduct his half for the lease of the land, and then deduct an amount of his own divination for the furnish. All too often, no matter how large the crop, no matter how high the going price of cotton, the cropper came up short.

Frustration with the inequities of the sharecropping system gave birth to a short-lived biracial alliance of farmers, who, at the turn of the century, joined forces with Populist Party advocates, seeking governmental assistance in bringing an end to the usurious system. Among the more vociferous advocates of such agricultural reform was Georgian Tom Watson. When opponents attempted to wreck the movement by pitting the races against one another, Watson intoned that, "the accident of color can make no difference in the interest of farmers, croppers, and laborers." No matter, the effort failed, and a defeated and dejected Watson was soon spouting the same racist rhetoric he had once decried.

## ■ NEW SOUTH, NEW DEAL

It would take more than 60 years and the accumulated effects of large infusions of Northern fiscal investment and federal legislative intrusion to transform the Georgia economy and by extension the lives of the Georgia people.

During the 1870s and 1880s, *Atlanta Constitution* editor Henry Grady sold Southerners and Northerners alike on the idea that a "New South" was emergent. The *New York Times* called him "the great interpreter of a new spirit which was awakening in the South, exhorting the people to concern themselves no longer about what they had lost, but to busy themselves with what they might find to do:

to put the whole strength of their minds and bodies into the building up of a New South."

Grady charmed the industrialists with his mellifluous speech and promises of eager, cheap labor, even while he chided General Sherman for being "kind of a careless man about fire." Under Grady's leadership, and with Atlanta at its center, a new South did begin to take shape. Between 1870 and 1910, almost $200 million was invested in Georgia manufacturing concerns. Yet Grady never lived to see his dream come to fruition. He died in 1889 at the age of 39.

*Henry W. Grady, seen here in bathing costume with Mrs. Bessie Johnson (left) daughter-in-law of President Andrew Johnson, in 1884. (Atlanta Historical Society)*

The late 19th and early 20th centuries saw Georgia prosper only modestly. Atlanta boomed with industry, but the rest of the state plodded along, suffering through boll weevil infestations that ruined cotton crops, and droughts that left farmlands parched and puckered.

In response, Georgians of all hues and hometowns lit out for the North, intent on securing manufacturing jobs in New York, Detroit, and Chicago. Between 1920 and 1925 alone, Georgia's farm population decreased by 375,000.

By the 1930s, Georgia, like the rest of the nation, was in the grip of the Great Depression. At a time when President Roosevelt was pledging to provide all possible aid to a South that he considered, "the nation's number one economic problem," Gov. Eugene Talmadge, Georgia's firebrand champion of the common man, was making every effort to resist Roosevelt's roster of relief and assistance programs on the grounds that they threatened "Georgia's way of life." For the first four years

*Farm Security Administration photographer Dorothea Lange took this picture of peach pickers during their lunch break in Muscella, Georgia, in 1936. (Library of Congress)*

of Roosevelt's administration, Talmadge successfully forestalled Roosevelt's agenda, but in 1936, Eurith D. "Ed" Rivers was elected governor, and Georgia fully embraced the New Deal.

Though the New Deal brought immediate relief to many Georgians, it was not until the outbreak of World War II that Georgia fully recovered from the ravages of the previous years. War brought true prosperity to Georgia as military bases opened across the state and manufacturing concerns geared up to produce airplanes, ships, and weapons. By the fall of 1943, 20,000 civilians were working at one new facility alone, the Bell Aircraft Corporation in Marietta. At the close of the war, the annual income of the average Georgian was twice what it had been when the Japanese bombed Pearl Harbor.

## ■ CIVIL RIGHTS MOVEMENT

For almost a century after the demise of slavery, African-American Georgians chafed under the yoke of a white majority intent on denying them the most basic of civil rights. A de facto system of segregation known as Jim Crow specified where blacks were allowed to study, eat, and work. In addition, steps were taken to ensure that black Georgians would be excluded from the electoral process, culminating in 1908 with the passage of a constitutional amendment that disenfranchised potential black voters by requiring proof of Confederate lineage and property ownership. But in 1946, the U.S. Supreme Court declared the "white only" primary illegal, paving the way for black inclusion in the electoral process. In 1954 the Supreme Court declared that separate but equal schools were inherently discriminatory.

The effects were not immediate, but by 1960, Atlanta—under the leadership of its remarkably progressive mayor, Ivan Allen—was admitting black students to previously all-white high schools. In 1961, against the strong protests of racist demagogues like Herman

*In 1964, Danny Lyon, staff photographer for the Student Nonviolent Coordinating Committee, took this photo of 17-year-old activist Taylor Washington being arrested at Lebs Delicatessen during a demonstration in Atlanta. (Library of Congress)*

Talmadge (Eugene's son) and Lester Maddox, the University of Georgia admitted its first two African-American students, Charlayne Hunter and Hamilton Holmes.

Meanwhile, in the southwest Georgia town of Albany, Student Nonviolent Coordinating Committee (SNCC) members organized a massive, grassroots voter-registration drive. In November of 1961, Martin Luther King Jr. came to their aid, but the local movement was ultimately frustrated by the efforts of police chief Laurie Pritchett. Though the Albany Movement did not achieve its goals, it did represent a turning point in the struggle of black Georgians to achieve equal rights under the law, as seasoned activists joined with students and members of the black middle class in a systemic effort of organized resistance that would set the precedent for similar efforts in Birmingham, Alabama, and elsewhere.

Across the state, the Civil Rights Movement spread. Leaders like Andrew Young, Julian Bond, and John Lewis led sit-ins and launched protests. Compared to states like Alabama and Mississippi, the Civil Rights Movement in Georgia was relatively peaceful. Cities like Atlanta and Augusta, faced with well-organized sit-in campaigns targeted at local restaurants and other public accommodations, negotiated compromises and quickly got back to work. Thanks to its comparatively tolerant racial policies and its reputation for business savvy, Atlanta was soon known as "the city too busy to hate."

Though the state would come close to riot at the news of the murder of favorite son Martin Luther King Jr.—and would flirt with racial demagoguery once again under the governorship of Lester Maddox—the 1970s held great promise for all Georgians.

*Before he became the governor of Georgia, Lester Maddox refused to serve two African-American divinity students in his cafeteria the day after Johnson signed the Civil Rights Act of 1964. Here he models a pair of water buffalo horns sent to him by a Georgia soldier serving in Vietnam. (UPI/Bettmann)*

*Like Lester Maddox, Jimmy Carter was a self-made man from rural Georgia who became governor—but their opinions on segregation could not have been more different. (Library of Congress)*

# ■ JIMMY CARTER AND MODERN TIMES

By the early 1970s, Henry Grady's vision of the New South was fast becoming a reality. In a fit of bravado worthy of the great Grady himself, newly elected Georgia governor Jimmy Carter declared in 1971 that, at the end of his term, "We shall be able to stand up anywhere in the world—in New York, California, or Florida—and say 'I'm a Georgian' and be proud of it." And much to the chagrin of some of the more conservative members of his own Democratic party, this onetime peanut farmer from Plains announced, "I say to you frankly that the time for racial discrimination is over."

With Carter at the helm, Georgia businesses boomed, Georgia schools received dramatic funding increases, and Georgia prisons were remodeled and reformed. By 1974, Carter was plotting a leap from the Georgia governor's mansion to the White House. In 1977 he took the oath of office as President of the United States.

*With its ever-increasing numbers of skyscrapers and highways, Atlanta is today the largest city in the South.*

While Carter was in the White House, change was afoot in Georgia. In search of manufacturing and service-industry employment, Georgians left farms in droves, moving to the urban center of the state—metropolitan Atlanta—in a trend that continues to this day. By 1990, metropolitan Atlanta accounted for more than 40 percent of the state's population.

Today, Atlanta is recognized as one of the world's premier corporate centers. Among the companies that call Atlanta home are such international powerhouses as Coca-Cola, CNN, UPS, and Delta Airlines.

Other regions of Georgia have also been affected by the booming economy. Change, in the form of urban sprawl, has come even to the hinterlands. Of modern north Georgia, Mary Hood writes: "Toward the interstate, pastures have been carved into streets. Oaks and horse barns have been shouldered out by apartments. It is only a matter of time before there will be a car wash, cleaners, convenience store, tanning salon, racquetball center, roller rink, and video rental club."

So is this progress? Are Georgians of today better off than they were a hundred years ago, a generation ago? Well, as a precocious child might say, that depends.

There is little debate as to whether Georgians are a different people than they were even a generation ago. No longer are we a segregated land of black and white, almost all of whom vote the Democratic ticket and live within a couple hours' drive of where we were raised.

No, we are all grown up now—so grown up that in 1996 we hosted the Summer Olympic Games. But that doesn't mean Georgia has lost its quirks. That doesn't mean our last shred of Southern distinctiveness has been mortgaged to build yet another strip mall. Should you doubt me, just point your car toward the little hamlet of Box Springs in western central Georgia. West of town, you'll spot the Giggle Box Cafe. Pull over, order yourself a mess of fried okra, and then tell me what you think.

*In 1996, Atlanta hosted the Summer Olympic Games. American track star Michael Johnson ran in the 200-meter heat shown here.*

HISTORY & CULTURE

# SOUTHERN WRITERS ON SOUTHERN CULTURE

*Visitors to Georgia encounter a variety of cultures. Life in Appalachian Georgia is a far cry from life in the university town of Athens, and Atlanta's old-money black elite has little in common with peanut or sugar-cane farmers in the south part of the state. And yet the idea that there exists such a thing as "Southern culture" has enormous staying power. Southerners themselves have no doubt made the largest contribution to the literature on the subject. The following excerpts offer glimpses of how Southerners see or have seen themselves.*

## ◆ SOUTHERN GENTLEMEN

*B*eside being of faultless pedigree, the Southern Gentleman is usually possessed of an equally faultless physical development. His average height is about six feet, yet he is rarely gawky in his movements, or in the least clumsily put together; and his entire *physique* conveys to the mind an impression of firmness united to flexibility…. the Northern people have been told so incessantly of the lazy habits of Southerners, that they honestly believe them to be delicate good-for-nothings, like their own brainless fops and nincompoops….The gentlemen of the South owe their physical perfectness in part, doubtless, to those mailed ancestors who followed Godfrey and bold Coeur de Lion to the rescue of the Holy Sepulchre….

Much more reasonably, however, we think we may attribute the good size and graceful carriage of the Southern Gentleman, to his out-of-doors and a-horseback mode of living. For we might as well here inform our readers, the genuine Southern Gentleman almost invariably lives in the country. But let them not conclude from from this circumstance that he is nothing more than the simple-hearted, swearing, hearty, and hospitable old English or Virginia Country Gentleman, of whom we have all heard so repeatedly.

—Daniel R. Hundley, *Social Relations in Our Southern States,* 186

*George Washington Lay (left) and his cousin, James Berry Lay, a couple of Southern gentlemen, photographed in 1855. (Georgia Department of Archives and History)*

*PHOTO BY KENNETH ROGERS*

## ◆ SOUTHERN LADIES

*In her 1975 collection of essays, titled* Southern Ladies and Gentlemen, *author Florence King explains the thrall in which Southern women hold many of us, writers included:*

𝒩ovelists prefer complex women for their protagonists, which is why the Southern woman has been the heroine of so many more novels than her Northern sister. The cult of Southern womanhood endowed her with at least five totally different images and asked her to be good enough to adopt all of them. She is required to be frigid, compassionate, sweet, bitchy, and scatterbrained—all at the same time. Her problems spring from the fact that she succeeds.

Antebellum Southern civilization was built upon the white woman's untouchable image. In order to keep her footing on the pedestal men had erected for her, she had to be aloof, aristocratic, and haughty. These qualities have always been required of women in societies based upon vast, entailed estates, but they were especially necessary in the South. They enabled the white woman to maintain her sanity when she saw light-skinned slave children, who were the very spirit of Old Massa, running around the plantation. By being sufficiently frosty and above it all, she was able to ignore and endure the evidence of intercaste sexuality that surrounded her.

—Florence King, *Southern Ladies and Gentlemen,* 1975

HISTORY & CULTURE

### ◆ SOUTHERN HOSPITALITY

Integral to the Southern mystique is the reputation Southerners enjoy for gracious accommodation. A distant relative, a neighbor, a statesman, or otherwise distinguished man, a stranger who came with letters of introduction from friends: all could be assured of a warm welcome. In his informal history, *Eating and Drinking in the South,* published in 1982, historian Joe Gray Taylor observes:

> *Of* the hospitality of the planters and well-to-do townsmen of the Old South there can be no doubt; the witnesses are too abundant. The story of the lonesome lord of many acres who at rifle point forced passersby to partake of his hospitality, is probably apocryphal, but it does make the point that life on the plantation could be isolated and lonely; the visit of a well-informed traveler could be a much welcomed break in the routine of the seasons."

Naturalist William Bartram was quite impressed by the cordial reception he received in Georgia in the 1770s. He noted that on one rice plantation he was entertained "in every respect as a worthy gentleman—A stranger spent the evening very agreeably and the day following (for I was not permitted to depart sooner)."

Bartram's observations were confirmed by another traveler of that era, Sir Charles Lyell, who noted that "they alone who have traveled in the southern states can appreciate the ease and politeness with which a stranger is received."

*A Southern-style family reunion circa 1900. (Georgia Department of Archives and History)*

*Baptism at Triplett Creek in 1940. (Library of Congress)*

#### ◆ SOUTHERN RELIGION

*Author Flannery O'Connor wrote that Georgia is "Christ-haunted." If a Georgian asks you what church you belong to, he's probably assumed you're either Baptist or Methodist. Here is O'Connor's evocation of a preacher:*

"*I* seen you cure a woman oncet!" a sudden high voice shouted from the hump of people. "Seen that woman git up and walk out straight where she had limped in!"

The preacher lifted one foot and then the other. He seemed almost but not quite to smile. "You might as well go home if that's what you come for," he said.

Then he lifted his head and arms and shouted, "Listen to what I got to say, you people! There ain't but one river and that's the River of Life, made out of Jesus' Blood. That's the river you have to lay your pain in, in the River of Faith, in the River of Life, in the River of Love, in the rich red river of Jesus' Blood, you people!"

His voice grew soft and musical. "All the rivers come from that one River and go back to it like it was the ocean sea and if you believe, you can lay your pain in that River and get rid of it because that's the River that was made to carry sin. It's a River full of pain itself, pain itself, moving toward the Kingdom of Christ, to be washed away, slow, you people, slow as this here old red water river round my feet."

—Flannery O'Connor, "The River," from *A Good Man is Hard to Find, and Other Stories,* 1955

# N O R T H W E S T

■ HIGHLIGHTS

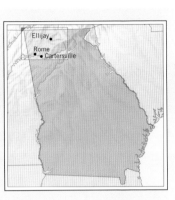

■ TRAVEL BASICS

Remote and relatively undeveloped, northwest Georgia is a delight. Natural beauty abounds, from Cloudland Canyon with its breathtaking views and waterfalls, to the rugged Cohutta Mountains and the rolling hills of the Civil War battlefield at Chickamauga. Vestiges of Native American life are well preserved at New Echota, the last eastern capital of the Cherokee nation, and at the Etowah Indian Mounds near Cartersville. For a glimpse at what man has wrought, make your way to visionary folk artist Howard Finster's Paradise Gardens, or to Fort Mountain, where an unexplained rock wall more than 800 feet long winds its way through the wilderness.

**Getting Around:** To appreciate the natural beauty of the region, head east or west from the I-75 corridor and wander the mountain roads. And by all means, get out of the car and take a hike. Rome, the largest town in north Georgia, can be toured on foot.

**Climate:** Cool and wet winters with temperatures ranging from the low 20s F to the mid-50s. Occasional snowfall possible. Summers are warm and humid with frequent thunderstorms; temperatures in the 80s. Fall is usually dry and pleasant. Spring peaks in April.

**Food & Lodging:** Good restaurants and inns are few and far between in this corner of Georgia. But there are a few surprises tucked away, including a suite for let in Pennsville that's situated in the gardens of a renowned visionary folk artist *(see page 67)*, and a tidy little diner in Rossville that serves near perfect cheeseburgers *(see page 65)*. Cabins are available at many state parks, including Cloudland Canyon *(see page 65)*, and Fort Mountain *(see page 72)*.

# NORTHWEST GEORGIA

Rich Mountain
Wilderness Area

**Elevation**
in feet

| 4,784 |
| 2,600 |
| 2,200 |
| 1,800 |
| 1,400 |
| 1,000 |
| Sea Level |

TENNESSEE

CAROLINA

ALABAMA

McCaysville
Epworth
Mineral Bluff
Morganton
Margret
Blue Ridge
Cherry Log

Tennga
Cisco
Crandall
Eton
Gregory
Ramhurst
Chatsworth
Spring Place
Holley
Dalton

Varnell
Ringgold
Tunnel Hill
Rocky Face
Rossville
Fort Oglethorpe
Chickamauga
Rock Spring
Noble
Catlett
Naomi
Cedar Grove
LaFayette
Center Post
Pennville
Villanow
Sugar Valley

Lookout Mtn
New England
Trenton
Rising Fawn
Cloudland
Menlo
Lyerly

Ellijay
Cartecay
Talking Rock
Jasper
Tate
Nelson
Sharp Top
Marblehill

Amicalola Falls
State Park
Dawsonville
Silver City
Coal Mountain
Cumming
Free Home
Birmingham
Lathemtown
Bluffington
Hickory Flat

Ball Ground
Canton
North Canton
Waleska
Fairmount
Funkhouser
White
Cartersville
Cassville
Kingston
Coosa
Six Mile
Rome

Oakman
Ranger
Carters
Redbud
Blackwood
Sonoraville
Folsom
Pine Log
Resaca
Calhoun
Adairsville
Shannon
Pinson
Armuchee
Holland

New Echota
Cherokee Capitol
& State Hist Site

Fort Mountain
State Park

Chief Vann House
State Hist Site

Etowah Indian Mounds
State Hist Site

Red Top Mtn State Park

Bansley Gardens

James H Floyd
State Park

Cloudland Canyon
State Park

Chickamauga &
Chattanooga
Nat'l Military Park

Cohutta
Wilderness Area

Gaylesville

Nottely
Lake

Blue Ridge
Lake

Carters
Lake

Lake Sidney
Lanier

Allatoona
Lake

Weiss
Lake

Summerville

N    E
W    S

# ■ OVERVIEW

Viewed in late fall, the mountains of northwest Georgia resemble a rumpled shag carpet of kaleidoscopic color, each tuft a different mix of russet and gold, purple and chocolate, dusky green and bleached black.

Here at the tail end of the Appalachian Mountains, the Cherokee nation once flourished. The settlement at New Echota—now a state historic site—is a testament to a valiant and ill-fated attempt to assimilate and survive in the face of European encroachment. Those first Europeans were for the most part Scotch-Irish settlers. Their descendants, living in the comparative isolation of these mountains, remain a people apart, friendly and welcoming, but not as likely to invite a stranger in as their low-country neighbors. Welcoming they are; gullible they are not.

Though the region remains remote, development is spreading north from Atlanta along the interstate highway system. From Calhoun to Dalton, north to Chattanooga, Tennessee, the I-75 corridor cuts a swath of development and industry that stands in stark contrast to the remote and comparatively unspoiled lands that lie to its east and west. Unlike the mountains of northeast Georgia, which were long ago claimed as vacation getaways by Atlantans, the Cohutta Mountains

*Thomas Hart Benton's* Arts of the South, *1932. (New Britain Museum of Art, New Britain, CT; © T. H. Benton and R. P. Benton Testamentary Trusts/Licensed by VAGA, New York, NY) (opposite) Cloudland Canyon State Park.*

and the remote canyons and cave-riddled ridges farther west are remarkably devoid of ticky-tacky tourist development. Here the land is unspoiled, the people unassuming and welcoming.

## ■ ROME  *map page 49, B-4*

On the southern fringe of the region is Rome. With a population of 30,000, this is the largest city in the state north of Atlanta. Once known as "the stove center of the South," modern-day Rome is still a manufacturing center, albeit one overshadowed by the behemoth that is Atlanta, located just an hour south. In 1863 the town was attacked by Union forces led by Col. Abel D. Streight, and the following year it was occupied by the Federals, and in November of 1864 its factories were destroyed.

*In Rome, Georgia, a replica of Rome, Italy's Etruscan Romulus and Remus guards City Hall.*

### ◆ THE CITY ON SEVEN HILLS

Perhaps because the founders realized they'd sited the city on seven rolling hills, they named their town for that other city on seven hills. Rome, Georgia, even claims a sculpture of Romulus and Remus and their lupine mother. In Rome, Italy, the original Etruscan sculpture sits atop Capitoline Hill; in Rome, Georgia, a replica guards the entrance to City Hall: a ferocious, almost fiendish she-wolf, fangs bared, protects the mythical boy twins, founders of the city. The inscription below is a bit unnerving: "From Ancient Rome to New Rome during the consulship of Benito Mussolini in the year 1928." *City Hall is located at the corner of Broad Street and Sixth Avenue.*

### Rome Area History Museum

Three blocks away from the City Hall is this greataunt's attic of a display space, stuffed to the gills with ephemera and homespun exhibits detailing local history in a provincial yet charming fashion. *305 Broad Street; 706-235-8051.*

### Clock Tower Museum

Up the hill at Fourth Avenue and Third Street is a brick water tower 100 feet tall topped with an 1871 clock. Inside, a spiral staircase leads to the top, where visitors may take in a sweeping view of the city's seven hills. *706-236-4430.*

### Myrtle Hill Cemetery

An equally lofty perspective on the city is offered at the cemetary on Rome's southwestern edge at the confluence of the Etowah and Oostanaula Rivers. Named for the hundreds of crepe myrtle bushes that grace the grounds and explode with purple each spring, the cemetery rises six terraced levels high and is the last resting place of Rome native Ellen Axson Wilson, first wife of President Woodrow Wilson.

Also of interest, if for nothing more than the florid prose, is the cemetery's **Women of the Confederacy Monument,** which pays homage to the women of Rome, "whose purity, whose fidelity, whose courage, whose genius in love and in counsel kept the home secure, the family a school of virtue, the state a court of honor, who made of war a season of heroism and of peace a time of healing, the guardians of tranquility and our strength." *South Broad and Myrtle Streets.*

### Chieftains Museum

Heritage of another sort is on display at the former home to Major Ridge, one of the leaders of the Cherokee nation. Ridge signed the U.S. removal act on behalf of the Cherokee people and followed them to Oklahoma. He was eventually executed by his tribe for having sold their tribal lands.

The clapboard museum houses an odd juxtaposition of Native American exhibits and gilded Victorian furniture, intended to convey the Cherokee people's attempts at assimilation. *A few miles north of town at 501 Riverside Parkway; 706-291-9494.*

### ◆ BERRY COLLEGE

On the northern outskirts of Rome is the beautiful campus of Berry College, founded in 1902 by Martha Berry. Near the entrance to the 28,000-acre campus (the world's largest in geographical size) is the cabin where Berry, daughter of a wealthy planter, first began teaching the sons and daughters of those less fortunate.

From here, the campus sprawls along Highway 27. Roadways are lined with towering oaks, and the pasture-like expanse of campus green space is dotted with Gothic stone halls and simple cabins. At the northern extreme, some three miles from the main campus, the Berry College Mountain Campus sits atop Lavender Mountain. Here the Old Mill Wheel still turns; the 1930 water wheel is one of the largest overshot wheels in the world. *Campus information: 706-232-5374.*

*The Old Mill Wheel at Berry College.*

Today, 2,000 students call the campus home. And thanks to Martha Berry's commitment to the interdependence of work and study, most students earn their keep by working at the college's farms and research facilities. Also on campus is the Berry family home, known as **Oak Hill**, a magnificent Georgian mansion filled with family mementos and ringed by boxwood gardens. And on this site is the newly renovated **Martha Berry Museum,** a tribute to Berry's life and legacy. *706-291-1883.*

◆ FURTHER SPLENDORS OF ROME

The **Claremont House**, a Victorian Gothic mansion built in 1882 and renovated in 1993, is a fine place to stay to soak in the culture of Rome, Georgia. Its proprietors offer champagne in the evening and a full breakfast every morning. The real attraction is the unique architecture of the house itself. Soaring 14-foot ceilings and period antiques lend a graceful air to the interior. *906 East Second Avenue, 706-291-0900.*

One important difference between Rome, Georgia and Rome, Italy would be barbecue. **Bubba's,** at the base of the Broad Street bridge, serves a hot sauce the proprietor claims is "neither fittin' for man nor beast." This smokeshack does a mostly takeout business, though a few picnic tables are set up. *One Broad Street; 706-291-0618.*

There are plenty of other excellent dining options. Try **La Scala Restaurant,** an Italian-inspired cafe, open for dinner. *513 Broad Street; 706-238-9000.*

The **Partridge Restaurant** is set in what was once the lobby of a downtown theater and exudes a '60s chic. Plate lunches are the draw, with offerings ranging from grilled chicken livers over rice and stewed tomatoes to chicken-and-dumplings and baked squash. Lunch and early dinner. *330 Broad Street; 706-291-4048.*

■ CARTERSVILLE AREA  *map page 49, D-4*

Thirty miles east of Rome (and 45 miles northwest of Atlanta via I-75) is Cartersville, a tidy town that boasts two quaint cafes and a bucolic business district. On the east wall of Main Street's Young Brothers Pharmacy, you can take a gander at the first outdoor sign painted to advertise Coca-Cola. These signs, once a ubiquitous a part of the Southern landscape, are now, in the words of a local, "scarce as chicken teeth."

Nearby are the **Etowah Indian Mounds,** a series of three large temple mounds and four smaller ones, constructed on the north bank of the Etowah River between A.D. 1250 and 1550. Constructed basket by dirt-filled basket, the largest of these flat-topped earthen knolls is more than six stories high, with a base covering three acres. Also of note are the restored fish traps built of stone and woven wood. When the river is low, these can be viewed from the riverbank. *Indian Mound Road, five miles from I-75, one-half mile from Dellinger Park; 770-387-3747.*

*Etowah Indian human figures dating from the Mississippian era, circa A.D. 1200–1400. (Georgia Department of Natural Resources)*

*The Etowah Mounds State Historic Site, south of Cartersville.*

Few towns the size of Cartersville can claim two venerable diners. **Ross's Diner,** open since 1945, is housed in a redbrick building, features a U-shaped counter at the center of the dining room. The biscuits and gravy breakfast, burgers, and chili are equally good. *17 Wall Street; 706-382-9159.*

**4-Way Lunch** is housed in a squat red frame building on the edge of downtown. Twelve chrome stools face the grill where an aged cook dishes out monstrous biscuits doused with cream gravy at breakfast, and beef stew for lunch. A great slice of Southern Americana. *West Main and Gilmer Streets; no phone.*

## ■ NORTH OF CARTERSVILLE

North of Cartersville along Highway 293 is the little village of **Kingston,** where in 1864 Union general William T. Sherman received permission from Ulysses S. Grant, commander of the Union Army, to begin his infamous March to the Sea.

Today, the village is but a ghost of its former self. In days past, the downtown business district teemed with shoppers on Saturday afternoons. Perhaps the sole diversion on a Saturday now is the **Church of the Lord Jesus Christ,** one of the few snake-handling churches in Georgia, which by evening comes alive with worshippers.

Dennis Covington, in his book *Salvation on Sand Mountain,* describes a service in this way:

> *It's* not true that you become used to the noise and confusion of a snake-handling Holiness service. On the contrary, you become enmeshed into it. It is theatre at its most intricate—improvisational, spiritual jazz. The younger the worshipper, the easier it seems to be for the Holy Ghost to descend and speak—lips loosened, tongue flapping, eyes rolling backward in the head....

At a typical service, three or four guitarists join a bassist and maybe a couple of drummers behind the altar. As they crank out a raucous back beat, the preacher begins his sermon, alternately chanting, shouting, praying, and singing as church members rise from their seats, some merely raising their hands in the air, others off on a jig of their own divination, while still others make their way to the pulpit, intent upon drinking "the deadly thing" (strychnine) or handling rattlesnakes, as prescribed in Mark 16:18: "They shall take up serpents."

Services can last upwards of three hours, and visitors should bear in mind that they are attending a religious ceremony. Potential guests are advised to write to the church in advance at General Delivery, Kingston, Georgia 30145.

■ BARNSLEY GARDENS   *map page 49, C-4*

A world away from the raw-boned life of Appalachia is Barnsley Gardens, once described by Union general James McPherson as being "one of the most beautiful spots on earth." The gardens were the site of a grand antebellum mansion built by British-born cotton exporter Godfrey Barnsley.

Today the house is but a shell, though the gardens, designed by pioneering landscape architect Andrew Jackson Downing, are a marvel of boxwood mazes and ancient gnarled rosebushes. The gardens and grounds have been reborn as a resort with a golf course, restaurants, a day spa, and suites with views of the ruins and gardens. *Located equidistant between Kingston and Adairsville, 10 minutes off I-75 at 597 Barnsley Gardens Road; 770-773-7480.*

NORTHWEST

*Early light on the ruins of the Barnsley Gardens estate, near Adairsville.*

■ New Echota   *map page 49, C-3*

Fifteen miles north of Barnsley Gardens, off Highway 225, is New Echota, the last eastern capital of the Cherokee nation, established on November 12, 1825. New Echota was a planned community, laid out by Cherokee surveyors and intended from its inception to serve as the seat of government. In the face of continuing pressure from the United States, the Cherokee adopted a system of government based on the U.S. model, dividing the nation into eight districts represented by a bicameral legislature.

It was here that a Cherokee named Sequoyah first devised a written language for his people—a syllabry of 86 characters, put to practical use in 1828 with the publication of a bilingual newspaper, the *Cherokee Phoenix.*

Despite such efforts to assimilate, the Cherokee nation came to an end when, on December 29, 1835, the Treaty of New Echota was signed, ceding all Cherokee lands east of the Mississippi River to the United States. In exchange, the Cherokee received $5,300,000 and a large parcel of Oklahoma land. In May 1836, over the objections of the many Cherokee who considered the treaty unjust, President Andrew Jackson signed the treaty into law, thus beginning the two-year-long removal along a route that came to be known as the Trail of Tears. Over the course of the 1,000-mile journey, more than 4,000 Cherokee lost their lives.

Faced with the prospect of removal, Elias Boudinot, first editor of the *Cherokee Phoenix,* composed this remarkably prescient statement in November of 1836:

*A Cherokee farmstead in spring at New Echota State Historic Site. A planned community, New Echota was the last eastern capital of the Cherokee nation.*

NORTHWEST

*T*he time will come when the few remnants of our once happy and improving nation will be viewed by posterity with curious and gazing interest as relics of a brave and noble race…perhaps only here and there a solitary being, walking as a ghost over the ashes of his fathers to remind a stranger that such a race once existed.

Soon after the Cherokee were installed in Oklahoma, the three principal signers of the treaty, the editor Elias Boudinot, Major Ridge, and his son John Ridge, were assassinated by their fellow tribesmen for selling tribal lands.

Today, New Echota is the living embodiment of Boudinot's words. Walking along the dusty lanes that crisscross the settlement, past the reconstructed print shop, courthouse, council house, and tavern, it seems the dwelling place of ghosts. H ere and there you come upon another visitor, but for the most part, the buildings are empty, their displays dust-covered. Eight major buildings are on view, and all save the Worchester house, home of a missionary who remained even after the removal, were the dwelling and meeting places of the Cherokee.

After a tour of the grounds, stop at the museum to see exhibits on Cherokee building techniques and language. Those interested in the Cherokee syllabry may listen to recordings of the language and gaze at an original copy of the Cherokee nation's newspaper.

◆ CHIEF VANN HOUSE

The opulent Chief Vann House, known as the "showplace of the Cherokee nation," was built by Chief James Vann in 1804. A two-story brick home, it stands in tribute to the great wealth the Vann family amassed farming cotton. At one point, Vann's 110 slaves

*Chief Vann House, built in 1804.*

worked 4,000 acres of land. The home sits on a grassy knoll, surrounded by a clump of trees with a log cabin behind. Inside, the mantelpieces are hand-carved, the staircase cantilevered, and the whole of the house painted a vibrant palate of iron-hued red, baby blue, earthy brown, and green.

Forced to leave their home in 1835 after the Treaty of New Echota was signed, Vann's descendants traveled in style, with a stint on a luxurious steamboat, on their way to the Cherokee reservation in Oklahoma. James Vann's son, Joseph, built a replica of his Georgia home in Weber Falls, Oklahoma.

Since 1958, the original Vann home has been managed by the state of Georgia as a historic site. *Located eighteen miles north of New Echota along Highway 225 in Spring Place; 706-695-2598.*

### ■ PIEDMONT HILLS AND CHICKAMAUGA

To the north, rolling hills give way to the stooped irregularity of the Piedmont-Plateau, and soon you are approaching Dalton, Georgia, the self-proclaimed "carpet capital of the world." Though there is little of interest in this city, its industrial might is changing the cultural face of northwest Georgia. Mexican immigrants are moving to the area in search of work in the plants, and in small towns like Dalton and Chatsworth, taquerias are now as common as cafes.

Close to the Tennessee border, the Piedmont erupts with geological complexity. Here, high plateaus long ago eroded into mountains, and gulleys deepened into gorges. On this rough, unforgiving terrain was fought the bloodiest two-day battle of the Civil War: Chickamauga.

On September 19 and 20 of 1863, 124,000 soldiers fought and 34,000 fell. Lt. Col. James Abernathy of Kansas remembered the battle this way:

> We advanced under a perfect shower of bullets, sometimes driving the enemy and in turn being driven by them, until we had fought over the ground over and over again, and almost half our number lay dead and wounded.

The battle, though a victory for Confederate forces, was quickly followed by a Union victory at the Battle of Lookout Mountain outside Chattanooga, Tennessee. That winter Union general Sherman plotted an attack on Atlanta from his Chattanooga lair.

◆ CHICKAMAUGA NATIONAL MILITARY PARK

Soon after the end of the Civil War, Chickamauga was established as a national military park, the first in the country. Today, more than 600 stone and brass monuments (most erected by Chickamauga veterans) stand in tribute to the battlefield losses of blue- and gray-clad boys and men.

A series of plaques—blue for Union, gray for Confederate—mark troop movements, while pyramids of cannonballs stand where brigade commanders were killed and headquarters established.

Deer now graze amid Chickamauga's monuments and children play games of tag, but reminders of the carnage of war are never far away. Though the setting is pleasing, the grounds of the park look like a vast graveyard filled with mausoleums and obelisks. Along Battle Line Road, the marble monuments face one another: the 90th Ohio Infantry squaring off against a Confederate unit from Alabama.

Among the most striking monuments is an imposing pedestal crowned with a statute of four soldiers and dedicated to Confederate soldiers from Georgia, "those who gave much and those who gave all."

*Florida Monument at Chickamauga and Chattanooga National Military Park.*

*The Battle of Chickamauga was one of the costliest Civil War battles for both sides.*
*(Library of Congress)*

Thanks to the miles of footpaths and roadways that wend their way through the park following old battle lines, this huge greensward can be explored at a leisurely pace. Spend an hour or so driving through, or an afternoon on foot, exploring some of the more remote sites.

A 30-minute introductory film offered at the graceful, flagstone **visitor center,** as well as an audiocassette-narrated tour of the park, put the battle in historical perspective and explain the major engagements. Also in the visitor center is the **Fuller Gun Collection,** a stockpile of rifles old and new, some of which feature fencing bayonets made from whalebone. *The military park is nine miles south of Chattanooga on US 27; 706-866-9241.*

During the Battle of Chickamauga the redbrick **Gordon Lee Mansion** served as headquarters for Union general Rosecrans. Today, four elegant rooms are available for overnight accommodations in the 1847 manor house, while two rooms are for let in the former slave quarters. There's a Civil War museum upstairs. *217 Cove Road; 706-375-4728.*

## CHICKAMAUGA VICTORY

*J*anuary and February of 1864 passed, full of cold rains and wild winds, clouded by pervasive gloom and depression. In addition to the defeats at Gettysburg and Vicksburg, the center of the Southern line had caved. After hard fighting, nearly all of Tennessee was now held by the Union troops. But even with this loss on the top of the others, the South's spirit was not broken. True, grim determination had taken the place of high-hearted hopes, but people could still find a silver lining in the cloud. For one thing, the Yankees had been stoutly repulsed in September when they had tried to follow up their victories in Tennessee by an advance into Georgia.

Here in the northwesternmost corner of the state at Chickamauga, serious fighting had occurred on Georgia soil for the first time since the war began. The Yankees had taken Chattanooga and then had marched through the mountain passes into Georgia, but they had been driven back with heavy losses.

Atlanta and its railroads had played a big part in making Chickamauga a great victory for the South. Over the railroads that led down from Virginia to Atlanta and then northward toward Tennessee, General Longstreet's corps had been rushed to the scene of the battle. Along the entire route of several hundred miles, the tracks had been cleared and all the available rolling stock in the Southeast had been assembled for the movement.

Atlanta had watched while train after train rolled through the town, hour after hour, passenger coaches, box cars, flat cars, filled with shouting men. They had come without food or sleep, without their horses, ambulances or supply trains and, without waiting for the rest, they had leaped from the trains and into the battle. And the Yankees had been driven out of Georgia, back into Tennessee.

It was the greatest feat of the war, and Atlanta took pride and personal satisfaction in the thought that its railroads had made the victory possible.

—Margaret Mitchell, *Gone With the Wind,* 1936

Those interested in Civil War sights may want to journey north to Chattanooga and the Point Park and Lookout Mountain battlefields. Unfortunately, the drive there is through a rather ugly commercial stretch.

## ■ CLOUDLAND CANYON STATE PARK *map page 49, A-1*

*A trail through Cloudland Canyon State Park.*

West of Chickamauga, almost at the Alabama border, is Cloudland Canyon State Park, perhaps the most remote spot in northern Georgia. Located on the western edge of Lookout Mountain, the park straddles a deep gorge cut in the mountain by Sitton Gulch Creek. Reached by way of an ear-popping climb on Highway 136, Cloudland Canyon offers sightseers unparalleled vistas from the parking lot, while hikers in search of more may take to two canyon-rim trails. *Highway 136, southwest of Trenton; park information: 706-657-4050.*

A variety of overnight accommodations are offered nearby, but most convenient for those wanting to soak in the natural beauty of the mountain and gorge would be the cottages at the state park. High above the world at an ear-popping altitude, these spacious, functional cottages are perched at the canyon rim. The best cabins are numbers 6 through 16, each with a screened porch and rocking chairs. There is also a lodge on-site that sleeps up to 40. *Located off Highway 136 West; information: 706-657-4050 or reservations: 800-864-7275.*

Outside the park, in nearby **Rossville** there is a blast from the past diner called **Roy's Grill**. Opened in 1934, this cleaner-than-clean diner serves hand-patted hamburgers on toasted buns and gutbomb chili to a loyal cadre of locals. *116 Chickamauga Avenue; 706-866-0290.*

## ■ PENNVILLE AND PARADISE GARDENS   *map page 49, B-3*

Down the mountain by way of Highway 27 is the little burg of Pennville, home to **Howard Finster's Paradise Gardens**. Situated on what was a patch of swampland, in the midst of a lower middle class neighborhood, this three-acre compound is a treasure trove of idiosyncratic architecture, religious iconography, and plain old funk.

Until 1976, the Rev. Howard Finster made his living as a Baptist preacher and bicycle repairman. But one spring day he had the first of several visions that changed his life forever. On that day, while fixing a bicycle, he glanced at his thumb, covered at the time with enamel paint, and saw a small, animate human face. The face spoke to him, saying, "Paint sacred art." Howard replied, "I can't!" The little face boomed back: "How do you know? How do you know? How do you know?!"

In desperation, Finster, using a one-dollar bill as a model, painted his first work, a portrait of George Washington. Soon after, Finster began to work nonstop. He painted on cars and cast-off tin, Nyquil bottles and paint lids, Coca-Cola bottles and coffin lids. Over time he began constructing a garden of sorts in his backyard, a jumble of towers made from bicycle parts and a four-story chapel made of scrap lumber. Concrete walkways embedded with shards of brightly colored glass criss-crossed the grounds. All, says Howard, was done for the greater glory of God.

Soon the press came calling. The Sunday *New York Times Magazine* called it "a garden of art that beats anything this side of Eden." Pop artist Keith Haring called it "a Disneyland of Art."

By the 1980s Finster was painting album covers for rock groups like the Talking Heads and REM, and advertisements for Absolut vodka. Asked why he would paint an album cover for a rock band, Finster replied, "I had 26 million verses go out and reach the world. That's more than I ever reached in the 45 years I was pastoring. The rock 'n' rollers are my missionaries."

*Paradise Gardens.*

RAILS.
FOR ACCIDENTS.
GES INSPIRE YOU
THROUGH THE
S BUILT BY THE
RD FINSTER.
S IS A REGISTERED
RPORATION.

*Howard Finster preaches/performs at Paradise Gardens on Sunday afternoons.*

Today, the septuagenarian still receives guests at Paradise Gardens on Sundays from 2 to 5 P.M., when he holds a ceremony that is equal parts religious service, art show, and gospel sing-along. The gardens, however, have seen better days. In 1996, many of Finster's better outdoor pieces were moved to the High Museum in Atlanta. Yet an hour-long stroll about the gardens still offers many an unexpected delight, like a six-foot-long high-top sneaker made of concrete and emblazoned with the words "Blessed are the feet of those who spread the gospel of peace," or a mirror-covered tree house perched in the pines.

At the entrance to the gardens, Finster's daughter Beverly now operates a gallery, selling art made by Howard and his many relatives as well as CDs of Howard preaching and singing. The ultimate experience is reserved for those who book a night's stay at the **Paradise Suite,** located in a cabin on the property. The floor is linoleum. And the furniture is faux maple. But for those who are fans of Howard Finster, this is the best room to rent in the region. Decorated with the work of Finster and his friends, admirers, and relatives, the suite is comfortable if not tasteful. *Located three miles north of Summerville on Highway 27; 706-857-2926.*

For local barbecue, drive to nearby **Summerville** and stop by **Armstrong's Barbecue**. Open since 1965, this white-tile building proffers a fine sliced barbecue sandwich as well as chili and burgers made from fresh ground chuck. Prices couldn't be more reasonable. *10480 North Commerce Street; 706-857-9900.*

## ■ COHUTTA MOUNTAINS

An alternate approach to the mountains of northwest Georgia can be made by way of I-575; at the terminus of this interstate spur, just 45 miles north of Atlanta, urban sprawl gives way to quaint, quiet small-town life, marble quarry country, and, finally, the mountains of Appalachia. Less traveled than mountainous regions to the east, the surrounding countryside as viewed from Highway 5 rewards travelers with glimpses of towering forests and numerous geological curiosities.

### ◆ BALL GROUND

Though Tate and Jasper are better known for their marble quarries, the little village of Ball Ground, located just an hour or so north of Atlanta, is a worthy detour for any rock hound: arrayed along the main drag, Gilmer Ferry Road, are eight brick storefronts, once home to hardware stores, grocery stores, and the like, and now given over to the display of rocks and minerals.

From the street, the **Rock Shop,** as the complex is called, doesn't look like much: some of the front windows are cracked, the sidewalk is a jumble of marble shards and boulders, and the whole of the block seems shrouded in a thick blanket of dust. But upon closer inspection, you come to see that the dirty display windows frame a collection of geodes, crystals, fossils, and assorted geologic whatnot worthy of a museum. Never mind that the displays are dotted with vaguely Chinese statuary and gaudy necklaces that hang from the ceiling like stalactites. If you can catch the proprietor on premises, step inside; if no one is home, window shopping will have to do.

**Two Brothers' Barbecue** has been open since 1974. This roadside white frame building has a couple of benches out front for those who like to lounge a bit after stuffing themselves with great, smoked pork and stew. The interior is festooned with old farm equipment. *1695 Old Canton Road; 770-735-2900.*

*Dogwood blooms in spring in Georgia's forests.*

◆ TATE AND JASPER *map page 49, E-3*

Just north of Ball Ground is Tate, the undisputed epicenter of the state's marble industry and home to the Georgia Marble Company. The company's founder, Col. Sam Tate, was an inveterate promoter of all things marble, working to ensure that Georgia marble was used in the building of the Lincoln Memorial in Washington, D.C., as well as in more plebeian projects like the local elementary school, a white marble wonder on Highway 53 just a half-mile or so outside the town.

On the same road is the pink marble palace Tate built in 1923, now doing business as a bed-and-breakfast inn. Known appropriately as the **Tate House,** it was built in 1925 and has five suites within the main building and a clutch of log cabins out back, each equipped with a fireplace and hot tub. *61 Marble Mansion Lane, Highway 53; 770-735-3122.*

Just down the hill from the mansion, the smokestacks of the **Georgia Marble Company** loom, spewing marble dust high in the air.

Highway 53 continues north to **Jasper.** The residents here have made studio space available to the **Finnish artist, Eino,** and he now displays his work around town.

Jasper is also home to the **Woodbridge Inn and Lodge** which from its inception in the middle years of the 19th century through the early years of the 20th century, was a railroad hotel. Now the original hotel is a frumpy but charming restaurant serving mountain trout and meatballs with horseradish sauce are and, surprizingly, no fried okra, a local staple. There's a lodge out back with 12 modern rooms, including the Eagle's Nest, with a second-story loft accessible by a spiral staircase. *44 Chambers Street, Jasper; 706-692-6072.*

◆ COOSAWATTEE RIVER AREA *map page 49, E-2*

Further north, route 5 draws near the Coosawattee River and the town of **Ellijay.** This is Gilmer County, the "Apple Capital" of Georgia. The nearby (and now dammed) Coosawattee River was the setting of James Dickey's horrifying novel *Deliverance.* Dickey took whitewater canoeing trips along the river in the early '70s while he was working for the Army Corps of Engineers. Though much of the novel (and the popular film that followed) dwells upon what befalls a group of suburbanites in the wilds of Appalachia, Dickey communicates a real love for the natural splendor of this corner of the state, as evidenced by this passage from early in the novel:

*There* was another bend up ahead, and the river seemed to strain to get there, and we with it. Around the turn it came into view, and broadened in the white. Everywhere we were going was filled with spring bubblings, with lively rufflings, not dangerous-looking but sprightly and vivid. There was not the sensation of the water's raging, but rather that of its alertness and resourcefulness as it split apart at rocks, frothed lightly, corkscrewed, fluted, fell, recovered, jostled into helmet-shapes over smothered stones, and ran out of sight down long garden-staircase steps around another turn.

Today, the biggest attraction around these parts is a roadside barbecue joint called **Colonel Poole's Bar-B-Q**, locally referred to as the "Taj Ma Hog." From humble origins, this little stand has grown to be one of the most visited 'cue spots in the state. And though the barbecue and Brunswick stew are indeed quite good, Poole's popularity is best attributed to the Colonel's flair for showmanship. Rising high on a raw red-clay hill behind the restaurant is the "Pig Hill of Fame," covered with thousands of plywood pigs, emblazoned with the names of patrons who paid $5 for the privilege to be so honored. Out front sits the Colonel's Pigmobile, a

*Colonel Poole's Bar-B-Q is hard to miss.*

retrofitted station wagon festooned with bright-red pig ears. It's a good laugh and—according to the Colonel—good business. Look for Colonel Poole's just south of Ellijay on Highway 515—as if you could miss it. *706-635-4100.*

The Democratic flip-side to Poole's is **The Pink Pig** in Cherry Log. This joint turns out better 'cue and, thanks to its more remote location, it isn't swamped by tourists. That said, the feel of this lunch and (early) dinner place is a bit drab compared to the circus atmosphere at Poole's. *824 Cherry Log Road; 706-276-3311.*

◆ FORT MOUNTAIN STATE PARK *map page 49, D-2*

West of Ellijay by way of Highway 52—perhaps the most beautiful stretch of highway in northwestern Georgia—is Fort Mountain State Park, a 3,200-acre wilderness refuge named for an 855-foot-long rock wall believed to have been built perhaps 4,000 years ago. Explanations for the wall's existence vary: some people believe it was used as a defensive barrier by Native Americans, while others opt for a more fantastic explanation, asserting that the wall was constructed by a Welsh prince whose travels predated those of Hernando de Soto. Either way, the wall is a marvel, zigzagging across the face of Fort Mountain. A stone observation tower affords a fine view of this edifice. *Information: 706-695-2621.*

Those wishing to explore the wilderness from the state park can stay at **Fort Mountain State Park Cottages,** where fifteen simple cottages ring the park. Pioneer trails lead off from the cottages into the woods, through thickets of blueberries and along meandering streams. *Reservations: 800-864-7275.*

Less rustic is the **Cohutta Lodge,** perched atop a hill with a commanding view of the surrounding countryside. This '70s–era lodge is clean and comfortable if a bit institutional in feel, but there's a heated pool as well as tennis courts and a mini-golf course. *500 Cochise Trail; 706-695-9601.*

◆ COHUTTA WILDERNESS *map page 49, D-1*

The Cohuttas are drier and more open than the Blue Ridge Mountains to the east. Hikers in the **Cohutta Wilderness Area** will find over 90 miles of trails, traversing both forest and wide-open vistas. Access points to this vast wilderness area are in the surrounding towns of Cisco, Crandall, Eton, Blue Ridge, and Ellijay.

At lovely Lake Conasauga, with its backdrop of Grassy Mountain, there is much wildlife to be seen. The 1.7-mile Songbird Trail crosses an area set aside to preserve habitat. Come here to see scarlet tanagers, red crossbills, and sandhill cranes, all visible at times from an observation platform. *To get to Lake Conasauga and the Songbird Trail, follow U.S. Highway 411 from Chatsworth north to Eton. Turn at the Lake Conasauga sign and continue to follow signs to the lake.*

■ BLUE RIDGE  *map page 49, E-1*

Northeast of Ellijay by way of Highway 515 is the little hamlet of Blue Ridge, a great jumping-off point for a tour of the Blue Ridge Mountains to the east or the Cohutta Mountains to the west. Friday through Monday, the **Blue Ridge Scenic Railway** makes a 26-mile round trip along the Toccoa River to McCaysville and back. *Information: 706-632-9833.*

With the exception of the rail depot, the town's commercial activity seems to focus on the sale of knickknacks and antiques.

To continue east along Highway 76, see "NORTHEAST GEORGIA," page 88.

*The Richard Russell Scenic Highway winds through northern Georgia.*

# N O R T H E A S T

■ HIGHLIGHTS

■ TRAVEL BASICS

The Blue Ridge Mountains themselves are the main attraction here in Appalachian Georgia. Rivers and waterfalls abound—some of the best whitewater rapids in the country are here—and the Chattahoochee National Forest covers most of the region. Former mill towns dot the mountains, and visitors can still pan for gold at Dahlonega. Numerous festivals highlight mountain music and crafts, yet except at these fairs, distinctive Appalachian folk culture can be hard for the outsider to come by.

**Getting Around:** Give yourself time to wander the back roads and soak up the quiet; inhale the scent of oak trees and sweet mountain laurel; listen to water running in the creeks. Opportunities abound for river trips and hiking; Springer Mountain has the southern trailhead of the Appalachian Trail, which winds its way through the region.

**Climate:** Cool and wet winters with snow above 3,000 feet in the mountains. Temperatures usually range from 20 degrees F to the mid-40s. Spring peaks in late April. Mild summers with highs in the mid-80s and frequent thunderstorms. Heavy rain falls year-round in the far northeast corner of the region. Fall colors peak in October.

**Food & Lodging:** Northeast Georgia is well equipped for tourists. Inns and clusters of cabins dot the mountains, and a passel of barbecue joints line the roads. Lodging is available at many state parks. To avoid country-cute tourist haunts, look for a mixture of pickup trucks and late-model sedans in restaurant parking lots, and steer clear of inns that spell country with a "K."

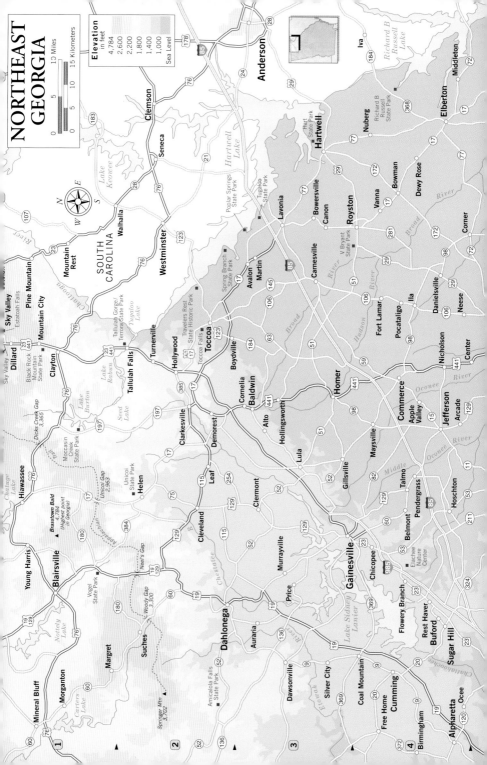

## ■ TOPOGRAPHY AND LANDSCAPE

The mountains of northeast Georgia are the tail end of the Blue Ridge Range, which extends north to Pennsylvania and is part of the Appalachian Mountains. Though the exurbs of Atlanta loom but an hour south, northeast Georgia feels far removed from city life. Instead, there are the broad valleys and timber-lined ridges of the foothills, followed by the increasingly knobby, increasingly high peaks (almost 5,000 feet) of Appalachia, where the roads wend their circuitous way along wooded slopes, bordered in the spring by a profusion of dove-white laurel blossoms, and in the fall by a blanket of leaves and a kaleidoscope of colors.

Northeast Georgia's Springer Mountain marks the southern end of the Appalachian Trail, a 2,100-mile hiker's path that extends through 14 states and seven national parks, ending at Mount Katahdin in Maine. Writing of the allure of the "AT," the initials by which hikers know the trail, Bill Bryson, author of *A Walk in the Woods,* describes it as wandering "through plump, comely hills whose very names—Blue Ridge, Smokies, Cumberlands, Green Mountains, White Mountains—seem an invitation to amble." Who could but pronounce the words, Bryson asks, "and not feel an urge, as the naturalist John Muir once put it, to 'throw a loaf of bread and a pound of tea in an old sack and jump over the back fence'?"

## ■ BACKWOODS HISTORY ·

In this comparatively remote corner of the state, economic and social isolation are less a choice than a physical reality. A writer at the turn of the 19th century referred to the people of Appalachia as "our contemporary ancestors." Perhaps he was on to something. Following old-time ways, in their sparsely populated hills and hollers, the hardy Scotch-Irish who came here in the early 19th century were rugged and unyielding.

When the Civil War erupted, pitting those who worked their land with slaves against the North, many of the inhabitants of Appalachia turned their back on both sides. It was not a war in which they had a stake. Instead, as the saying goes, they took to the hills, retreating farther into the mountains and contining to live as subsistence farmers, planting corn and beans for their families' larders. Some of that corn was converted into liquid, in the form of moonshine, while the majority was served up as hoecakes and hominy, corn pudding, and succotash. They lived in chinked log cabins, later improved with tin roofs; and well into the 20th century, they made their own clothes, musical instruments, and furniture (as reflected in the well-known *Foxfire* books).

It was not until the early years of the 20th century that the region began to feel the influence of the Industrial Revolution, as mills harnessed mountain streams and rural electrification programs pushed their way through the hills. Today, much of Appalachian Georgia teeters on the brink of modernity. Clapboard and brick homes now outnumber rough-hewn log cabins, and dirt roads are being paved. And yet the mountains still act as a buffer—separating hill folk from flatlanders, old-time ways from the insistent invasions of modernity. Things are slowly changing. A local man now wears the same mesh gimme cap as his cousin in Atlanta, and his wife shops at Wal-Mart. People watch television at night rather than sitting outside on their porches playing banjos, and most work days in small local industries rather than hoeing hilly cornfields. Yet a distinctive dialect, a culture of self-reliance, and a healthy suspicion of outsiders remain.

North of Atlanta, the roadways narrow and the sky opens up—loosed from the skyscrapers that boxed it in and the almost omnipresent shroud of Atlanta smog. Soon the artifacts of a unique culture begin to appear along the road. Near the spot where Interstate 985 intersects with the Old Cornelia Highway there stands a monstrous concrete bunny emblazoned with the slogan, "**Rabbittown**—A Hoppin' Little Place."

A hundred yards east, in the crook of an especially crooked turn of that old crooked road sits the home of R. A. Miller: "the fella down the road what makes them whirligigs," as the locals say. Nowadays, he's also known as an artist, and his works fetch hefty prices in galleries across the nation. From the road you can see the "whirligigs" high on a bluff, glinting in the afternoon sun. His creations spin: vibrant red and blue scraps of tin tacked to old bicycle wheels and perched atop spindly sticks; five-foot tin cutouts of blood-red devils, pitchforks in hand; three-foot renderings of Elvis, a guitar at his side.

This odd menagerie—standing just five miles down the road from Gainesville, the largest city in the region—is a testament to the ingenuity and idiosyncrasy that defines the people of northeast Georgia.

*(following pages) Spring in the Appalachians, as seen from the
Richard Russell Scenic Highway.*

NORTHEAST

NORTHEAST

■ GAINESVILLE  *map page 75, B-3*

Gainesville retains much of the feel of a county seat of yesteryear, with its redbrick business district and its tree-lined avenues bordered by columned homes. But this town on the southern fringe of Appalachian Georgia, was once a mill town. Here hosiery and denim were pieced and fitted, wood for furniture cut and lathed. For the people of the mountains, Gainesville also served as a market town, a center of commerce where eggs and corn, beans and buttermilk, might be bartered for flour and sugar or bolts of cloth. Today, the city remains a center of commerce, though the mills have been replaced by a new industry: poultry processing. Low-slung and bunker-like in appearance, poultry coops are everywhere, and the trucks that transport the chickens clog the roadways, trailing a cloud of downy feathers.

Thousands of workers have made their way up from Mexico in search of jobs, transforming many of the local cafes from joints where you get a platter of grits and eggs to taco stands where lengua and horchata are lunchtime offerings. Look for **Taqueria Los Rayos,** where the tacos al pastor are tasty and you can wash your meal down with a glass of horchata, a sweet rice-water drink *(323 Washington Street; 770-297-0905),* or **Two Dog Cafe,** for chicken and portabello mushroom quesadillas and an excellent the mojo-marinated pork sandwich. The cheerful room is decorated with colorful local art. *109 Bradford Street; 770-287-8384.*

◆ GAINSVILLE DIVERSIONS

**Brenau College**
On the city's northeastern edge, wedged between Brenau Avenue and Green Street, is the campus of Brenau College. Founded in 1879 as the Georgia Baptist Seminary, this liberal arts college for women boasts a museum that has featured shows by pop artist Jasper Johns.

**Georgia Mountains History Museum**
Nearby the college is a "grandma's attic" sort of museum where an eclectic collection of local ephemera includes a pie safe from which Union general Sherman presumably ate pies when he was billeted on a nearby farm. No record remains of the flavor,

though apple is a good bet, owing to the prevalence of apple trees in these parts. *311 Green Street; 770-536-0889.*

**Dunlap House**
Built in 1910, this nine-room B&B has a large, welcoming front porch shaded by a tasteful green-and-white awning. Renovated in 1985, the inn has all the modern conveniences and serves a full breakfast every morning. *635 Green Street; 770-536-0200.*

**Rudolph's on Green Street**
The finest dining room in these parts. Set in a handsome Tudor home, this continental restaurant features scallops en papillote

and beef filet in a béarnaise sauce, among other entrees. Children swoon over the deep-fried ice cream for dessert. *700 Green Street; 770-534-2226.*

**Lantern Inn**

In nearby Cumming on Brown Bridge Road, you'll find cooking and acting talent at the Lantern Inn. It's home to Mike Jones, a fry cook who does decent work with catfish, but whose real claim to fame—and the real reason to seek out this restaurant—is that, between batches of fish, he drops his apron, dons a cape, and slips on a pair of gaudy sunglasses, reappearing in full Elvisian garb. Between Mike's sets of "Hound Dog" and "Teddy Bear," his sister docs her own Patsy Cline act. *770-887-3080.*

**Luna's**

Dominican Republic native Juan Luna is the capable chef at the helm of this restaurant smack dab in the middle of downtown. The look is subdued and tasteful, almost hip. Try the paella or an innovative dish like a macadamia nut–crusted snapper. *200 Main; 770-531-0848.*

■ LAKE SIDNEY LANIER

Sprawling west and south of Gainesville is Lake Sidney Lanier, a man-made, 38,000-acre recreational lake created in the 1950s when the Chattahoochee River was damned for hydroelectric power. Today, the lake is favored by landlocked Atlantans who treat it like a third coast, flocking north on weekends to waterski and fish, or maybe just to tool around the lake on a party barge, dipping a fishing pole in the waters once in a while but for the most part just soaking up the sunshine. With more than 15 million annual visitors, Lake Lanier is the most visited Corps of Engineers lake in the country. Accordingly, during the prime spring and summer months, the waters can be choked with boaters. But even the roar of an outboard motor can't spoil the view afforded to canoeists and kayakers who paddle to the more isolated coves in search of a tranquil vantage point from which to take in the mountains rising just to the north.

■ DAHLONEGA  *map page 75, B-2*

Travel 20 miles northwest of Gainesville by way of Highway 60 and you are in Dahlonega, epicenter of America's first gold rush. According to local folklore, Benjamin Parks first discovered a chunk of gold, similar to "the yellow of an egg," while hunting deer in 1828. When word of his discovery began to circulate, he recounted that it "seemed within a few days, as if the whole world must have heard it; for men came from every state I ever heard of. They came afoot, on horseback, and in wagons, acting more like crazy men than anything else."

NORTHEAST

Soon the little town of Auraria, six miles south of present-day Dahlonega, was overrun with prospectors. By 1836 Dahlonega had won out over Auraria as the county seat, and a fine brick courthouse stood at the center of town.

### ◆ DAHLONEGA GOLD SIGHTS AND OTHER RICHES

Today, weekenders rather than prospectors throng the sidewalks during the fall and spring, shopping for antiques and visiting the gold mining exhibits. At two old mine sites on the outskirts of town you can pan for gold with a pie-tin–shaped plate, stooping and scooping gravel from the river bed.

**Dahlonega Gold Museum**

The old courthouse is now a museum with displays of gold pans for sifting gold dust, and coins from the days when Dahlonega was the site of one of the nation's first branch mints. By the time the mint closed in 1861, more than $6 million in gold coins had been minted here. *1 Public Square; 706-864-2257.*

**Jack's Cafe**

Across from the courthouse is the old Bank of Dahlonega, now a charming breakfast and lunch spot with great egg salad sandwiches, burgers, and salads. The place is a little history museum in itself, with photos and lithographs of historic Dahlonega and books by the proprietess's mother, historian Anne Amerson. *706-864-9169.*

*(above) A gold nugget panned near Dahlonega, epicenter of America's first gold rush.*
*(opposite) Gold-mining scenes at Dahlonega from a* Harper's Weekly *issue, circa 1870.*
*(Georgia Department of Archives & History)*

PANNING

STORE-HOUSE

THE CUT

STAMP MILL SHOWING WHERE GOLD PASSES OVER COPPER PLATES

### Crisson Gold Mine

This early strip mine has a still-functioning stamp mill. It crushes quartz into sand so that trace elements of gold can be spotted more easily. *Highway 19 at Cavender Creek Road; 706-864-6363.*

### Consolidated Gold Mine

This underground mine offers tours and gold panning. *185 Consolidated Gold Mine Road; 706-864-8473.*

### The Smith House

Just off the town square is the Smith House, a Victorian farmhouse with a shady front porch. The proprietors like to boast that it sits atop a rich vein of gold. Rooms upstairs are comfortable if not opulent. The Smith House has also been open as a boarding house since 1922, and the basement dining room still serves fried chicken, country ham, pole beans, fried okra, sweet potatoes, and the like from family-style platters passed from patron to patron. *84 South Chestatee Street; 706-867-7000.*

### Worley Homestead Inn

This 1845 farmhouse with a two-story front porch was renovated in 1984 by a

*Dockery Lake, just north of Dahlonega, lies near the southern end of the Appalachian Trail.*

descendant of the original owner, Capt. William Worley of the Confederate Army. Seven rooms are available, three of which have working fireplaces. A big country breakfast is served. *168 Main Street West; 706-864-7002 or 800-348-8094.*

**Blueberry Inn and Gardens**
Ten minutes north of town, this 1920s-style farmhouse offers a wonderful perch from which to survey the surrounding mountains. There are 12 rooms, each with private bath. And, yes, blueberries grow wild on the property and are yours for the picking. *400 Blueberry Hill; 706-219-4024.*

**Chestatee River**
The nearby Chestatee River is popular for **river trips** in this area. Try Appalachian Outfitters in Dahlonega; *706-864-7117.*

**Rick's Caricature Cafe**
This two-story, tin-roofed Victorian house is packed to the gills with folk art. The food ain't bad either. Offerings range from the time-honored (hot wings) to the innovative (a smoked chicken glazed with a delicious house Worchestershire sauce). *47 South Park Street; 706-219-2862.*

■ AMICALOLA FALLS STATE PARK *map page 75, A-2*

Twenty miles west of Dahlonega is Amicalola Falls State Park, a pristine 1,200-acre park highlighted by a dramatic 729-foot waterfall, four times as tall as famed Niagara Falls. For those intrepid few considering a journey up the **Appalachian Trail** (AT), this is the trailhead for the eight-plus-mile AT approach trail. A day's hike north is Springer Mountain, point of departure for the 2,100-mile trek to Maine.

The forest here is hardwood and wildflowers are abundant in spring. Beautiful, three-quarter-mile **Amicalola Falls Trail**, which begins at the parking lot at the end of the park road, climbs past cascading waterfalls to an observation deck. *Park information: 706-265-4703.*

The modern and airy **park lodge** is a pleasant place to stay. Some of its cabins are hidden away in the woods, others are set at the base of the falls. Bountiful buffets are served in a glass-walled dining room looking out over the trees atop the mountains. Look for Southern staples like grits and eggs at breakfast, and fried chicken and yams for lunch and dinner. *706-265-8888 or 800-864-7275.*

The park also offers a new, hike-in only lodge called the **Len Foote Hike Inn.** The inn is accessible only by foot over a moderate five-mile trail which originates at the top of the falls. *770-389-7275 or 800-864-7275.*

■ BLOOD MOUNTAIN AREA *map page 75, B-2*

Those who prefer burning fossil fuel to burning glucose should head north of Dahlonega on Highway 19, a serpentine two-lane switchback that leads up and around Blood Mountain—home in Cherokee mythology of the Nunnehi, spirit people known to look after wayward hunters and wanderers. At **Neel's Gap** is the Walasi-Yi Center, a Civilian Conservation Corps–era building of flagstone, now given over to hiker support and sale of camping gear. One-quarter of a mile north along the highway is a spur trail named in honor of Byron Herbert "Hub" Reece, Georgia's late lamented bard of the mountains.

■ VOGEL STATE PARK *map page 75, B-1*

Farther north still on Highway 19, you come upon Vogel State Park. Nestled in a valley with Lake Trahlyta at its center, this is one of Georgia's most scenic—and by extension most visited—state parks. In summer the place can be overrun with campers and their vehicles, but the park is nevertheless a great base from which to explore any number of hiking trails. In addition to the nearly 20 miles of trails within the park (including an easy, mile-long trail that loops the lake before leading off to a waterfall), there are a number of more strenuous hikes, including a nearly four-mile loop known as the Bear Hair Trail, that winds its way through thick, wet forest.

Vogel State Park has nearly 40 cottages for rent, the nicest being the lakeside flagstone and timber ones constructed by the Works Progress Administration in the '30s. *Highway 19 south of Blairsville. Reservations: 800-864-7275.*

Each August, the park hosts **Old Timers Day,** a festival of mountain music and handicrafts; *706-745-2628.*

■ BLAIRSVILLE *map page 75, B-1*

As Highway 19 winds through the Chattahoochee National Forest and heads (more or less) north toward the North Carolina border, the road is lined with signs advertising sorghum—a grassy crop that yields a sticky fluid similar to molasses. Soon you are in the hamlet of Blairsville, home each October to a **Sorghum Festival** that pits brother against brother, neighbor against neighbor, in biscuit-eating and syrup-sopping contests. *Festival information: 877-745-5789 or 706-745-5789.*

*Trahlyta Falls in Vogel State Park.*

If you come for the festival and want to stay nearby, try the **Blood Mountain Cabins**. They are hard by the roadside but somehow still remote in feel—perched high up on the side of the mountain as they are. *Located 14 miles south of Blairsville on Highway 19; 706-745-9454.*

**Southern Country Inn** is an English-style inn with unparalleled views of the surrounding mountains. Trails lead from the inn's back door into the surrounding countryside. *2592 Collins Lane; 706-379-1603 or 800-297-1603.*

## ■ BRASSTOWN BALD AREA RAMBLES   *map page 75, B-1*

Across the top of the state, Highway 76 cuts a four-lane swath eastward through beautiful rolling countryside framed by mountain peaks. Along the way it passes the bucolic little burg of **Young Harris,** hometown of former Georgia governor Zell Miller. Each summer the town hosts *The Reach of Song*—a folk play that evokes old ways of life in Georgia through storytelling and song.

Set amid a 500-acre forest is the **Brasstown Valley Resort**, a beautiful lodge with a soaring central hall lit by an antler chandelier. Rooms are filled with "nouveau mountain" furnishings and folk art. *6321 US-76; 706-379-9900.*

For the real thing in Georgia country food—breakfasts of hand-patted sausage, thick creamy grits, and ethereally light biscuits—drop by **Mary Ann's Country Kitchen,** on US 76, in the center of town. The setting is pure '50s, and plate lunch specials are offered at noontime. *706-379-2136.*

### ◆ BRASSTOWN BALD

One might expect Georgia's highest peak (at 4,784 feet) to be a treacherous, craggy mountain inhospitable to climbers, much less picnickers. Yet Brasstown Bald (properly called Mount Enotah), like many other so-called peaks in Georgia, is, in essence, a pasture perched atop a mountain. The Blue Ridge Range has many such "balds," and botanists have numerous theories but no definitive explanation for what has caused them.

Brasstown Bald rewards hikers who have traversed the steep half-mile trail from the parking lot with a sweeping view of four states, though the real treat may well be the mountain flora along the trail, including lush, pink rhododendron bushes that sometimes bloom late into the summer. *Located 10 miles southwest of Hiawassee by way of a spur road that cuts off Highway 180.*

*Snow-covered mountains viewed from Brasstown Bald.*

◆ CHATUGE LAKE  *map page 75, B-1*

Onward, the highway cuts across Chatuge Lake, a mountain-swaddled body of water that seems permanently shrouded in mist. Along the road, whitewashed gourds, now serving as birdhouses for tiny purple martins, stand like ghostly specters in the backyards of modest mountain homes, while billboards beckon the newly arrived—and the newly wealthy—to build luxurious log cabins in the subdivisions that are being carved deep into the woods.

Perched on the shore of Chatuge Lake is the crossroads town of **Hiawassee,** a popular stop with through travelers. For most of the year it is quiet enough to warrant the description sleepy. But each August the hills come alive when the **Georgia Mountain Fair** opens, a celebration of mountain music and traditional mountain crafts like split-oak basket weaving and pottery making. Though there is a good bit of hokum to be had, and the crowds can be daunting, a day's amble about the fairgrounds is, in effect, a crash course in mountain culture. *Fair information: 706-896-4191.*

## MOUNTAIN MUSIC

Contrary to what some may contend, the music of Appalachia is not solely a vestige of Elizabethan-era ballads, transported to these shores by Scotch-Irish settlers and performed in much the same style as was done in the motherland. Instead, much of what we know as mountain music owes its origins to a myriad of influences, ranging from the introduction of an African instrument, the banjo, to the innovations of a singularly talented individual, the late Bill Monroe, inventor of bluegrass music. That said, many of the ballads still plucked by mountain folks have at least a tenuous connection to Great Britain, especially graphically recounted murder ballads like "Knoxville Girl."

Aside from festival events, it can be difficult to find a place to hear mountain music in a setting that comes close to seeming authentic. There are a number of Georgia performers whose work is worth listening to on a record or CD. Among the early Hillbilly bands to make their mark were the Georgia Wildcats, Lowe Stoke's Georgia Potlikkers, and Gid Tanner and the Skillet Lickers. Of these, the most famous group was the latter. In 1924 the Skillet Lickers became the first Hillbilly band to cut an album for Columbia Records. Songs like "Boil the Cabbage Down," still ring out loud, true, and honest.

*Mountain musicians in Dillard, Georgia, playing banjo and guitar.*

*Queen Anne's lace fills a meadow in Sky Valley.*

If you come for the fair, you'll probably want barbecue. The best to be had in the area is at **The Ptiz**. Run by the Dorta family, it also serves thick Brunswick stew, and Cuban sandwiches juicy with mojo sauce. You won't find better Cuban food in the state. *595 North Main Street; 706-896-6232.*

Chatuge Lake has a marina where jet skis and powerboats are for rent adjacent to the modern **Fieldstone Inn**. Some rooms have private balconies and overlooking the lake. It's just west of the bridge. *3499 US-76; 706-896-2262.*

**Town Creek Cottages** are perched on a hillside overlooking a stream. From the porches are views of the mountain scenery. *4863 Seabolt Road; 706-745-8891.*

### ■ LAKES BURTON AND RABUN   *map page 75, C-1 and D-1*

East of Hiawassee on Highway 76 lap the waters of Lake Burton, one of many lakes created in the early years of the 20th century by the Georgia Power Company. In a program that would later serve as a model for the Tennessee Valley Authority's rural electrification efforts, the company dammed the Tallulah River in stair-step

*Fly-fishing on Cooper Creek in northeast Georgia.*

## JAMES DICKEY'S *DELIVERANCE*

"*D*o you know where you're going?" she said.

"Not exactly. Lewis does. Somewhere up in the northeast part of the state, where he's been fishing. If everything goes off OK, we ought to be back late Sunday."

"Why wouldn't it go off OK?"

"It will, but you can't predict. Listen, if I thought there was anything dangerous about it, I wouldn't go...."

*Thus begins* Deliverance, *James Dickey's 1970 horror novel about Georgian Appalachia, in which the darkest of the stereotypes foisted upon the people of Appalachia fuel the plot:*

*A*n old man with a straw hat and work shirt appeared at Lewis' [car] window, talking in. He looked like a hillbilly in some badly cast movie, a character actor too much in character to be believed. I wondered where the excitement was that intrigued Lewis so much; everything in Oree was sleepy and hookwormy and ugly, and most of all, inconsequential. Nobody worth a damn could ever come from such a place.

*As it unfolds, Dickey's drama documents what befalls four suburban Atlantans on a whitewater canoe trip down a river that everyone in these parts recognized as the Chattooga, but that Dickey called the Cahulawasee. Over the course of a weekend, the Atlantans are beset by a cast of depraved Appalachian characters, defined by their physical deformities and violence:*

*E*very family I've ever met up here has at least one relative in the penitentiary. Some of them are in for making liquor or running it, but most of them are in for murder. They don't think a whole lot about killing people up here.

*After Dickey's novel became a bestseller and was made into an equally horrific movie, it seemed the whole of the United States became aware of Appalachian Georgia and believed it was peopled by maniacs. Some folks in northern Georgia, where Dickey once worked for the Army Corps of Engineers, still haven't forgiven him.*

fashion, creating a string of lakes including Burton and nearby Lake Rabun. Today, the lakes look as though they have been a part of the landscape for eons.

Both lakes are popular with Atlantans, who treat them as weekend getaways. Rabun is the tonier of the two, a Catskill-like enclave of cathedral-ceilinged lodges and sleek boat. Burton, to the northeast, is more the fisherman's favorite. Both are home to unique mountain inns, where accommodations harken back to simpler days and the food (cornmeal-crusted catfish and bacon-wrapped trout are favorites) is never frou-frou.

### Lake Rabun Hotel

This classic hotel was built in 1922. In its lobby, a massive stone fireplace gives a cozy glow and rooms are decorated with locally made twig furniture. There are fresh-baked muffins and coffeecake in the morning. *Lake Rabun Road; 706-782-4946.*

### LaPadre's

Set right on the lake is a sprawling green timber structure built in 1916 to house workers who were in the area building hydroelectric dams. Today, LaPadre's is both a first-class country-cooking restaurant famed for its fried chicken and country ham with red-eye gravy, and a dreamy fish camp with cabins and cottages. *Highway 197; 706-947-3312.*

### Burton Woods

Tucked away a half mile from the lake in a remote, heavily wooded area, **Burton Woods** cabins seem a far remove from civilization. With their stone fireplaces, they are rustic to say the least. But in a day of chain hotels, their quaint charm is refreshing. *155 Fox Valley Road; 706-754-7442.*

## ■ BLACK ROCK MOUNTAIN AREA  *map page 75, D-1*

East and north of the lakes is a wedge of Appalachian Georgia sandwiched between the Chattooga River and the North Carolina border. Here you will find **Black Rock Mountain State Park,** the highest park in the state of Georgia. There are 10 simple cottages for let at the park, but make reservations early as they are among the most sought-after cabins in the mountains. *Highway 411; 800-864-7275.*

Also off Highway 441 is the oldest inn in Georgia in continuous operation. In business since 1896, the **York House** began as a two-room cabin. It is ringed by a wonderful veranda dotted with rocking chairs. *York House Road; 706-746-2068.*

**Sky Valley,** Georgia's only ski resort, is nearby. This is where many Georgians try their luck at skiing. The slopes are often ice-slicked rather than powder-packed, and not a few first-timers can be seen making their way down the mountain on their backsides rather than on their skis. *706-746-5302.*

*Sunset view from the eastern continental divide at Black Rock Mountain State Park.*

◆ FOXFIRE

Perhaps the most influential educational institution in the mountains of northeast Georgia is headquartered in the shadow of Black Rock Mountain, along busy Highway 441 in Mountain City. Foxfire—established as a literary magazine of the same name in the early 1970s by local teacher Eliot Wigginton and his students— has become an educational phenomenon of sorts, spurring a series of best-selling books, a television movie, and a new wave of interest in the ways and means of Appalachia.

Originally conceived by Wigginton as a device to motivate his high school students, the Foxfire project encouraged schoolchildren to interview their elders about such crafts as log-home construction, hominy making, and the weaving of white-oak chair bottoms. Under Wigginton's direction, the interviews were transcribed and the results published for an increasingly attentive audience. Soon, Foxfire became an educational institution of its own, sponsoring seminars throughout the country where students and elders worked together, sharing Appalachian knowledge and lore with outlanders.

Among the Foxfire Center's recent publications is the *Foxfire Book of Appalachian Cookery*, wherein aged local "Granny" Gibson recounts the process by which hard kernels of dried corn are made into hominy, the big brother to fine-ground grits:

> People used to tie the ashes and corn in a sack and boil them a pretty long time in an old iron pot. The water going through the ashes makes lye. That's what makes the outer part of the corn scale off, and what you have left is hominy. You just wash it and wash it to get the lye out, and then you put it back in the pot with just pure water and cook it until it gets tender. Keep adding water to it because it just keeps swelling. Then you take it out, put some grease in it and fry it. It takes all day to make, but it was good.

Today, the facility houses a museum, a reconstructed Appalachian village, and a bookstore and gift shop. By special arrangement, you can arrange a tour of the entire facility. *706-746-5828.*

◆ DILLARD

Seven miles north of the intersection of Highways 76 and 441 is the burg of Dillard, founded in 1794 by Revolutionary War veteran John Dillard. Dillard's descendants now run a resort and classic country dining establishment called **The**

## PUTTING UP TOMATOES FOR WINTER

*Hillard Green was almost 80 when the first Foxfire book was published, in 1969. He lived by himself in the mountains near the North Carolina border, in a one-room cabin with a wood stove. He still grew his own food and got his water from a spring next to the cabin. The students who compiled the book were so moved by the time they spent interviewing and photographing him that they chose to close the book with his words. On the students' last visit, Hillard Green was canning tomatoes:*

People'll look at those pictures and say, "What is that crazy old man a'doin'?" You tell 'em I'm puttin' up 'maters for th'winter, that's what. People might laugh at such stuff as this, but I'll tell y', I'm not about t'let 'em rot. And when you've got old, you're not a'goin't'lay down and die just because you're old. Feller's got t'have somethin' t'do. Well, this is one of th' things I do, and I'm proud I can. Let 'em laugh. I'll be eatin' good this winter and laughin' back.

Everyone ought t'learn how to do such as this. One a'these days, times might get back hard again, and then what will they do? Nobody not knowin' how t'do nothin'. Might have t'live off th' land again, one day. We never had nothin' fer th' winter only what we put up. What we put up was what we had. Goin't'be a lot of hungry people someday.

Lotsa people don't even know how t'cook any more. They just go t'th' store and get it fixed already. These girls nowadays go off t'school and learn about everything but what's really important. Get home and still can't even cook a meal. If your woman can't cook whenever you get married, let me know and I'll come cook fer y'!

*About his life in the mountains, Hillard Green had this to say:*

[There's] nobody t'ask you where you're goin', when you'll be back, or where you've been. I do just as I please. Tomorrow? Who knows? I might put up 'maters again.

—Hillard Green, from *Foxfire*, 1969

**Dillard House.** An odd mixture of country farmhouse and glassed-roof solarium, the restaurant serves meals family style. Servers, in their rush to clear tables, raise a clatter—so much so that the din in the dining room can reach deafening levels — but the food satisfies. Among the best of the meats and vegetables to be piled on each table are rosy-hued country ham, gooey sweet-potato soufflé, fat green beans, and some of the tenderest, smokiest barbecue chicken you will ever taste. Tea, served in ersatz Mason jar mugs, is so sweet it'll cave in your teeth. Also on the grounds are a cluster of cabins and a lodge, where the rooms are plain but clean. From almost any vantage point, nearby Black Rock Mountain looms magisterial. *678 Franklin Street, off Highway 441; 706-746-5348.*

Across the valley from this flagstone-and-glass temple of country cooking, and perched on a grassy hill, are the redbrick Colonial-style buildings that are home to the **Rabun Gap–Nacoochee School.** Founded in 1900 as the Rabun Gap Industrial School by Andrew Jackson Ritchie (a Harvard alumnus and one of the area's first college graduates) the private academy was the first to introduce the Farm Family Plan of education, whereby entire families worked their way through a course of industrial and agricultural instruction. The school continues to serve mountain families.

Nearby, on Betty's Creek Road, is the **Hambidge Center**, an artists' retreat in operation since 1934. In addition to regular art shows and occasional concerts, the center hosts guided nature walks throughout the fall and spring. *706-746-5718.*

To the south, Highway 441 passes through **Clayton**, seat of government for Rabun County and the largest commercial center in the area. Hard by Old Highway 441, and serving the pinnacle of mountain cookery, you'll find **Green Shutters**. This is the real thing: Georgia local—the perfect, crisp little biscuits for breakfast and the fried chicken, mashed potatoes, and splendid peach cobbler for lunch. Open Friday through Sunday. *706-782-3342.*

Past Clayton, Highway 441 dips down through Tallulah Falls, connecting to a number of smaller roads that lead westward to Clarkesville, Cleveland, and Helen.

■ TALLULAH FALLS AND WEST  *map page 75, D-2*

Once the summer playground of Athens and Atlanta residents who took trains north in search of a respite from the heat, Tallulah Falls was, until the damming of the Tallulah River in 1913, site of one of the highest and most spectacular waterfalls in North America. And Tallulah Gorge, spanning more than three miles in length and plunging more than 600 feet, has long been a gawker's delight and a thrill seeker's challenge. (In 1970, tightrope artist Karl Wallenda crossed the gorge balanced on a thin wire cable, without the security of a net stretched beneath.) Today, few buildings remain from the end of the 19th century, save the old rail station, now operated as an artists' cooperative and stocked with local honey, hand-carved toys, and the like. Most visitors are white-water enthusiasts who have come to run the recently reopened river gorge.

*George Cooke's painting* Tallulah Falls, *circa 1840, depicts a view that no longer exists.*
*(Georgia Museum of Art, University of Georgia, gift of Mrs. Will Moss)*

◆ CLARKESVILLE   *map page 75, C-2*

Clarkesville, southwest of Tallulah Falls along Highway 115, was once a summer resort destination. Today air conditioners stay the sultry heat of August, but city folks still take to the hills around Clarkesville in search of clean mountain air and a heaping helping of solitude; the town itself beckons with country-cute shops.

On the town square, **The Trolley** is a casual lunch spot, but at dinnertime, the menu gets more adventerous—jerk-glazed pork chops and sautéed shrimp with white beans and basil over polenta are but two of the recent specials. *146 Washington Street; 706-754-5566.*

Perhaps the best white-tablecloth restaurant in the mountains can be found at Clarksville's **Glen-Ella Springs Inn.** Dinner might include smoked pork tenderloin with Vidalia onion chutney, or low-country shrimp and gravy over fried grits cakes. The restaurant's cuisine has been featured at New York's prestigious James Beard House. The century-old inn has 16 rooms overlooking a peaceful meadow, and there is a large pool for summertime frolics. Beyond the meadow, Panther Creek trickles by. The complimentary breakfast befits an inn with such a fine dining room. *1789 Bear Gap Road; 706-754-7295.*

◆ CORNELIA AND "ELVISIANA"   *map page 75, C-3*

Just south of Clarkesville is the little village of Cornelia, site of an attraction that's as unlikely as any you'll find in Georgia. On a quiet side street the graceful white clapboard **Loudermilk Boardinghouse and Museum** houses one of the world's foremost collections of Elvisian memorabilia and art. In other words, this is the best spot east of Graceland for Presley pilgrims. The displays are unconventional, to say the least. Come here to gaze upon a wart removed from Elvis, or a toenail fished from the shag carpet in Graceland's Jungle Room. Or just come here on the off chance that you will catch the proprietor, Joni Mabe, in residence. Joni is a font of Elvis lore, not to mention a talented artist in her own right, whose collages and paintings fill her home. (Her work can be found in the permanent collection of the Museum of Modern Art in New York and in the private collection of the late Andy Warhol.) Also on site is what Joni terms a bed-and-Elvis, a comfortable suite in the downstairs of the home, available to let for a reasonable price. *271 Foreacre Street; 706-778-2001.*

◆ HELEN   *map page 75, C-2*

The faux-Alpine village of Helen owes its origins to a bit of hucksterism. Faced, in the late 1960s, with a faltering lumber industry and a moribund economy, town fathers hit upon a scheme to breathe life into their town: paint building broadsides in the business district with murals of the snow-capped peaks of Germany, and tack gingerbread trim to the eaves of every house in town. In short order, a tourist attraction was born.

Today Helen, 10 miles north of Cleveland on Highway 75, sells as much baloney as bratwurst. But no one seems to mind; it's all in good fun, and it's all good for business. The primary draws in Helen are shopping, eating, drinking beer, and clogging to the incessant sound of oompah bands. Here even the local purveyor of grease, the Huddle House, is gussied up in Bavarian trim. Despite the decorations, the main strip of shops feels more like the midway at a Midwestern state fair than an Alpine village.

Helen is not a great town in which to sample German food. Most of the restaurants serve Americanized dishes, and the selection of German beers proffered is no better than you will find in a good Atlanta pub. But for those intent on eating German, **The Hofbrauhaus Inn** at number one Main Street does sling schnitzel and spaetzel and has a pleasant outdoor beer garden. If you might be inclined to stay too long in the garden, the inn also offers a place to lay your head. *706-878-2248.*

#### ◆ CHATTAHOOCHEE RIVER

Truth be told, Helen is such a spectacle that you almost fail to notice the Chattahoochee River rippling through the middle of town. Just up the road from downtown, perched on the banks of the shallow Chattahoochee is the low-slung **Chattahoochee Riverfront Motel**. This place is a far remove from the hubbub of Alpine Helen. *8849 North Main Street; 706-878-2184 or 800 830-3977.*

For **river trips** on the Chattahoochee River try Wildewood Outfitters in Helen; *706-878-1700.*

North of Helen, the Chattahoochee is the spectacular, fresh-running stream it's supposed to be. At **Anna Ruby Falls Scenic Area** double waterfalls crash over rocky cliffs, and a pleasant walking trail (that leads from the parking lot), will take you past mountain laurel and rhododendron. Possibly one the wild turkeys, deer, or squirrels who live in this area will step out of the woods. *Turn off Highway 75 one mile north of Helen onto Highway 356 and follow signs.*

Three miles downstream on Highway 17 is the **Norah Mill Granary**, where grits are ground from corn on the same stones that were in place when the mill opened in 1876. Here you will receive an informal education in Southern grains, learning the difference between whole-grain grits like these and the version made from ground, dried hominy. *7107 S Main Street; 706-878-2375.*

The white clapboard house just across the street from the granery is home to the **Habersham Winery**. A tasting bar pours samples of the dry whites and reds the company now bottles. Of special note is their port-like Chambourcin variety, a surprisingly supple and tasty dessert wine with a spicy nose. *7025 South Main Street; 770-983-1973.*

◆ CLEVELAND AND HANDICRAFTS  *map page 75, B-2*

The town of Cleveland is ancestral home to the Meaders clan, Georgia's most celebrated family of potters. At a little settlement just south of town called Mossy Creek, the Meaders family has been "turning and burning" pottery, fashioning functional butter churns and fanciful face jugs (influenced by West African memory vessels and English Toby jugs) since the 1890s. Though the family's patriarch and most accomplished potter, Lanier Meaders, passed away in late 1998, a new generation of Meaders has taken to the wheel and are now selling their hand-glazed, wood-fired wares throughout the South.

Down the road in Gillsville, the Hewell family still turns and burns too, making utilitarian ware like strawberry pots and, thanks to the increasingly high prices that face jugs command, oddities such as a two-faced jugs with a candelabra sprouting from the top.

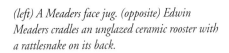

Locally, **Rosehips Gallery** sells the work of the Meaders family as well as that of many other area potters. *Highway 129; 706-865-6345.*

Handicrafts of another sort are on display for a sel-guided tour at **Babyland General Hospital,** an "adoption center" where the folks who brought you that late-'70s fad, the Cabbage Patch Kid, fight valiantly to rescue their product from anonymity in the face of subsequent fads, such as the Beanie Baby onslaught. *73 West Underwood Street; 706-865-2171.*

*(left) A Meaders face jug. (opposite) Edwin Meaders cradles an unglazed ceramic rooster with a rattlesnake on its back.*

# ATLANTA

## HIGHLIGHTS



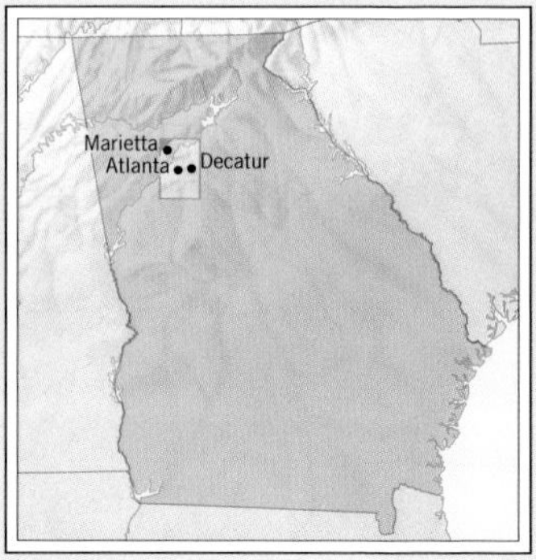




## TRAVEL BASICS

Atlanta is the citadel of both the mythical and the modern South. It's a place where old and new Georgia manage to coexist socially, but where older, graceful buildings are being overwhelmed by massive highrises encircled by freeways, at the expense of a comfortable civic life. Often, visitors who come to stay at big downtown hotels feel Atlanta is uninteresting, as street life, local restaurants, and stores aren't much in evidence. Even Midtown can be daunting, although the blocks of huge buildings do rise alongside older, walkable streets where charming façades and cafes still exist. To enjoy Atlanta, you must get in a car and drive out to the older neighborhoods, where you'll find lovely old homes, vital commercial districts with funky stores, and restaurants serving good Southern cooking.

**Getting Around:** Atlanta is not easily explored on foot—you'll be best off in a car. Central Atlanta is known to locals as I.P. (inside the perimeter highway), new suburban Atlanta as O.P. (or outside the perimeter freeway).

**Climate:** Cool and wet winters with temperatures ranging from the low 20s F to the mid-50s. Occasional snowfall possible. Summers are warm and humid with frequent thunderstorms; temperatures in the upper 80s. Fall is usually dry and pleasant. Spring peaks in April.

**Food & Lodging:** Atlanta offers an array of world-class restaurants and hotels, palaces of haute cuisine like Seeger's, and temples of luxury like the flagship Ritz-Carlton Hotel Buckhead. But there are bargains to be had as well, in unassuming neighborhood haunts where the fried chicken is crunchy and the tea (in the Southern tradition) is tooth-achingly sweet.

*(above) Gridlock, suburban Atlanta, 1998.*
*(below) Gridlock, suburban Atlanta, 1908.*
*(below photo, Georgia Department of Archives & History)*

ATLANTA

## ■ OVERVIEW

Natives of genteel Savannah like to dismiss the bustle and boosterism of Atlanta, citing an oft-repeated bit of doggerel: "If Atlanta could suck as hard as it can blow, it would be a seaport." True, such sentiment seems mean-spirited, but compared to historic, refined Savannah, Atlanta is indeed an upstart, a city built on salesmanship and speculation rather than tradition.

According to the prevailing wisdom, Atlanta is the quintessential modern American city, sprawling outward from a threatened inner core. Its roadways are choked with commuters, its borders ringed by a barrier of glass and steel skyscrapers, its population mostly newly arrived, its identity in question. In a recent *New York Times* story, Atlanta was deemed (and damned) the "new Los Angeles." Though the *Times* article referred to Atlanta's burgeoning traffic problems, the observation might well be applied to many aspects of life in what critics are now labeling a loosely connected series of exurbs and suburbs rather than a cohesive collection of neighborhoods.

*Downtown skyline at night: Atlanta has grown into a sprawling city that many have compared to Los Angeles.*

*Springtime visitors to Atlanta's Carter Presidential Center can enjoy blooming cherry trees and azaleas as well as historic exhibits.*

ATLANTA

And yet, there exists another Atlanta, far removed from suburban blight. This Atlanta remains approachable, enjoyable, swaddled in green spaces, and shaded by the boughs of towering oak and pine trees. In the springtime, when dogwood trees and azaleas burst forth from their dull winter slumber, Atlanta is a magical place, awash in pastel-hued splendor. In the fall, a patchwork of orange and russet blankets the hills.

■ HISTORY

Located atop the Piedmont Plateau, 50 miles or so south of the Appalachian Mountains, this city of three million is an anomaly among Georgia cities. Most Georgia cities of import grew up along navigable waterways or natural harbors. Not so Atlanta, a latter-day arrival on the Georgia map. Atlanta owes its birth to the coming of the railroad and to the trade and prosperity that followed in its wake.

In 1836 the state of Georgia chartered a rail line that would cross the northern part of the state, connecting the market towns of Augusta and Savannah with the transportation hub of Chattanooga, Tennessee. In September of 1837 civil engineer Stephen Long drove a surveyor's stake into the ground at a location just east of what is now known as Underground Atlanta, marking the spot as the terminus for the railroad. Around this stake grew a town known first simply as Terminus, then as Marthasville, and finally, in 1845, as Atlanta.

Atlanta grew quickly. By the time Georgia seceded from the Union in 1861, Atlanta was the primary transportation hub for the Deep South. The city's strategic importance attracted the eye and ire of Union commanding general Ulysses S. Grant, who in 1864 dispatched Gen. William Sherman and nearly 100,000 men on a mission to sever all Confederate rail and supply lines. From early May until the city's surrender on September 2, Sherman fought Confederate forces in and

*This painting from the Atlanta Cyclorama depicts the fierce fighting around the Troup Hurd House during the Battle of Atlanta.*

*Union troops move into Atlanta's Public Square on September 2, 1864. (Library of Congress)*

ATLANTA

around Atlanta. Sherman wreaked havoc, pummeling the Confederates at every turn. Fighting raged across what is now the neighborhood of Buckhead, through modern-day Inman Park, and south to Jonesboro.

At the Battle of Atlanta, the culmination of the campaign, over 7,000 boys in gray were killed along with nearly 2,000 in blue. The streets were lined with maimed and mortally wounded soldiers. Gutters ran red with blood. Churches were pressed into service as temporary triage stations. The city was decimated. In the weeks that followed, Sherman pounded the city with artillery, leveling most of the business and residential districts.

Confederate troops fled the city on September 1. On September 7, the remaining 1,500 or so civilians were removed. And in a final blow, upon departing for Savannah on November 16, Sherman ordered the destruction of all but 400 of the remaining 3,600 homes and buildings that had survived the initial onslaught.

Despite the carnage, Atlanta recovered quickly in the years following the Civil War. Fueled by Northern investment and buoyed by journalist Henry Grady's civic salesmanship, Atlanta emerged as an economic force to be reckoned with. Again, transportation proved to be the primary impetus for Atlanta's prosperity. But the real story is that of Grady and his selling of the New South.

*By 1890 Atlanta was rebuilt and had begun to prosper, as this photograph of Union Station in that year shows. (Georgia Department of Archives & History)*

In the 1880s, Grady preached a gospel of economic deliverance exhorting Southerners to raise their region up by the bootstraps. Rather than advocating isolationism, Grady sought Northern investment. "Every dollar of Northern money reinvested in the South gives us a new friend in that section," he intoned.

Today, Henry Grady is remembered as the primary proponent of the New South and of a new Atlanta. It was a role in which the Georgia native took great pride. "From the ashes left us in 1864, we have built a brave and beautiful city," he told a gathering of Northern civic leaders in 1886.

◆ CAPITAL OF THE MODERN NEW SOUTH

Although the South prospered to some degree in the late 19th and early 20th centuries, much of the region remained rural, agricultural, and poor. At the onset of the Second World War in the early 1940s, the construction of new military bases and an influx of American men from all over the country infused new life into the region. In the 1960s, the Civil Rights Movement shook Georgia's culture to the core, challenging the long-held values and ushering forth a New South of which

Henry Grady could not have even conceived. With the emergence of this modern New South, Atlanta came to the fore as the region's most visible, prosperous, and vital city.

### ◆ RACE RELATIONS

Atlanta has not been without its problems. Race riots swept Atlanta for four days in 1906; anti-Semitism reared its ugly head in 1915 and in 1958; and many blacks were unable to vote well into the 1960s. Yet for the most part, Atlanta's white citizens declined to become involved in the sort of ugly events that stigmatized cities like Birmingham, and much of the credit for Atlanta's ascension is attributable to its relatively stable race relations. This was due in part to the stabilizing influence of Atlanta's well-educated and comparatively wealthy black middle class. Since 1867, Atlanta has been home to a number of the nation's finest black colleges and universities, including such renowned institutions as Spelman College and Morehouse College. African-American businesses have long thrived along Auburn Avenue, once dubbed "the wealthiest Negro street in America."

*Martin Luther King Jr. preaching at Ebenezer Baptist Church, where his father also served as pastor. (Library of Congress)*

ATLANTA

During the Civil Rights era, the greatest positive influence was that exerted by the local religious community. The Reverend Martin Luther King Jr. (a co-pastor in Atlanta from 1960 to 1968) may have been the most famous advocate of African-American equality, but he was by no means the sole architect. As the Civil Rights Movement gained momentum in the 1960s, preachers and rabbis took to pulpits like politicians to stumps, rallying support among parishioners for what was expected to be a protracted struggle. The right to vote was but one of the issues; there were also neighborhoods, schools, and workplaces to integrate. While Watts and Chicago erupted in riots, Atlanta leaders, black and white, negotiated closed-door settlements, paving the way for an integrated city.

In 1973, Atlanta elected the first African-American mayor of a major Southern city, Maynard Jackson. Jackson served two terms before giving way to Andrew Young, who had made his mark as one of Dr. King's assistants before serving as head of the U.S. delegation to the United Nations during the Carter Administration.

## ◆ PREMIER SOUTHERN CITY

By the 1970s Atlanta was known for its progressive social policies—which resulted from the synergistic efforts of the black and white business and political communities. Success followed success. Corporation after corporation moved to Atlanta, believing that this Southern city had reason to remain above the fray of racial strife and to focus instead on closing deals and making money. Homegrown businesses like Coca-Cola, Delta Airlines, and Turner Broadcasting grew by leaps and bounds. Soon Atlanta was touting itself as "the hometown of the American dream." Anything, it seemed, was possible.

Perhaps the crowning glory in the Atlanta story came in 1996 when the city hosted the centennial Olympic Games. In preparation, Atlanta embarked on a massive public works campaign, building new stadiums, refurbishing old ones, converting urban wasteland into parkland, and installing a good measure of public art. By the time of the opening ceremonies—a spectacle capped by the lighting of the Olympic cauldron by boxing champion Muhammad Ali—Atlanta stood in the klieg lights of the international press and declared its transformation from citadel of the Old South to capital of the New South, a fait accompli.

*The gold-domed Georgia State Capitol was constructed in 1889 at a cost of $1 million. Today it serves as the focus of activity in downtown Atlanta.*

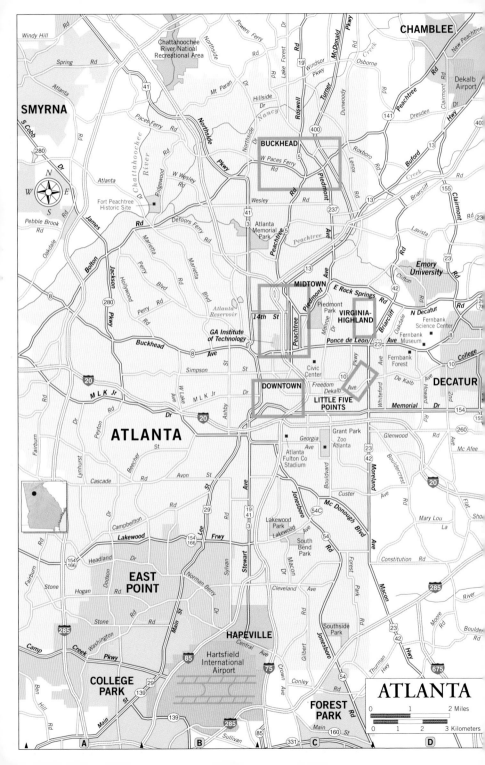

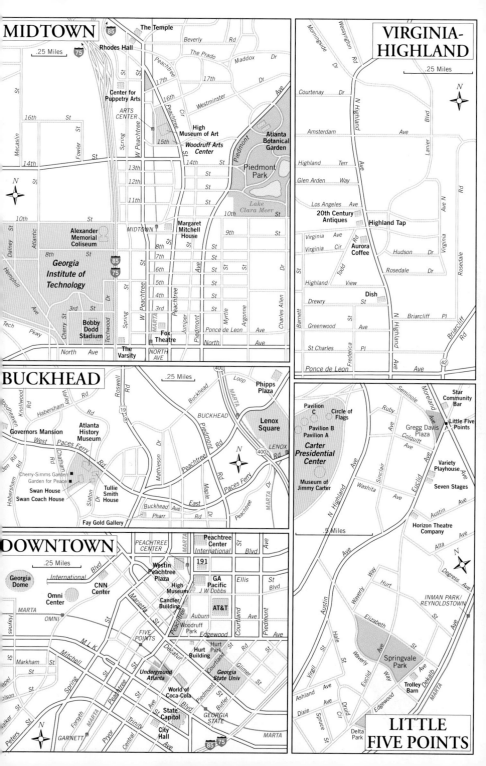

Over the years Atlanta has reinvented itself a good half-dozen times, never shy about broadcasting its merits (and sometimes selling its soul) in pursuit of the almighty dollar. Today, that huckster spirit prevails. Atlantans will build a strip mall in the middle of far-flung Alpharetta, name it Peachtree Brook, and tell the world what a fine thing they have wrought. Don't buy the bull. Instead, make your way to the in-town neighborhoods that are at the spiritual heart of the city. There you will meet an interesting and diverse cast of Atlantans, and there, along the sun-dappled sidewalks and tree-shaded avenues, you will discover the city's charm.

If you find yourself confused as you make your way around the city, it might be due to the proliferation of roads, areas, and destinations containing the name "Peachtree." Peachtree Street has long been a center of commerce in Atlanta, and it became such a desirable address that, as the city grew, more and more roads and developments were given the name. Adding to the confusion is the fact that, in recent years, several downtown streets have even been *renamed* to provide influential tenants with a Peachtree address.

## ■ INMAN PARK AND LITTLE FIVE POINTS    *map page 115*

*map page 115*

Inman Park was Atlanta's first suburb. Established early in the 20th century by developer Joel Hurt, the planned community was linked to downtown Atlanta (three miles to the west) by means of the country's first electrically powered streetcar line. During those years, Inman Park was the most exclusive community in Atlanta, home to, among others, the Candlers and Woodruffs of Coca-Cola fame *(see page 139).* And yet, with the advent of the automobile age, Inman Park's gilded Victorian mansions lost favor as the moneyed elite made use of their new conveyances, moving farther east and north to the emerging au courant neighborhoods.

By the middle years of the 20th century, Inman Park was a wreck. The adjacent business district known as Little Five Points fared no better. As the neighborhood folk tell it, that all changed when the "hippies showed up in the late '60s," looking for cheap housing close to the city center. Pouring "sweat equity" into the old Victorians, these urban pioneers made Inman Park fashionable once again. Alas, the neighborhood's greatest threat may come from success. Today, Inman Park is one of the city's hippest addresses. To hear the aging urban pioneers tell it, what was once a bohemian enclave is fast becoming a yuppie haven where you can get a great latte, but buying a lug wrench requires a trip across town.

## ◆ LITTLE FIVE POINTS

### Greg Davis Plaza

Named for a police officer slain in the line of duty during the early 1990s, Greg Davis Plaza is the heart of Little Five Points and Atlanta's answer to New York's East Village. It is here that Moreland, Euclid, and Seminole Avenues intersect, and it is here that the nose-ring set and the terminally hip mix and mingle with low-key locals. Avant-garde businesses line Moreland and Euclid Avenues and include **Stefan's**, an upscale vintage clothing store; **Wax 'n' Facts**, the city's premier source for used records and CDs; and **A Capella**, a used bookstore that's well stocked with Beat-era novels as well as classics.

### Euclid Avenue Food, Drink and Nightlife

The **Bridgetown Grill** was serving jerk chicken before jerk was cool. Join the hipper-than-thou and slumming suburbanites for a supper of slightly Americanized Jamaican fare. Stick to the basics and you will be well rewarded. The brightly painted courtyard booms with the sound of reggae music. *1156 Euclid Avenue; 404-653-0110.*

**La Fonda Latina** serves a great skilletful of cheap paella: yellow rice studded with squid, chorizo sausage, shrimp, and various vegetables. The setting—a courtyard facing on an alley—is either scruffy or charmingly funky, depending on your perspective. *1150-B Euclid Avenue; 404-577-8317.*

*Little Five Points is known as a prime shopping area for the hipster set.*

*A rockabilly couple at Atlanta's Star Community Bar. (photo by Kelly Duane)*

Live music is a big draw in Little Five Points, ranging from the rockabilly bands featured at the **Star Community Bar** *(437 Moreland Avenue; 404-681-9018)* to an eclectic schedule of touring acts at the **Variety Playhouse** *(1099 Euclid Avenue; 404-521-1786)*. Two theater groups call Little Five Points home: the **Horizon Theatre Company** *(1083 Austin Avenue; 404-584-7450)*, often a showcase for local productions of seasoned Off-Broadway fare, and **Seven Stages Theatre** *(1105 Euclid Avenue; 404-523-7647)*, Atlanta's most consistently innovative, multicultural theater.

L5P is more a place to drink and play than eat. There are two drinking establishments with great bar food.

The **Euclid Avenue Yacht Club** is a neighborhood institution, famous for its great beer selection and superior bar food. The bar draws an eclectic crowd, from local politicos to bikers, and visitors of all hometowns and hues are always welcomed. *1136 Euclid Avenue; 404-688-2582.*

Just down the street and around the corner is **The Vortex** with its huge, two-story skull, eyes oscillating wildly, on the façade. Inside, servers dish attitude and great burgers, and the beer selection is outstanding. *438 Moreland Avenue; 404-688-1828.*

◆ CARTER PRESIDENTIAL CENTER

Three blocks west of Little Five Points is the **Carter Presidential Center,** home to the Museum of the Jimmy Carter Library and the offices of the former President's numerous philanthropic and ambassadorial operations. Although much of this complex of interconnected concrete pavilions is off-limits, exhibits dealing with the Carter presidency are open to the public. *441 Freedom Parkway (at Highland Avenue); 404-331-3942.*

At the rear of the complex, on a ridge overlooking downtown, is a terraced Japanese-style garden and a grassy slope popular with dog lovers, who convene to let their canine companions romp and play.

◆ INMAN PARK

A 10-minute walk southwest of Little Five Points down Euclid Avenue—along sidewalks shaded by towering oaks—takes you to Inman Park. A few hours wandering the neighborhood is time well spent. Among the highlights are the homes along Edgewood Avenue, Elizabeth Street, and Waverly Way, built in a hodgepodge of architectural styles and including a number of brick-turreted Victorian follies.

The green- and red-shingled **Trolley Barn,** a High Victorian wonder located in the 900 block of Edgewood Avenue, is the only vestige of Inman Park's days as a trolley-car suburb. It now serves as a community center and special event facility.

Two nice bed-and-breakfast inns are located in the neighborhood. The **King-Keith House,** a Victorian "painted lady" with five guestrooms has twelve-foot ceilings and ornate carved fireplaces that give this inn a regal, if a bit dowdy, air. A full breakfast is included in the tariff. *889 Edgewood NE; 404-688-7330.*

The **Sugar Magnolia** is the most opulent B&B south of Buckhead. Built in 1892, this Victorian has a rooftop deck that offers a panoramic view of downtown Atlanta, and each of the three rooms has a working fireplace. *804 Edgewood; 404-222-0226.*

For traditional southern food in the neighborhood try **Son's Place** *(See description on page 153).*

## ■ VIRGINIA-HIGHLAND    *map page 115*

Just a mile or so north of Little Five Points, across Ponce de Leon Avenue (pronounced by Atlantans without a trace of a Spanish lilt), is a neighborhood of comfortable bungalow homes known as Virginia-Highland, so named for the intersection of Virginia and Highland Avenues at its epicenter.

Once a slightly down-at-the-heels, middle-class enclave, the neighborhood now bustles with young professionals—jogging, biking, or pushing the latest model designer stroller down the narrow sidewalks. Some of Atlanta's most eclectic shops and innovative restaurants are grouped along the one-and-a-half-mile stretch of Highland Avenue from Ponce de Leon north to University Avenue. Take the time to wander the back streets of what many believe to be Atlanta's most engaging intown neighborhood.

### ◆ NORTH HIGHLAND AVENUE GOURMANDIZING

**Ground Zero and South**

At the intersection of Highland and Virginia is the **Highland Tap**, Atlanta's den of drinking iniquity where the city's best martinis are served alongside well-marbled steaks in a cool subterranean setting, but perhaps a better way to start a Virginia-Highland tour would be to head across the intersection to #922 for a cup of joe from **Aurora Coffee**. If the coffee cries out for a bagel, head down another block to #832 where **Highland Bagel** is housed in a former laundromat.

Just beyond the bagle shop is **Dish**, a futuristic fusion restaurant housed in a former filling station. *870 N Highland; 404-897-3463.*

**On Ponce de Leon**

There's always a late-night scene at the 24-hour joint called **Majestic Food Shop** where clientele and waitstaff provide the show. When it comes to people-watching,

the Majestic has it all: snippy waitresses, beat cops, and local freaks galore. *1031 Ponce de Leon; 404-875-0276.*

**North of Virginia on Highland**

For a sidewalk table that may be the best perch in the city try **Moe's and Joe's** at 1033 N. Highland. They've been around since 1947, long before Virginia-Highland became in-town Atlanta's most popular neighborhood. The burgers and fries are just okay, but the Pabst is cold and the service is friendly.

A favorite shopping stop near Moe's and Joe's is **20th Century Antiques**, chockablock with chrome-trimmed and leopard-spotted furnishings from the not too distant past. *1044 N Highland.*

To satisfy that aching sweet-tooth, continue on up to the 1300 block for Atlanta's best cookies at **Alon's Bakery**, or the best key lime pie at **Indigo**, a funky fish camp for urbane in-towners. *1397 N Highland.*

*The neon sign at the Majestic Food Shop reads "FOOD TO TAKE HOME" on one side and "FOOD THAT PLEASES" around the corner.*

ATLANTA

Two homey, bungalows offer lodging in the Virginia-Highland area. The **Gaslight Inn,** *1001 St. Charles Avenue; 404-876-1001,* and **Virginia-Highland Bed-and-Breakfast Inn**. *630 Orme Circle; 404-892-2735.*

## ■ DRUID HILLS

Druid Hills, just east of Virginia-Highland, was a late-1890s project of developer Joel Hurt (who also developed Inman Park) and America's foremost landscape architect, Frederic Law Olmsted. The neighborhood is a tangle of looping lanes wedged between two main thoroughfares, Briarcliff Road and Ponce de Leon Avenue (just Ponce to locals). Lushly landscaped and grand in scale, the homes of Druid Hills are among the most imposing in the Atlanta area.

Though planned as a residential enclave, Druid Hills is also home to some of the city's most vital cultural and educational institutions.

Tucked into a bank of hardwoods just off Ponce is the **Fernbank Museum of Natural History**. Opened in 1992, this is the largest museum of natural history constructed since the Roosevelt era. The building itself is a wonder, featuring lime-stone floors studded with fossils, but the real treats are the permanent exhibits, including "A Walk Through Time in Georgia," a fascinating account of the natural history of Georgia and the Southeast. Also on the premises is a giant IMAX theater. *767 Clifton Road; 404-378-0127.*

Adjacent to the Fernbank Museum is **Fernbank Forest,** a 65-acre woodland preserve just a small remove from the traffic snarl of Ponce de Leon Avenue. Now maintained by Dekalb County as a teaching center, the forest is home to the **Fernbank Science Center,** which includes a 500-seat planetarium and an observatory that boasts a 36-inch telescope. *156 Heaton Park Drive NE; 404-378-4311.*

■ MIDTOWN    *map page 115*

A diverse, dispersed collection of shops, restaurants, and homes spreading north and south along Peachtree Street between Buckhead and Downtown, Midtown is the center of Atlanta's thriving gay and lesbian community as well as home to the city's premier cultural institutions. Once a jumble of lovely bungalow homes and neighborhood businesses, Midtown's main thoroughfares are increasingly shadowed by postmodern skyscrapers, but side streets remain relatively undisturbed.

◆ MIDTOWN HIGHLIGHTS

**Piedmont Park**

At the center of Midtown, sandwiched between Piedmont Avenue and Monroe Drive, is Piedmont Park, Atlanta's largest public green space. Designed in part by Frederic Law Olmsted, the 185-acre park was once the race ground for the Piedmont Driving Club, Atlanta's most exclusive social club. Today, the lakes and lawns are given over to biking, sunbathing, and Rollerblading. At the park's southeastern corner is a cafe serving cold beers and sandwiches, the perfect respite from a dog day summer afternoon.

**Atlanta Botanical Garden**

Northwest of the park is the Atlanta Botanical Garden, a 30-acre oasis of meandering paths and vast swaths of grass. The gardens are punctuated by the **Fuqua Conservatory** and a new children's playscape, the most arresting feature of which is a wrought steel Butterfly Pavilion, designed and constructed by up-and-coming Atlanta sculptor David Landis. A variety of plants within the structure attract butterflies, and the pavilion is less a cage to contain the kaleidoscope of winged creatures than it is a focal point around which they gather, flitting in and out among the foliage. *1345 Piedmont Avenue NE; 404-876-5859.*

## Fox Theatre

Almost directly across the street from the Georgia Terrace Hotel is the Fox Theatre, Atlanta's singular architectural jewel. A gaudy mix of faux Moorish and Egyptian architecture, this 1929 theater was initially intended to be the Yaarab Temple of the Ancient Order of the Nobles of the Mystic Shrine. But a financial shortfall forced the Nobles to turn the temple over to movie impresario William Fox, who retrofitted the building to serve as a movie palace.

Threatened with condemnation in the 1970s, today the Fox has been completely restored. As the curtain rises, the ceiling above comes alive with a galaxy of stars, and the trompe l'oeil Moorish-style courtyard that surrounds the seating area echoes with the sounds of Mighty Mo, the Fox's 3,600-pound Moller organ.

Tours are offered most mornings. Performances are scheduled throughout the year. *660 Peachtree Street NE; 404-881-2100.*

## Georgia Tech

East of the Fox, across the interstate highway chasm that locals call "the Downtown Connector," is the campus of the Georgia Institute of Technology, known to most everyone as Georgia Tech. One of the premier scientific institutions in the nation, Georgia Tech, like its sister state campuses, has benefited immensely from the influx of dollars courtesy of the Georgia Lottery. During the 1996 Olympic Games, Georgia Tech was the site of Olympic Village, housing more than 15,000 athletes and personnel. The dorms they inhabited are visible from the interstate, directly across the way from **The Varsity,** opened in 1928 by

*The Fuqua Conservatory in the Atlanta Botanical Garden.*

Georgia Tech dropout Frank Gordy. The Varsity lays claim to the title "world's largest drive-in." Carhops still work the parking lot, though most folk eat inside these days. *61 North Avenue; 404-881-1706.*

## Woodruff Arts Center

A couple of miles north of Georgia Tech is the Woodruff Arts Center complex, Atlanta's version of New York's Lincoln Center. The Arts Center building serves as home base for the **Atlanta Symphony Orchestra**, the **Alliance Theatre Company**, and the **Atlanta College of Art**. *1280 Peachtree Street; 404-733-4200.*

## High Museum of Art

Adjacent to the Arts Center building is the High Museum, which opened in 1983.

Designed by Richard Meier, the High Museum has won rave reviews from architecture critics across the country. Blockbuster exhibits that once bypassed Atlanta now make a stop at the High, and retrospectives on Picasso, Monet, and Pop art have all attracted large audiences. Out front on the lawn, an Alexander Calder stabile whirls, a kinetic study in primary colors. *1080 Peachtree Street; 404-733-4400.*

## Center for Puppetry Arts

Headquartered in an old schoolhouse, this is one of the few museum and performance spaces devoted solely to puppetry. Though the museum displays vintage puppets from around the globe, the biggest draws are its shows for adults. These range from renditions of theater classics to avant-garde

*The High Museum of Art, designed by Richard Meier, hosts large touring exhibits as well as its own substantial collection.*

performance pieces that stretch the bounds of puppetry propriety and have been known to raise the ire of self-appointed art critic Jesse Helms. *1410 Spring Street; 404-873-3089.*

### Rhodes Hall

There was a time in the not too distant past when Peachtree was a residential street rather than a busy thoroughfare. Rhodes Hall is a vestige of that time. This graceful, turreted granite home, completed in 1904, now houses the Georgia Trust for Historic Preservation and is open daily, except Saturday. *1516 Peachtree Street NW; 404-881-9980.*

### The Temple

Also on Peachtree, just a few blocks north, is the Temple, home of Atlanta's oldest Jewish congregation. The exterior may be neo-classical, but the interior is a rendering of King Solomon's temple in Jerusalem as envisioned by the late Phillip Trammel Shutze, favorite architect of the Atlanta elite. In 1958 the Temple was blown apart by a 50-stick dynamite charge. Intended to intimidate Jews, the blast was set by that era's well-known cast of malcontents—the guys in the long white robes and pointy hoods. Bombing suspects were quickly apprehended and sent to trial, where they were represented by (among others) defense attorney Jimmy Venable, Imperial Wizard of the National Knights of the Ku Klux Klan. The defendants were not convicted and the trial was a circus, but today the rebuilt Temple remains the focal point of Jewish religious life in Atlanta. *1589 Peachtree Street NE; 404-873-1731.*

### ◆ GONE WITH THE WIND SITES *map page 115*

A few blocks west of Piedmont Park is the **Margaret Mitchell House,** a rather ordinary building where the author of *Gone With the Wind* and her husband, John Marsh, lived from 1925 to 1932. Mitchell, disdainful of her onetime digs, often referred to the apartment house as "the Dump." Nevertheless, preservationists have recently restored the house, now home to an exhibit that details the life of Atlanta's most famous author. Unfortunately, the house seems out of place amid the unappealing new highrise developments all around it. *Intersection of 10th and Peachtree Streets; 404-249-7012.*

In 1934, five years before the movie version of *Gone With the Wind* premiered in Atlanta, Mitchell handed over the as-yet-uncompleted manuscript for the novel to literary scout Harold Latham of the Macmillan publishing house in the marble-lined lobby of the **Georgian Terrace Hotel.** Located nine blocks south of the Margaret Mitchell House, at the corner of Peachtree and Ponce, the hotel was the host hostelry for the movie's stars and it still receives guests. *659 Peachtree Street NE; 404-897-1991.*

## GONE WITH THE WIND PHENOMENA

*One of the most popular books in American publishing history,* Gone With the Wind *remains a terrific read and a national embarrassment. If Margaret Mitchell's Scarlett O'Hara and Rhett Butler move through the Civil War era with an unforgettable panache, both the author and her characters treat slavery with nonchalance. And yet few who begin to read this story can put it down. Tom Wolfe (whose 1998 novel,* A Man in Full, *centers on Atlanta) recently observed: "I love being in the same paragraph as Margaret Mitchell. In literary circles, you're not supposed to say that. But you could argue, and I would if anyone would listen, that* Gone With the Wind *is the greatest American novel ever written." Whatever its merits,* Gone With the Wind *is irrevocably linked with the state of Georgia.*

cꙮↄ ꙮↄ

*The year is 1861 and 16-year-old Scarlett O'Hara appears in all her vivid glory:*

Scarlett intended to marry…and she was willing to appear demure, pliable and scatterbrained, if those were the qualities that attracted men. Just why men should be this way, she did not know. She only knew that such methods worked. It never interested her enough to try to think out the reason for it, for she knew nothing of the inner workings of any human being's mind, not even her own. She knew only that if she did or said thus-and-so, men would unerringly respond with the complementary thus-and-so. It was like a mathematical formula….

If she knew little about men's minds, she knew even less about the minds of women, for they interested her less. She had never had a girl friend, and she never felt any lack on that account. To her, all women, including her two sisters, were natural enemies in pursuit of the same prey—man.

*Scarlett meets her match in blockade runner Rhett Butler:*

He was dressed in black broadcloth, a tall man, towering over the officers who stood near him, bulky in the shoulders but tapering to a small waist and absurdly small feet in varnished boots. His severe black suit, with fine ruffled shirt and trousers smartly strapped beneath high insteps, was oddly at variance with his physique and face, for he was foppishly groomed, the clothes of a dandy on a body that was powerful and latently dangerous in its lazy grace. His hair was jet black, and his black mustache was small and closely clipped, almost foreign looking compared with the dashing, swooping mustaches of the cavalrymen near by. He looked, and was, a man of lusty and unashamed appetites. He had an air of utter assurance, of displeasing insolence about him, and there was a twinkle of malice in his bold eyes as he stared at Scarlett, until finally, feeling his gaze, she looked toward him.

*Later, the upstanding Dr. Meade confronts Rhett on his lack of patriotic sentiment.*

𝒟r. Meade's brows were thunderous.

"Nothing may be sacred to you, young man," he said, in the voice he always used when making speeches. "But there are many things sacred to the patriotic men and ladies of the South. And the freedom of our land from the usurper is one and States' Rights in another and—"

Rhett looked lazy and his voice had a silky, almost bored, note.

"All wars are sacred," he said. "To those who have to fight them. If the people who started wars didn't make them sacred, who would be foolish enough to fight?"

~ଉ ଚ୨~

*The movie premiere of* Gone With the Wind *was a national event, and for years people remembered the night of the film's premiere as if it was a high holy day in Atlanta history. In Rebecca Well's 1996 novel,* The Divine Secrets of the YaYa Sisterhood, *a young girl from Louisiana who has made a trip to Atlanta to see the opening writes to a friend:*

𝒲e have just come from the premiere of the greatest movie ever made. …Vivien Leigh *is* Scarlett.…The minute I saw Miss Leigh there on the steps of the porch at Tara with the Tarleton twins at her side… well, I was a goner….

I want to live in this movie, Necie! This is the kind of drama I was born for.

*The Loew's Grand Theatre hosted the world premiere of* Gone With the Wind *on December 15, 1939.*

*(Atlanta Historical Society)*

## ◆ Surviving in Midtown . . .

. . . is hardly a problem with so many fine eateries, late-night spots, and good lodging options in the neighborhood. See pages 152-157 for some of the most notable restaurants.

### Good Eats

At **Agnes and Muriel's** place, *1514 Monroe Drive; 404-885-1000,* you'll find comfort food served amidst Jetson's decor. **Zócalo,** *187 10th Street; 404-249-7576,* offers authentic regional Mexican, a sunny patio, and a great tequilla selection. Try **Pasta da Pulcinella,** *1123 Peachtree Road; 404-892-6195,* for regional Italian food at a bargain price, or **Vickery's,** *1106 Crescent Avenue; 404-881-1106,* for great outdoor dining, a late-night bar scene, and a Cuban-influenced menu.

### Quick Treats

For more basic survival there's a 24 hour **Krispy Kreme Donuts,** *295 Ponce de Leon Avenue,* and a scruffy grocery store lunch spot called **Kool Korner** with great Cuban sandwiches and good mojo. *349 14th Street.*

### B&Bs

In exclusive Ansley Park you'll find the **Ansley Inn.** Once the home of retailing magnate George Muse, this 1907 Tudor home is now one of the best B&Bs in town. *253 15th Street; 404-872-9000 or 800-446-5416.*

On the southern fringe of Midtown is the **Woodruff Bed-and-Breakfast.** Once a house of ill repute, the inn is no longer occupied by ladies of the evening but by visitors seeking an alternative to the chains. *223 Ponce de Leon Avenue; 404-875-9449.*

A little more upscale is the **Shellmont Bed-and-Breakfast,** located a few blocks from Piedmont Park in a 1891 mansion with a carriage house in the rear. It's decorated with Victorian-era antiques. *821 Piedmont Avenue; 404-872-9290.*

### Hotels

Midtown also offers a supurb collection of hotels: the swanky **Four Seasons Hotel,** *75 14th Street; 404-881-9898,* the convenient **Sheraton Colony Square,** *188 14th Street; 404-892-6000,* and the surprising **Days Inn,** decorated like a 19th-century men's club, with a charm rarely, if ever, associated with a Days Inn. *683 Peachtree Street; 404-874-9200.*

## ■ Buckhead *map page 115*

Situated five or so miles north of Downtown, spreading outward from the nexus of Peachtree Street, Roswell Road, and West Paces Ferry Road, Buckhead is Atlanta's wealthiest neighborhood. Home to the city's toniest nightclubs, swankest shops, and most refined restaurants, Buckhead serves as the de facto capital of

Southern glitz and glamour. And yet its origins are altogether humble. The community earned its moniker in the late 1830s when a deer hunter mounted the head of a buck on a post somewhere near the site of a tavern built by the area's first inhabitant, Henry Irby. Visitors today will be hard pressed to detect a trace of such frontier style in this mannered, moneyed neighborhood, home to the Georgia governor and a passel of the city's power brokers. Author Tom Wolfe wrote of Buckhead in his 1998 novel, *A Man in Full:*

> *H*ere in the gloaming, the white blossoms, arranged in their distinctive planes, swept from green breast, from mansion to mansion, estate to estate, as if some divine artist had adorned the heavenly air itself with them to show that the residents of Buckhead, off West Paces Ferry Road, were the elect, the anointed, the rightful hand-grabbers of whatever Atlanta, Georgia had to offer.

Detractors are quick to point out that Buckhead seems to reinvent itself every couple of years in a feverish pursuit of the almighty dollar. And they do have a point. Rest assured, if it's in vogue you will be sure to find it in Buckhead. Atlanta's largest collection of upscale retailers and restaurants is grouped along Peachtree Street between Roswell Road and two of the South's most prestigious and luxurious malls, **Lenox Square** and **Phipps Plaza.**

To see where the beautiful people live, turn off West Paces Ferry Road onto a side street such as Blackland or Cherokee, roll your windows down, and drink in the wealth. Among the bigwigs who call Buckhead home is the governor of Georgia. The **Governor's Mansion**, built in 1968 in the Greek revival style, is an imposing edifice surrounded by 18 acres of landscaped grounds. Tours by reservation, Tuesday through Thursday. *391 West Paces Ferry Road; 404-261-1776.*

Also on West Paces Ferry Road, close to the intersection with Peachtree, is what may be Atlanta's prime attraction, the **Atlanta History Center.** On the grounds you will find the **Atlanta History Museum,** a decidedly multicultural introduction to Atlanta that opened in 1993, as well as the **Tullie Smith House,** a working farm (complete with outbuildings) where during late summer and fall you will find a cotton crop growing.

Another home on the grounds, the 1928 **Swan House,** occupies the opposite end of the economic spectrum from the unassuming clapboard Smith House. Designed by noted Atlanta architect Philip Trammel Crow—and named for the

*The Swan House, a historic mansion in the Buckhead area.*

recurring swan motif used throughout the 1928 mansion—the Swan House is the centerpiece of the Atlanta History Complex. This storybook mansion casts an imposing, almost baronial shadow over the landscaped grounds. The Swan House is open for tours. Adjacent is the **Swan Coach House Restaurant,** long popular with the Ladies Who Lunch set who flock here for pimento cheese and chicken salad served in a chintz-flocked tea room. *Atlanta History Center, 130 West Paces Ferry Road; 404-814-4000, Swan Coach House Restaurant; 404-261-0636.*

Most of Atlanta's premier **art galleries** are located in Buckhead. These include Timothy Tew Gallery, Jane Jackson Fine Art, and Fay Gold Gallery, all of which are tucked away in a warren of side streets between Peachtree Street and East Paces Ferry Road. At night, particularly on weekends, a young and rowdy crowd descends upon Buckhead, enticed by its lively bar scene. Those with a taste for a good Moroccan lamb kabob accompanied by authentic belly dancing should head for **Imperial Fez,** *2285 Peachtree Road; 404-351-0870.*

Many of Atlanta's temples of haute cuisine are found here in Buckhead: the pricy, but highly lauded **Seeger's,** the oh-so-French destination restaurant,

**Brasserie Le Coze**, great sushi at **Soto Japanese**, and the clubby **Bone's**. *(These restaurants are described further on pages 156-157.)*

In addition, look for the unpretentious little **Anis Café**, serving the cuisine of Provence to a loyal cadre of French expats and in-the-know Atlantans, *2974 Grandview Avenue; 404-233-9889,* and **Prime**, *3393 Peachtree; 404-812-0555,* where a latter-day version of surf-and-turf offers sushi for the surf half of the concept. Here you will also find **La Grotta Ristorante Italiano,** Atlanta's oldest grand Italian restaurant. *2637 Peachtree Road; 404-231-1368.*

Stop in to the **Buckhead Bread Company** , *3070 Piedmont,* for breakfast or a loaf of artisinal bread, and for lunch, try the **Buckhorn Diner** just across the street. *3073 Piedmont.*

Those wanting to dig in for a few days at a good address will find that Buckhead is well supplied with a full spectrum of hotels with respectable, familiar names. The **Ritz-Carlton Buckhead** is the flagship of its chain, and the level of service here ranks perennially among the best in the world. Atlanta's power brokers gather in the lobby bar for early evening cocktails. *3434 Peachtree Road NE; 404-237-2700.*

## ■ WEST END

A couple miles southwest of Downtown, West End—like Buckhead—grew up around a crossroads tavern. Once home to a wealthy white population, the beautiful Victorian houses at the center of this neighborhood are now home to a thriving black middle class, many of whom teach at the nearby Atlanta University Complex.

Born a slave in 1858 near Social Circle, Georgia, Alonzo Herndon was an early black Atlanta entrepreneur who founded the Atlanta Life Insurance Company, the largest black-owned business of the early 20th century. Even before founding Atlanta Life, Herndon had been a successful businessman; his Peachtree Street barber shop, which employed only black barbers and catered to an affluent white clientele, was the largest and fanciest in Atlanta, featuring leather benches, marble floors, and crystal chandeliers. Today **Herndon Home,** the house he built in 1910, is open for tours Tuesday through Saturday. Of Beaux-Arts design, this imposing brick home features many of the original furnishings as well as exhibits that detail the life of this influential member of Atlanta's black leadership, the group W. E. B. Du Bois deemed the "talented tenth." *587 University Place; NW 404-581-9813.*

Named for a family of birds that once nested in the mailbox, **Wren's Nest**, a Victorian jewel of a house, was home to journalist Joel Chandler Harris, best known for his interpretations of African-American folklore collected as the *Uncle Remus Tales*. Soon after Chandler passed away in 1908, the house was opened to the public, making it Atlanta's first house museum. Among the items on display are first editions of many of Chandler's books. Those curious about Chandler's childhood should journey to Eatonton *(see page 184),* where he was born in 1848. *1050 Ralph David Abernathy Boulevard; 404-753-7735.*

◆ ATLANTA UNIVERSITY

The **Atlanta University Complex** is the heart and soul of Atlanta's west side. Here, more than 19,000 students matriculate at six separate institutions of higher learning, among which are Spelman College, the country's oldest college for black

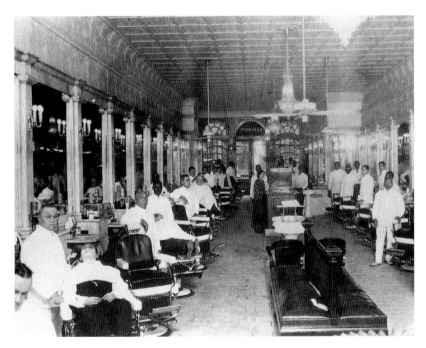

*Among Alonzo Herndon's businesses was this opulent barber shop on Peachtree Street.
(courtesy of the Herndon Foundation)*

women, and Morehouse College, alma mater of the late Dr. Martin Luther King Jr.

Atlanta University, founded in 1865 and once under the direction of W. E. B. Du Bois, was an early citadel of African-American education. Morris Brown College was built in 1867 and Spelman in 1881. Morehouse Medical School and the Interdenominational Theological Seminary followed, after the turn of the century.

Long the bastion of the South's middle-class and upper-class blacks, these colleges have fueled Atlanta's growth as a mecca for black entrepreneurs, religious leaders, and educators. Among the redbrick Italianate buildings that comprise the campuses, there stands, on the Morehouse lawn, a modern

*Atlanta University students William Anders, Rashad Boatwright, and Andre Tucker pause for a break between classes.*

chapel dedicated to King and fronted by a two-story statue of the slain leader. *James P. Brawley Drive at Martin Luther King Jr. Drive.*

One of Atlanta's most venerable 'cue shacks, **Harold's Barbecue,** is here in the West End. The smoked pork and Brunswick stew have been drawing fans here from all over the city since the business began in 1947. The cracklin' cornbread is without peer. The setting—within sight of the federal pen—only heightens the thrill for true pilgrims. *171 McDonough Boulevard; 404-627-9268.*

While you are in the neighborhood, you will want to belly up to the steam table at **Heath's Grocery** for some of the best collard greens and cornbread on the planet. *787 Cascade Avenue SW; 404-755-0543.*

■ GRANT PARK    *map page 114, C-4*

Named not for the Union general but for one of Atlanta's founding fathers, Lemuel Pratt Grant (who in 1883 donated 100 acres of parkland to the city), Grant Park is a work in progress, a neighborhood of lovingly restored, grand old Victorians homes and sagging Victorian eyesores awaiting the restorer's kind touch. At its center is the eponymous park, home to the Cyclorama and Zoo Atlanta. On its fringes are Atlanta's fabled burying ground, Oakland Cemetery, and Cabbagetown, a onetime mill village now in the throes of restoration.

**Fulton Bag and Mill** is the concrete-and- brick behemoth that sits at the center of Atlanta's **Cabbagetown** neighborhood. An outpost of Appalachia in the midst of the city, the mill once employed workers who moved south from the mountains in search of jobs. And in typical mill town fashion, the company built the small frame houses that ring the plant for the workers. When the mill closed in 1977 after almost 100 years of operation, the neighborhood went into a tailspin, though most of the residents stayed put. Today, this enclave of narrow streets lined with shotgun houses is experiencing a renaissance of sorts. The old mill has reopened as a mixed-use apartment and retail complex, after suffering a major fire in 1999. *Memorial Drive at Boulevard Road.*

**Oakland Cemetery** is the final resting place of Atlantans both famous—author Margaret Mitchell and golfer Bobby Jones—and unknown. Established in 1850 and covering more than 85 acres, the cemetery is integrated by both race and religion. A favorite of picnicking urban pioneers from nearby Cabbagetown, the cemetery is open to the public daily. *Memorial Drive at Oakland Avenue.*

Long one of the nation's worst zoos, **Zoo Atlanta** received a major face lift in the mid-'80s, when natural habitats replaced cages and Willie B, the city's prized silverback gorilla, emerged from what amounted to solitary confinement. Today, the zoo is considered to be one of the best in the nation. *800 Cherokee Avenue; 404-624-5600.*

There was a time in the late 1800s when cycloramas, circular paintings that depicted some momentous event, were transported from city to city and displayed with great aplomb. They were, in essence, the IMAX theaters of an earlier time. One of the few still in existence is the **Atlanta Cyclorama,** a three-ton-plus painting of the Battle of Atlanta that revolves around the viewer. The realism is heightened by a two-dimensional diorama that fades from the foreground into the

## THE GREAT LOCOMOTIVE CHASE

Georgia is particularly proud of its role in an episode of Civil War history that seems straight out of a Buster Keaton movie. On April 12, 1862, a group of Union raiders boarded a train in Marietta. The passengers and crew, unaware of the Federals in their midst, got off at Kennesaw for a snack, and the raiders departed in the train, planning to destroy the bridges between Kennesaw and Chattanooga. They were foiled, though, by the train's heroic engineer, who doggedly chased his train—first on foot, then by polecar, and finally by commandeering three other engines. Two of these he ran in reverse, since there weren't roundhouses nearby. At one point, the raiders let go two cars, thinking the cars would slam into the pursuers; but the Confederates were able to couple the loose cars with their engine. After 87 miles and eight hours, the raiders were caught. And thus was born the legend of the Great Locomotive Chase.

painting. Also on display is the locomotive *Texas*, one of the two engines involved in the Great Locomotive Chase of the Civil War. *800 Cherokee Avenue in the park; 404-658-7625.*

■ EAST ATLANTA *map page 114*

Those in pursuit of the "next big thing" should make their way east from Grant Park and across Moreland Avenue to the neighborhood of East Atlanta, where funk and food are now the big draws. Over the past few years, urban speculators have begun opening shops and restaurants along Flat Shoals and Glenwood Avenues, drawing a young crowd presumably turned off by the gentrification of Little Five Points. Though there are no "sights" to see, the six-block commercial center is in an almost constant state of entrepreneurial upheaval. Who knows what the future holds?

If you venture into the area, look for innovatine burritos at **Burrito Art,** *1259 Glenwood Avenue; 404-627-4433.* One of the pioneering businesses in this emerging neighborhood is **Heaping Bowl and Brew.** They serve stews and jumbles of rice and vegetables from a somewhat funky kitchen. *469 Flat Shoals Road NE; 404-523-8030.*

■ DOWNTOWN  *map page 115*

Despite the best efforts of boosters, Downtown is where Atlanta works rather than lives or plays. Home to the headquarters of CNN, Georgia-Pacific, and Coca-Cola, downtown Atlanta is, unfortunately, an after-dark desert, populated primarily by conventioneers plying the streets on weekday nights in search of diversion.

Three distinct districts stretch from north to south along Peachtree Street: Peachtree Center, architect John Portman's skyscraper complex; Five Points (as distinguished from Little Five Points, described on pages 117–118), the onetime heart of the city, now sliding into decline; and Underground Atlanta, formerly a unique subterranean entertainment district, now an urban shopping mall.

◆ PEACHTREE CENTER AND ENVIRONS

Architect John Portman, arguably the man most responsible for reshaping the Atlanta cityscape, was also one of the first architects in the country to aspire to be a developer. Portman's 1961 Atlanta Merchandise Mart was followed in succeeding years by a raft of building projects that sprawled up and down Peachtree Street from its intersection with International Boulevard in a loose assemblage of seven office towers, three hotels, and an urban shopping mall.

Known today as **Peachtree Center,** the complex is showing its age, maybe even looking a bit kitschy, as evidenced by early buildings like the Hyatt Regency Hotel with its soaring atrium and blue-domed restaurant spinning away up top. The Westin Peachtree Plaza, however—at 720 feet high the tallest hotel in the country—still looks nearly as futuristic as it did when it opened in the mid-1970s. *265 Peachtree Street NE; 404-577-1234.*

The complex is interconnected by a series of aboveground passageways that look like little mole tunnels leading from habitat to habitat. There are some that criticize the scale of Portman's master plan. Others take issue with an aesthetic focused on glass and concrete. But none can deny that his developmental zeal played a large part in fueling the building boom that vaulted Atlanta into the top tier of international business centers.

Just west of Peachtree Center is **Centennial Olympic Park.** At its heart is a fountain fashioned in the shape of the Olympic rings, a gathering spot that is

*Employees gather for lunch in the atrium of the CNN Center.*

especially popular in the summer months, when children play in the intermittent sprays of water that shoot upward. Walkways leading from the fountain fan out into the park and are paved with commemorative bricks inscribed with the names of the thousands of people who paid $35 for the privilege. A performance pavilion is also on-site, and an Olympic museum is to be built. *Between Marietta Street and Techwood Drive, north to Baker Street.*

After the closing ceremonies of the 1996 Olympic Games, the track and field stadium built for the occasion was remade into **Turner Field,** home of the Atlanta Braves, the winningest major-league baseball team of the 1990s. The field is now known to most locals as simply the Ted, in deference to team owner and media mogul Ted Turner. As much an arcade as a ball field, the stadium offers batting cages and a Braves museum, not to mention numerous spots to eat and drink. That said, it's also a great spot to see a ball game, an intimate facility with great site lines and televisions mounted on the walls at about every five feet to ensure that you won't miss a thing, even if you're in line for a hot dog when someone crushes a home run over the centerfield fence. *755 Hank Aaron Drive at Ralph David Abernathy Drive. Tour information: 404-614-2311. Tickets: 404-249-6400.*

Just south of Olympic Park by way of Techwood Avenue is CNN **Center.** Once home to an indoor theme park—the World of Sid and Marty Krofft—this glass-and-steel behemoth with a soaring atrium at its center now serves as the headquarters for one of the world's largest news organizations, beaming breaking stories to more than 200 countries around the globe. Studio tours, despite their promotional bluster, provide an entertaining glimpse into the workings of a news-gathering organization. VIP tours, priced at a premium, put you on the newsroom floor and offer the opportunity to grab a snack at the company commissary, where you may just catch a glimpse of Bernard Kalb or Wolf Blitzer. *Corner of Techwood Drive and Marietta Street; 404-827-2300.*

Atlanta's other downtown green space, facing on Peachtree Street between Edgewood and Auburn Avenues, is **Woodruff Park,** a pocket oasis among the skyscrapers. On weekdays, park benches are filled with business people toting brown bags, while on weekends, skateboarders rip down the walkways. At the southwestern corner of the park, facing Peachtree Street, stands Atlanta's preeminent symbol: a bronze statue of a woman bearing a phoenix on high, titled *Up From the Ashes.* The sculpture pays homage to the city of Atlanta, which, after the Civil War, arose like the mythical phoenix from the ashes of destruction.

◆ UNDERGROUND ATLANTA  *map page 115*

In the late 19th century a series of bridges were built across the center of Atlanta to ease congestion caused by the expansion of the railyards. Over time, the bridges evolved into streets at the second-floor level of the old redbrick buildings in the area; the ground floor was now essentially underground. Merchants moved their operations to the second floor, leaving the first floor to spiders and mice.

In the early 1970s, hedonistic hotspots and subterranean hideaways began flourishing in these cellars, attracting tourists and Atlantans alike to what became known as Underground Atlanta. Clubs like Dante's Down the Hatch hopped 'til the wee hours of the morning. But by the late '70s, the thrill was gone, the nightlife almost nonexistent. In 1981, Underground Atlanta was shuttered, returning to its former state as a dark and dank city beneath a city

But the concept was too good, the appeal too great to let the entertainment district lie fallow. Entrepreneurs reopened Underground Atlanta in 1989 as a mixed-use, family-friendly complex of shops, restaurants, and a few bars. Though there is still an air of mystery about the place, it now feels less like an urban grotto and more like a mall in a semi-subterranean setting. Though the convention trade throngs the area on a good night, Atlantans, for the most part, aren't buying it.

◆ WORLD OF COCO-COLA

Just east of the Kenny's Alley entrance to Underground Atlanta, the World of Coca-Cola is housed in a stucco jukebox of a building erected in tribute to that fizzy liquid sold the world over. Inside you will find a replica of a 1930s soda fountain and learn of the role that Coca-Cola Company print advertising played in fashioning our national conception of what Santa Claus looks like. And of course there's plenty of free Coke all around. *55 Martin Luther King Jr. Drive; 404-676-5151.*

*A Coca-Cola advertisement dating from 1898.*

*The museum inside the State Capitol is open to all visitors free of charge.*

◆ GEORGIA CAPITOL

The gold-domed Georgia capitol was constructed in 1889 at a cost of more than $1 million. Visitors are free to roam the marble halls, perhaps making their way to the odd Georgia Museum of Science and History on the fourth floor, where an unlikely assortment of Georgia ephemera is assembled: mounted fish beside meteorites, big ole cotton bales, and—everyone's favorite—the two-headed calf known among some of the lobbyists as Janus.

But the real sights to see are on the grounds that surround the limestone edifice. Here you will come face to face with statues of old-school politicians the Talmadges, both father and son, as well as a compelling sculpture titled *Expelled Because of Color.* Erected in the 1970s on the northeast lawn of the capitol, the artwork is dedicated to the 33 African-American lawmakers who served in the state legislature during Reconstruction before being ousted with the coming of Redemption. The bronze depicts the ascendance of black Georgians from slaves to equals in a participatory democracy. *206 Washington Street; 404-656-2844.*

■ SWEET AUBURN

Once the economic, social, and spiritual heart of segregated black Atlanta, Sweet Auburn gave birth to the nation's first black-owned newspaper, the *Atlanta Daily World;* the first black-owned radio station, WERD; and the largest black-owned business to emerge from the South, Alonzo Herndon's Atlanta Life Insurance Company. In 1957, *Fortune* magazine deemed Auburn Avenue "the richest Negro street in the world."

Located just a mile or so east of Five Points (not to be confused with Little Five Points), the 12-block stretch along Auburn Avenue declined in the years following

## ATLANTA'S BLACK ELITE

*M*any members of the city's old guard—people like Ella Yates and the men and women she knows—would probably acknowledge that part of Atlanta has become known for its ability to remake itself: to tear up its historical roots every few years and erect a shiny new facade that reflects little of what preceded it....

Yates is old Atlanta. She's fourth-generation. She's Spelman College. She lives in the right neighborhood. She's earned the right graduate degrees, held the right jobs, and married into the right family. She even belongs to the right literary club—one that includes a small and elite group of black Atlanta's old-guard women who have met once a month, without fail, for eighty-nine consecutive years. Yates is the real thing, and she knows where the bones are buried.

But there are many new wealthy blacks in Atlanta who wouldn't know that. Some of the new black money that has landed in Stone Mountain, in Guilford Forest, in Buckhead, or in Dunwoody wouldn't know about the Yates family, or the bank or the drugstore they founded. The wouldn't know about the book party that was just given for Julian Bond's mother...or about the medical contributions of Asa Yancey or the business accomplishment of the Blayton family.... In fact, many members of the new elite don't live within the city limits. They are not among the 260,000 blacks that make the city only one-third white. The new black elite are on the outskirts of old Atlanta—both geographically and socially.

—Lawrence Otis Graham,
*Our Kind of People: Inside
America's Black Upper Class,* 1999

*Judie Dobbs, photographed here
around 1885, was the matriarch
of what became one of Atlanta's
celebrated black families. Born a
slave in the 1840s, she is said to
have lived to be 101.
(Muriel Gassett James files,
Sacramento, CA)*

desegregation as African Americans, free to work and live in areas not specifically consigned to them, moved their businesses and residences to other parts of the city.

Today, Sweet Auburn retains its role as the spiritual heart of Atlanta's African-American community. It was here that Martin Luther King Jr., arguably the most influential American religious leader of the 20th century, was born. Here were the headquarters of the Southern Christian Leadership Conference, the civil rights organization King headed during the 1960s. And it is here that King's body rests, in a white marble tomb beside a reflecting pool, on the grounds of the Martin Luther King Center for Nonviolent Social Change.

Wheat Street Baptist, Big Bethel African Methodist Episcopal, and Ebenezer Baptist: these are the churches that form the backbone of Auburn Avenue. **Big Bethel,** established in 1847 by slave owners for their slaves, was once the political hub of black Atlanta. A huge "Jesus Saves" sign, tacked to the steeple in the 1920s, advertises the church's philosophy in no uncertain terms. *220 Auburn Avenue; 404-659-0248.*

**Wheat Street Baptist Church** owes its name to the former name of Auburn Avenue. From the late 1930s to 1988, the humble but influential Rev. William Holmes was pastor of this congregation. *359 Auburn Avenue; 404-659-4328.*

But the best known of Sweet Auburn's churches is undoubtedly **Ebenezer Baptist,** the somber brick-and-masonry building where Martin Luther King Jr. took to the pulpit, and in so doing raised our nation's awareness about the inherent inequity of a segregated society. It was here that a 17-year-old King preached his first sermon, under the watchful eyes of his father, the pastor known to everyone as Daddy King. Here the younger King convened the Southern Christian Leadership Conference, one of the organizations that led the efforts to end segregation. And here was held the memorial service after his 1968 assassination. A recorded program in the sanctuary tells the story of the church and its favorite son. But the best way to gain an understanding of the importance of this church—or Big Bethel or Wheat Street—is to come to a Sunday morning service. As the gospel music rises to a crescendo, and the pews themselves seem to shake with the power of the pastor's message, you will come to appreciate how churches served as places of both solace and strength during the Civil Rights Movement. No matter your religious belief, you will be moved. A newer, larger Ebenezer was recently built nearby. *407 Auburn Avenue; 404-688-7263.*

APEX museum, formally known as the African-American Panoramic Experience, seeks to trace the lineage of black Atlantans from Africa to the modern day. The most compelling parts of the museum are the exhibits dedicated to the little postage stamp of urban Atlanta known as Sweet Auburn, including a re-creation of Yates & Milton, the drugstore that was once a gathering place for black Atlanta. Open Tuesday through Saturday. *135 Auburn Avenue; 404-521-2739.*

◆ MARTIN LUTHER KING JR.

The National Park Service now manages a complex of interrelated buildings with the **Martin Luther King Jr. Center for Nonviolent Social Change** at its core. Founded in 1968 by Coretta Scott King, wife of the assassinated civil rights leader, the center was intended to serve as an organ of change, to further King's agenda of racial and social reform. In years past, the center has sponsored concerts that were cross-booked with rap and rock bands in order to draw a racially mixed crowd. And through the years Mrs. King and her children have remained staunch defenders of Martin Luther King's legacy. But today, the center is not as much an organ of change as a representation of it, a place for reflection rather than activism.

The focal point of the center is King's final resting place, a simple white marble tomb surrounded by a reflecting pool and framed by a stepped waterfall. The inscription repeats King's prescient pronouncement from a civil rights speech:

FREE AT LAST
FREE AT LAST
THANK GOD ALMIGHTY
I'M FREE AT LAST

Inside the main building is a small exhibition hall displaying mementos from King's short and turbulent public life. There are plans afoot to expand the center's displays. *339 Auburn Avenue; 404-524-1956.*

One block west is the clapboard and shingle house where King was born on January 25, 1929. Unadorned, simple even, the nine-room house was home to Daddy King and his wife, Alberta, for the first 12 years of young Martin's life. National Park Service rangers now lead tours through the home as well as up and down this stretch of Auburn Avenue, providing visitors with a lively narrative of King's life. **Martin Luther King Jr. National Historic Site:** *501 Auburn Avenue; 404-331-5190.*

◆ DOWNTOWN CREATURE COMFORTS

If it's lunchtime and you find yourself downtown, you can queue up with the office workers at the closest **Barker's Charbroiled Red Hots** cart for heaven on a bun. There's a cart at the corner of Peachtree and Ellis, and more are scattered, strategically in various locations. Another downtown lunch tradition that is not to be missed is **Thelma's Kitchen** *(see page 153)*. For a more stylish taste of Downtown, try **City Grill** *(see page 154)* or **Mumbo Jumbo**, run by one of Guenter Seeger's protégés. The interior is an urbane mix of gothic and modern, trendy and tasteful. At night, the beautiful-people-in-black make this their haunt. *89 Park Avenue; 404-523-0330.*

With the major hotels lined up along Peachtree Street, and the Omni at CNN Center, visitors wishing to stay in downtown are well served. *Contact the Atlanta Convention & Visitors Bureau, 233 Peachtree Street N.E., Suite 100, Atlanta, Georgia 30303; 404-521-6600 or www.acvb.com.*

■ GREATER METROPOLITAN ATLANTA

Spreading outward from Atlanta's core, the interstate highway system hurtles travelers north, south, east, and west. Come quitting time, the roadways are thronged with commuters, cell phones in hand, hopping from lane to lane, their horns blaring out a chorus of frustration.

For the most part, the towns that ring metropolitan Atlanta are bedroom communities, their identities long lost to suburban sprawl that reaches across 18 counties and more than 5,000 square miles. But there are a few exceptions, communities of charm and diversity that boast attractions worthy of a detour, like Stone Mountain, Decatur, Kennesaw Mountain, and Moreland. Also of interest, though not detailed here, are Roswell, an old mill community turned toney suburb; Newnan, a thriving town centered on a courthouse square; and Jonesboro, a southside community chockablock with antebellum homes. Just don't venture out at rush hour!

◆ MARIETTA *map page 145, A-2*

Marietta, on the northwestern fringe of Atlanta, retains an attractive square with a grass-ringed gazebo at center. Gathered around the green space is a collection of lively shops and restaurants. But most visitors never make it this far; they're still stopped out on Cobb Parkway, gawking at the Big Chicken, a hen-shaped edifice erected during the heyday of roadside excess. With its rolling eyes and pecking yellow beak, it's a favorite of children, and thanks to it height of nearly 60 feet, pilots use it as a landmark. (Today, Kentucky Fried Chicken has the Big Chicken franchise.)

◆ KENNESAW MOUNTAIN NATIONAL BATTLEFIELD
*map page 145, A-2*

West of Marietta, down Highway 120, is the Kennesaw Mountain National Battlefield. Part of the Atlanta Campaign *(see page 108-109)* was waged here, and more than 11 miles of earthen breastworks remain. Though Union General Sherman would eventually push through Confederate defenses, at Kennesaw Mountain his advance was stalled for more than two weeks. His victory came with a stunning price: the lives of more than 3,000 Union troops.

*"The Big Chicken"—a Cobb County landmark in Marietta.*

*Two young drummers at a Civil War battle re-enactment.*

Today the spot is popular with day hikers and picnickers alike who explore the trails that wend through the park. *900 Kennesaw Mountain Drive; 770-427-4686.*

Closer to downtown Marietta, the National Cemetery on Washington Drive is the final resting place of more than 10,000 boys in blue who lost their lives in the Atlanta Campaign. Nearby, the Confederate Cemetery on Cemetery Street is home to more than 3,000 boys in gray, a full third of whom remain unknown.

◆ STONE MOUNTAIN    *map page 145, D-3*

Located just 15 miles east of Atlanta, this 825-foot-tall dome of stone rises from the Piedmont like an apparition. Though quarrying operations over the years have removed some of the granite for use in projects as varied as the Panama Canal and the U.S. Capitol, what stuns the first-time viewer is what remains: a massive rock, gray and imposing, with tufts of greenery jutting out improbably from the sides and top.

## UNCONQUERABLE KENNESAW MOUNTAIN

*I*n the warm wet summer nights, Atlanta's homes stood open to the soldiers, the town's defenders. The big houses from Washington Street to Peachtree Street blazed with lights, as the muddy fighters in from the rifle pits were entertained, and the sound of banjo and fiddle and the scrape of dancing feet and light laughter carried far on the night air. Groups hung over pianos and voices sang lustily the sad words of "Your Letter Came but Came Too Late" while ragged gallants looked meaningly at girls who laughed from behind turkey-tail fans, begging them not to wait until it was too late. None of the girls waited, if they could help it. With the tide of hysterical gaiety and excitement flooding the city, they rushed into matrimony. There were so many marriages that month while Johnston was holding the enemy at Kennesaw Mountain, marriages with the bride turned out in blushing happiness and the hastily borrowed finery of a dozen friends and the groom with saber banging at patched knees. So much excitement, so many parties, so many thrills! Hurrah! Johnston is holding the Yanks twenty-two miles away!

Yes, the lines around Kennesaw Mountain were impregnable....

With the loss of the supposedly unconquerable position, a fresh wave of terror swept the town. For twenty-five wild, happy days, everyone had assured everyone else that this could not possibly happen. And now it had happened! But surely the General would hold the Yankees on the opposite bank of the river. Though God knows the river was close enough, only seven miles away!

—Margaret Mitchell, *Gone With the Wind,* 1936

*Carving of Confederate generals Robert E. Lee and Stonewall Jackson and of Confederate president Jefferson Davis on the side of Stone Mountain.*

At the foot of the rock is the town of Stone Mountain, which, despite its obvious tourist bent, exudes a great deal of charm. Old storefronts face on the railroad tracks. White clapboard homes line the narrow streets. The city was late to develop, but by 1839 a settlement had begun to grow at the base of the mountain, soon becoming home to stonecutters and other laborers.

In the early years of the 20th century, when the South was awash in efforts to commemorate the Lost Cause, Helen Plane, a charter member of the United Daughters of the Confederacy, began what would be a nearly 60-year campaign to honor the Confederate heroes with a grand sculpture. The result of her efforts is a 90-foot-tall bas-relief on the face of Stone Mountain depicting Confederate president Jefferson Davis and Generals Stonewall Jackson and Robert E. Lee. Among the early sculptors to work on the project was Gutzon Borglum, who designed the carving on Mount Rushmore. When finally completed in the 1970s, this sculpture became the world's largest bas-relief.

Today, the effect of the sculpture is somewhat peculiar—what with Davis, Lee, and Jackson mounted on horseback and presiding over a metropolitan Atlanta area so far removed from its Old South. Beneath them, the park teems with visitors who have come to ride the railway, hike the 1.3-mile trail to the summit, view the antique cars on display, or bask on a white-sand beach and swim and fish in the lakes that ring the mountain. *Stone Mountain Park is 16 miles east of downtown Atlanta, off Highway 78; 770-498-5600.*

◆ DECATUR AND EMORY UNIVERSITY   *map page 145, C-3&4*

Six miles west of Stone Mountain—six miles closer to Atlanta—is the graceful town of Decatur. At once antiquated and up to date, Decatur is a great mix of yesterday's charm and today's attitudes. Suburban sprawl seems not so much absent as arrested here. At the center of town stands the imposing Old Dekalb County Courthouse, built in 1898, while the surrounding blocks are filled with sidewalk cafes, antique shops, and galleries. Ponce de Leon Avenue, the same thoroughfare that cuts slices through Atlanta's in-town neighborhoods, is the main drag.

Home to a sizeable contingent of post-hippies, longhair intellectuals, and college students—the latter attending Emory University or Agnes Scott, a women's college—the town has a reputation as the most tolerant of Atlanta's suburban communities. For evidence, look no further than the local gardening and social club, The Digging Dykes of Decatur, who have been known to march in local parades, pushing toy lawnmowers and chanting playfully, "We're here. We're queer. We garden!"

Just west of Decatur and north of Fernbank Forest, is the main campus of **Emory University**. Founded at Oxford, Georgia, in 1836, Emory moved to Atlanta in 1915, lured by a grant of of 75 acres of land and a one-million dollar endowment from Coca-Cola magnate Asa Candler. Ties to the Coca-Cola Corporation remain important to the school, as evidenced by the new Goizuetta School of Business, named for the company's former chief executive.

Today the campus covers almost 600 acres and attracts a liberal student body, many of whom, in the Georgia vernacular, "ain't from around here." Indeed, the university is home to a large international population and, thanks to its sterling academic reputation, has attracted to a good number of students from Northern states lured by the mild winter weather, as well as excellent academics and generous scholarships.

The university's **Michael C. Carlos Museum,** houses the largest collection of ancient art in the South—from Mesopotamian cuneiform tablets to pre-Columbian pottery. The building itself is a delight, an architectural marvel that somehow manages to mix Italian Renaissance and postmodernist styles. *571 Kilgo Drive; 404-727-4282.*

The university community helps support a plethora of shops and restaurants in the area. Among the most noteworthy eaterys are: **Burrito Art,** *1451 Oxford; 404-377-7786,* the **Floataway Cafe,** a warehouse area hotspot, *1123 Zonolite Road; 404-892-1414,* and **Violette** with hearty French fare, *2948 Clairmont Road; 404-633-3363.*

And then there's **Twelve Oaks Barbecue,** a Kosher restaurant operated by a Jewish native of New York and serving, of course, beef instead of pork. Every table is set with a copy of *Gone With the Wind,* presumably so that you might quickly re-read the Twelve Oak barbecue scene while awaiting your order. The barbecue, by the way, is not in the same league as some of the standard-bearers. *1451 Scott Boulevard; 404-377-0120.*

*Sunset over Atlanta, as seen from the top of Stone Mountain.*

◆ MORELAND   *map page 159, A/B-2/3*

At the lower end of the socioeconomic scale is the little burg of Moreland, some 25 or so miles southwest of Atlanta. The village center is a forlorn place where simple storefronts look as timeworn as the stray dogs that loll about on the front porches of the town's simple clapboard homes. Hard by the railroad tracks is writer Erskine Caldwell's birthplace, known as the **Little Manse**. Caldwell, author of such works as *Tobacco Road* and *God's Little Acre*, was one of the most popular novelists of the first half of the 20th century; his 55 novels sold more than 80 million copies altogether.

Caldwell used his bully pulpit to decry the harshness of rural life. In *You Have Seen Their Faces*, a project he undertook with his wife, photographer Margaret Bourke White, he wrote: "Tobacco Road is a thoroughfare of indeterminable length through every state in the Union. Sometimes it is an alley, sometimes it is a paved highway; now it is a dirt road through Arkansas, now it is a boulevard through Massachusetts." *Erskine Caldwell Birthplace Museum: One East Camp Street; 770-251-4438.*

## ATLANTA DINING—A TO Z

Atlanta has it all—from cutting edge cuisine to basic southern comforts.

### ◆ ATLANTA'S TRADITIONAL SOUTHERN RESTAURANTS

Atlanta may well be the citadel of the New South. But when stomachs growl at lunch, even the carpetbaggers among us are prone to sit down to a plate lunch of fried chicken and stewed squash, candied yams and corn pone. Anthropologists tell us that eating habits are among our most conservative habits. Atlanta's old-line purveyors are living proof—and destinations worthy of a cultural tourist in search of a taste of the Old South. Among the best are:

**The French Quarter Food Shop Too.** The original, midtown location went out of business, but you can still get the same good muffulettas, po-boys, and etoufée out on Johnson Ferry Road. Unlike many of the restaurants that pretend to serve Crescent City cuisine, this busy eatery is short on pretense and long on authentic flavor. *2144 Johnson Ferry Road; 770-458-2148.*

ATLANTA

**Heath's Grocery.** A few miles south of West End—but worth the drive. Belly up to the steam table for some of the best collard greens and cornbread on the planet. Decor is nonexistent and the food is available for takeout only, but if you wanted something fancy, you wouldn't be here in the first place. *787 Cascade Road; 404-755-0543.*

**Mary Mac's Tea Room.** A long-lived Atlanta institution—the place to come in midtown for a cup of potlikker or a platter of country-fried steak with mashed potatoes and gravy. You fill out your own ticket, hand it to the waitress, and, quick as a wink, she's back with your order. *224 Ponce de Leon Avenue; 404-876-1800.*

**Our Way Cafe.** These folks do vegetables proud. Cream corn is a paragon of flavor: fresh-scraped kernels simmered in a sauce tasting of butter and cream and little else. Squash casserole and butter beans are without peer in the city. Not to neglect the fried chicken or meatloaf, both of which are platonic entrees sure to satisfy. The cafe recently moved a mile east from its original Decatur location, but the atmosphere is still tidy and unfussy, like a classic small town cafe. *2831 E College Avenue; 404-292-9356.*

**The Silver Grill.** This classic, midtown grill has survived the gentrification of the surrounding neighborhood. Plate lunches and dinners are still served by waitresses who call you honey —without the least hint of affectation. The monstrous fried chicken breasts are the most popular items on the menu. *900 Monroe Drive; 404-876-8145.*

**Son's Place.** This Inman Park institution is run by Lenn Story, heir to the legacy of Atlanta's fabled fry cook, Deacon Burton. Some say Story's fried chicken is almost as good as the late Deacon's. If that's so, it's surely the best in town. For breakfast, try a salmon croquette-stuffed biscuit. For lunch, sop up your potlikker with a hoecake. Service is by cafeteria line service. *100 Hurt Street; 404-581-0530.*

**Thelma's Kitchen.** Owner Thelma Spurlock is famous for her okra patties—and rightly so. Truth be told, just about everything that emerges from her tidy, downtown kitchen is a paragon of soul food excellence. Locals grumble that the $7-plus per head price tag is steeper than it should be. *768 Marietta Street; 404-688-5855.*

◆ ATLANTA'S NEW SOUTHERN CUISINE: A SIX-PACK OF TASTES

What is New Southern Cuisine? At its best this school of cookery constitutes a return to roots, a rededication to cooking with local ingredients, albeit while complying techniques that owe much to French and various Mediterranean influences.

Many of the restauranteurs at the forefront of New Southern cooking - people like Robert Waggoner of Charleston, South Carolina who has been known to serve foie gras with fig-stuffed hushpuppies and pomegranate cream, or Jimmy Sneed of Richmond, Virginia who makes a Redneck Risotto from grits and shiitake mushrooms - dish up plates that challenge the longtime dismissal of Southern foods as being nothing more than grits, greens, and grease. As befits the capitol of the New South, Atlanta has its own stars, its own constellation of great restaurants.

**City Grill.** This elegant oasis in the middle of downtown, is housed in the former lobby of a landmark neo-classical granite building, with an interior graced by pastoral murals. Among recent favorites are crab cakes atop a bed of lemon linguini and Georgia mountain trout stuffed with sage-scented cornbread dressing and napped with a brown butter vinaigrette. *50 Hurt Plaza; 404-524-2489.*

**Horseradish Grill.** Arguably, Atlanta's premier purveyor of New Southern cuisine. This Buckhead restaurant draws its name from its setting—a converted livery barn. A veteran of the Atlanta restaurant scene, it also boasts a proud pedigree—Edna Lewis, the grande dame of Southern culinary arts, helped design the menu, and remnants of her signature dishes, like sherry-scented shrimp paste over stone ground grits, are still offered. *4320 Powers Ferry Road, facing on Chastain Park; 404-255-7277.*

**Justin's.** Owned by rap impresario Sean Puff Daddy Combs, this is the city's premier Nouveau Soul outpost. Though the setting is opulent Mediterranean palazzo-style, the cooking is straightforward. Sure, they gussy up some dishes, adding chipotle peppers to the tartar sauce that accompanies an appetizer of fried catfish fingers, napping a red velvet cake with a vanilla crème anglaise. But unlike many of the restauranteurs at the forefront of New Southern cooking the chefs at the helm of

Justin's tend to be down-home traditionalists at heart. Menu mainstays are of two types: Southern standards like smothered pork chops and seafood gumbo, fried catfish and braised short ribs of beef; and country club fare like batter-fried lobster tails and New York strip steak. *Located between Buckhead and Midtown at 2200 Peachtree Road; 404-603-5353.*

**South City Kitchen.** A twist on Southern traditions and a fillip up of such standards as fried green tomatoes with a bit of goat cheese. The chefs use stone ground grits as a foil for everything from pork to fish. Sometimes they stretch the bounds of New Southern convention, as in a curious take on the Reuben sandwich tradition: fried catfish, country ham, and coleslaw between two slices of toasted country bread. For dessert, try the white chocolate banana cream pie. South City Kitchen occupies a renovated two-story bungalow just off Peachtree Street in midtown. *1144 Crescent Avenue; 404-873-7358.*

**Taqueria Del Sol.** Be not deceived—if at first glance this looks like nothing more than a hip take on a traditional taco stand, take a close look at Eddie Hernandez's menu. This is ethnic Mexican-Southern assimilation at its best. The Memphis taco is filled with honest-to-goodness smoked pork and topped with jalapeno coleslaw; the fried chicken taco benefits from a jolt of lime mayonnaise; and the side order of turnip greens swim in a smoked chicken stock. On spring days, they pull up the garage doors and let the sun shine in. *Located on the west side of midtown at 1200-B Howell Mill Road; 404-352-5811.*

**Watershed.** As much a gourmet grocery as a restaurant. But with Indigo Girl Emily Saliers at the helm and consulting chef Scott Peacock around the stove, this relatively new arrival on the Decatur dining scene has quickly won its place in the Southern firmament. The culinary cognoscenti make their appearances on Tuesday nights when Peacock serves up cathead biscuits and pluperfect fried chicken, which taste mighty fine with a nice bottle of Syrah from the onsite wine store. *406 W Ponce de Leon Avenue; 404-378-4900.*

◆ Dining: Atlanta Chic

Atlanta's dining scene, like the city itself, is ever changing, ever evolving. Thanks to an influx of New South cash—and not a few restauranteurs from points beyond—Atlanta now claims its berth in the upper tier of America's restaurant cities. The following restaurants constitute a representative, if a tad quirky, sample of the city's best: a bit of French, a taste of Italian, a smidgen of Japanese, and a surfeit of great modern American cookery.

To find out about the hottest new spot in town, pick up a copy of Atlanta magazine at a local newsstand, and look for the reviews written by Christiane Lauterbach, the city's ablest, and, at times, most acerbic critic.

**The Atlanta Fish Market.** In a unique building that looks like an old railroad station passenger shed, this is the place to go in Buckhead for impeccably fresh seafood, simply prepared. If available, try the grilled grouper cheeks—they have the consistency and sweetness of lobster—served atop a bowl of grits. *265 Pharr Road; 404-262-3165.*

**Bacchnalia.** A table at this premier Buckhead establishment, located in a refurbished Snapper Lawnmower plant, is one of the hardest-won in town. A prix-fixe menu of such delights as a crab fritter in orange broth and foie gras atop charred scallops is well paired to the inventive, and exclusively American wine list. For desert try a cheese plate, featuring the best from regional American fromageries. The restaurant shares space, and ownership, with Star Provisions, a high end purveyor of all thing culinary. *1198 Howell Mill Road; 404-365-0410.*

**Bone's.** Regulars are treated to a car wash while dining at this clubby, Buckhead steakhouse. Thick cuts of beef are dry-aged, and the service is attentive but not fawning. You enter through the bar where blue-suited swells swill martinis and smoke bootlegged Cuban cigars. *3130 Piedmont Road; 404-237-2663.*

**Brasserie Le Coze.** Another Buckhead destination, Brasserie Le Coze is set in the midst of a shopping mall. The mirrors that line the walls and the oh-so-French menu give this stylish restaurant—first cousin to New Yorks' Le Bernadin—a look and feel that is the most genuinely Gallic in Atlanta. Cassoulet, rillettes, and fish dishes are best bets. *Lenox Square; 404-266-1440.*

**Eno.** This stylish, midtown newcomer to the wine bar scene serves nearly 100 wines by two-ounce tastes, and prices are reasonable—it's not one of those fussy late-80's places where the pubescent waiter trills his R's and doesn't deign it worthy of effort to serve anything less than a first growth, tagged with a first class price. Look for the Spanish reserve wines. Full meals are available, but grazing is best. Bar snacks include a great Provencal onion tart and a variety of rustic pâtés. *800 Peachtree Street; 404-685-3191.*

**Seeger's.** When chef Guenter Seeger left his longtime post at the Ritz Carlton Dining Room, he made headlines in the local paper. Set in a converted home on the edge of the Buckhead business district, his new restaurant, Seeger's, is decorated in a style that fuses austerity and opulence, old and new. The prix-fixe menu features such seasonal offerings as a beet salad with shrimp and champagne and sea urchin soup. Since the first day it opened, the national food press has fallen at Seeger's knees, heaping accolade upon accolade, award upon award. But all this excellence and opulence comes with a price: the tariff for three and six course dinners is the highest of any restaurant in Atlanta. *111 W Paces Ferry Drive; 404-846-9779.*

**Soto.** The best sushi in Atlanta—perhaps one of the top five sushi restaurants in America, and of course, it's in Buckhead. The interior is drab, but behind the bar, chef Sotohiro Kosugi sparkles. In addition to impeccably prepared, and artfully arranged, maki and sashimi, this quiet perfectionist creates daily specials that look almost jewel-like. The fatty tuna is always exceptional. And he's not adverse to getting a little wacky, working in Western style ingredients like truffle oil. *3330 Piedmont Road; 404-233-2005.*

**The Supper Club.** An unexpectedly romantic enclave, tucked into a strip shopping center just off the square in Decatur. Take one step inside the door of this intimate cafe and leave reality behind. The lighting is soft; the decorations are a charming, ever so avant garde mix, of opulent ornamentation and flea market bric-a-brac. The wine list is an engaging showcase for lesser known varietal like Syrahs and Malbecs. And the menu features such delights as savory crepes laced with cheese and ethereal steamed mussels perfumed with citrus. *308 Ponce de Leon Place; 404-370-1207.*

**Veni Vidi Vici.** Originally opened by the Hazan family of famed Italian food writers. Northern Italian food served in a swank, midtown setting is the draw here. Try the gnocchi in pesto or the rotisserie-cooked suckling pig. Or just order an appetizer and a cocktail and enjoy a night out on the patio. *41 14th Street; 404-875-8424.*

# MIDDLE GEORGIA

■ TRAVEL BASICS

Running in a line east to west across Middle Georgia are the cities of Augusta, Macon, and Columbus; along with the state's academic citadel of Athens, located to the north, these cities are the heart and soul of the region. Their revitalized downtowns are flanked by lovely tree-shaded boulevards and graceful homes. On the outskirts of each, urban life quickly recedes as you enter pine forests and trace your way down roadways lined with red clay. The region has two significant Native American sites.

**Getting Around:** Wander the back roads that link the cities. Middle Georgia's towns are all easily explored on foot, so get out of the car and meander the back streets lined with bungalows and Victorian painted ladies.

**Climate:** Mild winters with occasional cold outbreaks; temperatures in the 50s F; snow rare. Very hot and humid summers with frequent thunderstorms; temperatures in the low to mid-90s. Fall is usually dry and pleasant .

**Food & Lodging:** With a few notable exceptions, Middle Georgia is not the home of haute cuisine and high-falutin' hotels. That is not to say the region is without charm. There are antebellum inns that have been lovingly restored, and grand old hotels that still sparkle with the charms of yesteryear. And you'll find plenty of wonderful cafes where country cooking is raised to an art form, and roadside barbecue joints where pork is smoldered for hours before being pulled from the bone and napped with a thin sauce tasting of peppers, vinegar, and just the slightest hint of tomato. Three of Middle Georgia's prized barbecue establishments are, in layman's terms, out in the boonies. They may be far afield, but they're worth the drive. All three are between Atlanta and Macon. *(See pages 245-246 to read about about barbecue across the state.)*

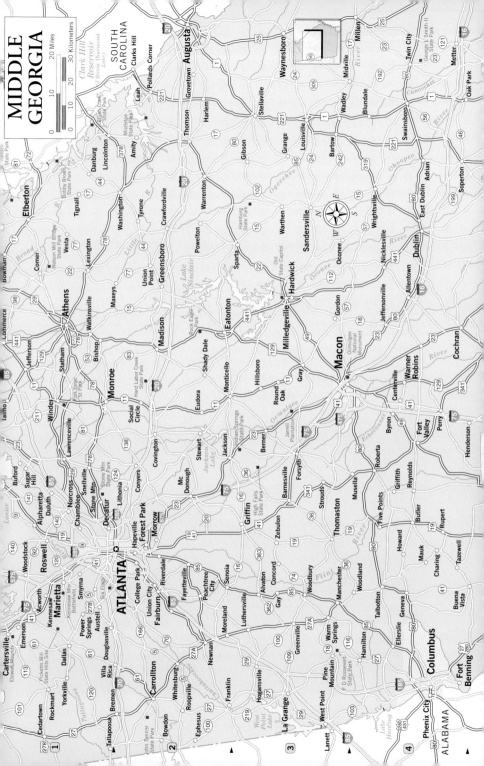

■ OVERVIEW

The region of Middle Georgia cuts across the center of the state, separating the bustle and boosterism of metropolitan Atlanta from the languor of southern Georgia. At its core are the towns of Augusta, Macon, and Columbus, urban outcroppings in an otherwise rural region.

North and south of the urban corridor that stretches from Augusta on the east, through Macon, and on into Columbus on the state's western border, there are little-populated burgs and vast, open expanses of pine forests. Both can be found just a short detour down narrow two-lane blacktops that snake their way along the state's belly, past roadside produce stands and kudzu-shrouded trees that, in the heat of a sultry summer afternoon, look more like dada topiary than an unfortunate attempt to arrest soil erosion.

It is a region where the past and present seem locked in a slow and fitful dance, where billboards beckoning "Sons of Confederate Veterans Join Now!" share the roadside with the tumbledown houses of the sons of slaves, where ancient wizened women still sweep their dirt yards with handmade brooms and tend day lilies planted in old truck tires.

*Along a Georgia two-lane blacktop between Atlanta and Athens. (photo by Kelly Duane)*

Georgia Red Clay, *Nell Choate Jones, 1946. (Morris Museum of Art, Augusta)*

In the summer, the sweet perfume of honeysuckle can be almost overwhelming. In the winter, the roadsides bleed red with each heavy rain as the iron-rich soil washes onto the bleached gray pavement.

Though most Native Americans were removed to Oklahoma in the early 19th century, Middle Georgia is awash in physical reminders of a time when they were the sole inhabitants of the area. Near Eatonton stands the Rock Eagle Effigy Mound, a quartz-rock figure believed to date from the Woodland period, which began 3,000 years ago and ended 1,000 years ago. In Macon, the Ocmulgee Indian Mounds stand in mute tribute to the city-building efforts of the Late Mississippian-era people who thrived on the site around 1,000 years ago (the mounds area was settled again by members of the Creek Confederacy by the 1700s).

European settlement of Middle Georgia began in 1736 when settlers made their way up the river from Savannah to establish a trading outpost on the banks of the Savannah River. Like other towns established in the early years of the colony,

Augusta was founded at the fall line, the point at which rapid flowing rivers turn to churning torrents, signaling the end of the Savannah River as a navigable waterway. With the coming of the Industrial Revolution, the choice would prove to be prescient, as the rushing rivers could be harnessed to generate power for mills.

From Augusta, the population moved inland in search of fertile land. And with the people moved the seat of Georgia government, first from Savannah to Augusta in 1784, then west to Louisville, and later to Milledgeville, where it would remain throughout the Civil War.

At the beginning of the Civil War, Augusta, Macon, and Columbus were among the most prosperous towns in the state. Cotton, shipped by rail and river, was traded in local markets or woven by mills into cloth. During the war, munitions plants and other industries thrived. Though much of the region would wither under the onslaught of General Sherman's March to the Sea, the major towns escaped virtually unscathed.

## SLEEPLESS NIGHTS—JULY 1864

*From the diary of Dolly Burge, who lived on a central Georgia plantation at the time of Sherman's March to the Sea.*

29TH

Last night was a sleepless one. At two o'clock I had the carriage at the door. Miss Mary took me out & showed me where she had buried the silver, then she, her brother, & Sally took the carriage for Madison, leaving me all alone again. I feel very much alarmed about them, fearing they will be molested.

All day I have walked about…. The Yankees left Covington for Macon headed by Stoneman to release prisoners held there. They robbed every house on the road of provisions, sometimes taking every piece of meat, blankets, & wearing apparel, silver & arms of every description. They would take silk dresses & put them under their saddles & things for which they had no use. Is this the way to make us love them & their union?

31ST

I slept scarcely none last night. We heard the enemy were below Sandtown destroying everything & that Wheeler was in pursuit. I was looking for them all night. I could hear their cannon. Sadai had the toothache. Mr. Rakestraw come in to dinner & wanted me to send him to Rutledge. I am so very lonely, no one passing.

—Dolly Lunt Burge, 1864, from *Diary of Dolly Lunt Burge*

After the war, rural areas returned to the business of cotton farming while the people of Athens set to work rebuilding a University, scarred by the decimation of its student population and a lack of capital. Through a cycle of boom and bust that lasted until World War II, the landscape and lifestyle remained little changed. But as tenant farmers left the farms for the lure of life in the North, small towns began to sink into oblivion, and the larger cities of Middle Georgia ceased to grow.

The sole economic savior during those bleak years was the U.S. military. Augusta's Fort Gordon, Fort Benning near Columbus, and Warner Robins Air Force Base, just down the road from Macon, boomed during the Cold War years. But their growth, coupled with "white flight" to the suburbs in the 1970s, meant that city centers were virtual ghost towns.

Soon manufacturing concerns were deserting the core as well. Mills closed. Jobs were moved overseas. Until the late 1980s, Middle Georgia was stuck in a rut. At the end of the 20th century, however, the region took on a new vitality, as cities redeveloped their downtown core and manufacturing companies began building plants in the South, lured by the promise of cheap, nonunion labor, inexpensive land, and easy access to the growing distribution network that emanated outward from Atlanta.

Today, the same blacktop road that winds past a row of tumbledown houses—or past a gimme-capped farmer sitting in the shade of an oak tree, selling boiled peanuts—is likely to continue on past a sleek brick-and-steel manufacturing facility perched amid the old cotton fields.

■ AUGUSTA *map page 159, F-2*

Augusta is a city seduced by ghosts, where lineage matters more than acreage and the local genealogical society is housed in finer, more spacious quarters than the main public library. Here, upon encountering a native Augustan of a certain age, you are likely to be greeted with the question, "Who are your people?" rather than, "What do you do for a living?" In Augusta, say some detractors, you had best count three generations of ancestors as natives or be branded an interloper.

That is a far remove from Augusta's birth in 1736 as a frontier trading town and military outpost. At the behest of colonial governor James Oglethorpe, troops were stationed at the post in hopes of better regulating trade with Native American tribes, a venture so successful that by 1740 construction had begun on a road linking Augusta with the colony's other trading center, Savannah.

Sibley Cotton Mill, Augusta, Ga.

*Hand-painted photograph postcard of the Sibley Cotton Mill, Augusta, circa 1900. (Augusta-Richmond County Museum, Augusta, collection of Joseph M. Lee, III)*

Augusta's role as a center of trade would sustain it through the colonial, antebellum, and Reconstruction eras, as it grew to be the Deep South's largest inland cotton market. By the late 1800s Augusta was also a manufacturing center, boasting a newly built canal that serviced mills and other plants with water-driven power. Concurrently, thanks to the availability of rail travel and Augusta's temperate climate, the city became a vacation destination for frostbitten Northerners and malaria-threatened coastal Southerners.

Today, Augusta is indeed a town that revels in its past and pageantry, eager to showcase the grand mansions of the Summerville neighborhood and inclined to wax poetic about the beauty of the Augusta National Golf Course, home of the yearly Master's Tournament. And yes, there is a drowsy quality to life in this, the second largest city in Georgia.

But that is not the whole story. For an earful of the other Augusta, point your radio dial to native son James Brown's 94.7 FM as you take a turn though the heart of town—down the length of Broad Street, the primary artery of Augusta's urban renaissance. Serenaded by the soulful sounds of Ray Charles or the "hardest working man in show business" himself, you will discover a downtown on the upswing, rich with diversity and cultural adventure, where funky bars and burrito stands coexist with one of the South's great art museums, the Morris Museum of Art.

◆ Riverwalk

The focal point of downtown Augusta's revitalization is the Riverwalk, a five-block promenade stretching along the Savannah River between Fifth and Tenth Streets. Atop the old levee and at water's edge, walkways wend past lush gardens, connecting many of the city's major cultural attractions. *Visitors Bureau: 32 Eighth Street; 706-823-6600.*

*The Cotton Exchange.*

**Cotton Exchange**
Centerpiece of the Riverwalk, the graceful, brick-turreted Cotton Exchange was built in 1836 and renovated in 1988. Now serving as both a museum of cotton culture and a visitor's center, this is the place to take a gander at a sample box and learn the difference between fair and middling grades of cotton. Along the back wall, a 45-foot-high chalkboard uncovered during renovations still displays turn-of-the-century market quotes for everything from cotton futures to picnic hams. *Reynolds and Eighth Streets; 706-724-4067.*

*Farmers bringing cotton to market, circa 1890. (Georgia Department of Archives & History)*

## Augusta Museum of History

Two blocks east of the Cotton Exchange is the museum affectionately known as "Augusta's Attic". Its redbrick seams bulge with an assortment of ephemera that tells the story of the region from prehistoric Indians through the 1970s. Children will delight in the 1914 steam locomotive and tender. *560 Reynolds Street at 6th; 706-722-8454.*

## Morris Museum of Art

Also along the Riverwalk is the Morris, the only museum in the world dedicated solely to the art of the American South. Ten intimate galleries are filled with works by, among others, Ida Kohlmeyer, Lamar Dodd, John McCrady, and Benny Andrews. Among the most arresting pieces is a curved, 1868 mural by John Mooney entitled *Surprise Attack Near Harper's Ferry.* It depicts Union soldiers bathing nude in the river, as seen through the eyes of a Confederate soldier just moments prior to attack. *One 10th Street; 706-724-7501.*

## National Science Center: Fort Discovery

Facing on the river itself, Fort Discovery uses virtual reality and other interactive technologies to teach children about natural phenomena such as lightening bolts. *One Seventh Street (at Reynolds); 706-821-0200.*

## Radisson Hotel Augusta

Right next door to the Morris, the swank Radisson has sweeping views of the Savannah River below. *706-722-8900.*

*The Morris Museum in Augusta is one of the finest art museums in the South.*

*The Sacred Heart Cultural Center now hosts several Augusta performing arts organizations.*

## ◆ MORE AUGUSTA TREASURES

The most stunning building in this architecturally inviting city may well be the **Sacred Heart Cultural Center,** a onetime Catholic church that now hosts the Augusta ballet, symphony and other arts organizations. The twin tin-tipped spires of this awe-inspiring, 1900 Romanesque revival building, shine brighter than any other spot on the Augusta skyline. *1301 Greene Street; 706-826-4700.*

### Old Town

To the east of the Cultural Center is an enclave of restored Victorian homes known as "painted ladies" for their bright color schemes. Here you will find the **Azalea Inn,** an eggplant-hued bed-and-breakfast where the ceilings soar to dramatic heights. *312 Greene Street; 706-724-3454.*

### Enterprise Mill

A concrete neoclassical bridge spans the Augusta Canal at 15th Street. Here the old Enterprise Mill stands as a testament to Augusta's past and future. Built in 1848 as a flour mill and later converted to a cotton mill, the 260,000-square-foot brick complex is now a mixed-use facility.

### Confederate Powder Works Chimney

Located along the canal on the site of the present-day Sibley Mill, this towering brick edifice is another fixture on the Augusta industrial skyline.

### Meadow Gardens

While Augustans bemoan the loss of some of city's grand old buildings, many fine homes survive, including Meadow Gardens (circa 1791), onetime home of Declaration of Independence signer George Walton. Sandwiched as it is between the Augusta Canal and a hospital parking lot, the white frame home looks threatened, but rest assured, it has been in the safe hands of the Daughters of the American Revolution since 1901. *706-724-4174.*

### Springfield Baptist Church

African Americans, brought to Augusta for cotton cultivation, have been an integral part of Augusta since its founding. Springfield Baptist Church, founded by freedmen in 1787 and perhaps the oldest independent African-American church in America, gave birth to what is now Atlanta's Morehouse University, one of the nation's finest universities. Today, the congregation worships in a brick building crowned with a copper cupola, and welcomes all comers to Sunday morning services. *Corner of Reynolds and 12th Streets; 706-724-1056.*

## ◆ BROAD STREET

A few blocks south of the river, Broad Street has been undergoing a renaissance of sorts, from Eighth Street west to 13th Street. (On the lower end of Broad, signs still beckon servicemen into bars with names like Lucifer's Follies.) Art galleries and restaurants are the primary draw, but the architecturally inclined will want to take note of graceful old theaters like the candy-striped **Modjeska** and retrofitted skyscrapers like the **Lamar Building**. The Lamar is a 16-story hodgepodge of Gothic and Italianate styles, built in 1913 and topped in 1973 by a two-story concrete pyramid designed by architect I. M. Pei.

### Soul

Pilgrims of soul, hoping for a James Brown sighting, may seek out **94.7** FM ("The Boss"), the family radio station at Broad and Ninth, or head down the street for a beer at the **Soul Bar,** where the walls are lined with posters and ephemera.

### Sunshine Bakery

Opened in 1946 by the Greenburg faimly, formerly of Minsk, Russia, this simple restaurant, with brick walls, and gold vinyl booths serves egg salad sandwiches and Rubens on house-baked sourdough rye. *1209 Broad Street; 706-722-9419.*

### Luigi's

A vestige of yesteryear, Luigi's Italian grotto still has booths of red leatherette and Tony Bennett playing on the jukebox. There's toasted ravioli, lasagna, moussaka, and spaghetti with fried chicken livers, and Chianti, in those little straw-encased bottles for a bargain price. *590 Broad Street; 706-722-4056.*

### The Pizza Joint

Exposed duct work looms above and hardwood floors run beneath. The pizzas, calzones, and strombolies are first rate. *1245 Broad Street; 706-774-0037.*

**White Elephant**
Come to this charming, plant filled dining room for good homemade chicken sausage, grilled fish, or Cuban sandwiches. An ele-phant tusk juts out from behind the bar like a prop in a child's dream. *1135 Broad Street; 706-722-8614.*

## ◆ AUGUSTA NATIONAL GOLF COURSE

In the suburbs, along busy Washington Road, is the Augusta National Golf Course. An impenetrable curtain of green foliage separates it from the concrete wasteland of fast-food franchises and gas stations. Conceived as an indigo plantation known as Fruitland, and in later years the site of a nursery, this complex is home each April to the world's most exclusive and prestigious golf event, the Master's Tournament.

A phalanx of chain motels, one as nondescript as the next, lines Washington Road near the golf club. But should your travel plans coincide with the annual Master's Golf Tournament, be forewarned: rooms will be as scarce as chicken teeth.

*Crowds gather around the sixth hole at the Augusta National Golf Course during the Masters Tournament.*

MIDDLE GEORGIA

◆ SUMMERVILLE AND THE PARTRIDGE INN

During the late 19th century, before Augusta was protected from flood by levees, the community of Summerville began to prosper, since it has a higher elevation than riverside downtown Augusta. Though many of Summerville's frame structures have since burned, two of the crown jewels from the area's heyday as a resort getaway still stand at the crest of the hill on Walton Way: the huge Mediterranean-style Bon Air, and the **Partridge Inn,** a charming hotel that remains at the center of Augusta social life.

The Partridge was built in 1890 and in its second century it still shines with the opulence of old. Perched high on a hill and fronted by a wide and welcoming veranda, it features a wonderful little courtyard pool at its center and a great bar on the second floor. *2110 Walton Way; 706-737-8888.*

◆ AUGUSTA DINING

**Delta Sandwich Shop**
In this tiny nook of a lunch spot tucked behind a now closed drugstore, the Whitaker family has been frying great burgers on a solid-top grill since 1978. Try one slathered with pimento cheese or capped with coleslaw. *1208 Wilson Street; 706-738-5221.*

**Duke Restaurant**
The local greasy spoon—and politico's haunt—where plate lunches of country fried steak, creamed corn, and lima beans draw the faithful. Breakfast is especially tasty, and the grits are good enough, as they say, to make you slap your mama. *1920 Walton Way; 706-868-1078.*

**Treybon**
The place to go if you can't decide what sort of barbecue you like best. There's a large selection of sauces, ranging from the ketchupy stuff they serve in western Tennessee to the mustard-laced sauce popular in South Carolina. Chili, Brunswick stew, and a few Cajun specialties round out the menu at this simple downtown roadhouse. *520 Reynolds Street; 706-724-0632.*

**Sconyers Barbecue**
Opened in 1956 in a two-story log cabin and operated by Augusta mayor Larry Sconyers who cooks his pork over oak and hickory chips and serves up sides of hash and rice as well as coleslaw. *2250 Sconyers Way; 706-790-5411.*

**La Maison on Telfair**
In this candlelit Victorian mansion Austrian native Heinz Sowinski does wonders with wild game and seafood. *404 Telfair Street; 706-722-4805.*

**Le Café du Teau**
A plush dining room where escargot, lamb, and venison are prepared with a flair that borders on pretension. *1855 Central Avenue; 706-733-3505.*

*The Confederate Memorial in Augusta at sunset.*

## ■ WASHINGTON AND ENVIRONS  *map page 159, E-2*

Surely there is not another town in all of Georgia with as many historical markers per capita as Washington. Washingtonians are a proud people, proud of their picturesque town and its picaresque history. Chartered in 1780, the town was the first to be named in honor of President George Washington, yet its most significant moment in history did not come until the close of the Civil War.

It was here that in May of 1865 Confederate president Jefferson Davis, while fleeing from Union troops, signed the last official acts of the Confederate government. In effect, it was here that the Confederacy came to an end. And it was near here that the remaining gold from the Confederate coffers was last seen. Treasure hunters still take to the woods each fall in search of the half a million dollars that is believed to have been buried in the red clay of Wilkes County.

Today the town exudes a prosperous air. Spend a few minutes wandering the sun-dappled streets where Victorian painted ladies and Greek revival mansions stand abreast the redbrick façades of stores selling antiques and hardware. There's a brisk efficiency in the air, as though Washington never succumbed to the drowsiness that defines many of Middle Georgia's bucolic little burgs.

MIDDLE GEORGIA

At the time of Georgia's secession from the Union, the primary challenger to Jefferson Davis for the Confederate presidency was Washingtonian **Robert Toombs** (1810-1895). Though Toombs would serve as the Confederate secretary of state and as commander of a Georgia brigade at Antietam, he is remembered today more for his firebrand oratory than his political acumen. Rather than accept a pardon and regain Union citizenship, Toombs reveled in his status as an "unreconstructed rebel," boasting in 1880, "I am not loyal to the existing government of the United States and do not wish to be suspected of loyalty."

His imposing home, built between 1794 and 1801 and purchased by Toombs in 1837, is supported by two-story Doric columns that line up across the broad front of the house; French windows open into high-ceilinged rooms. Toombs, an avid practitioner of Southern hospitality, always welcomed guests and when, after the Civil War, a hotel was proposed for Washington, Toombs opposed it. "If a respectable man comes to town," Toombs said, "he can stay at my house. If he isn't respectable, we don't want him here."

*The Campbell Historic Home is one of Washington's many well-maintained Greek revival mansions.*

*The living room of the Robert Toombs House, where the "respectable" were welcome.*

Today the house is open for tours; the best part is a brief film in which an actor playing Toombs tells his life story to a cub reporter. *216 East Robert Toombs Avenue; 706-678-2226.*

Just a block down Robert Toombs Avenue, the **Washington Historical Museum** offers a fascinating, chauvinistic introduction to local history. The museum is filled with Reconstruction-era carpetbags ("Those Yankees used them to cart away all our silver," says one of the tour guides), a cotton gin from the late 18th century, assorted Civil War ephemera, and a collection of fine furnishings. *308 East Robert Toombs Avenue; 706-678-2105.*

Sitting in the vestibule of the redbrick **Mary Willis Library** is a battered old chest thought to have once held some of the lost Confederate gold. Though the chest is empty, the graceful, high Victorian building, built in 1888 and home to the first free library in Georgia, is filled with treasures including a floor-to-ceiling stained glass window by Louis Comfort Tiffany. *204 East Liberty Street; 706-678-7736.*

Like much of Georgia, Wilkes County owed its wealth to cotton. **Callaway Plantation** stands in tribute to the halcyon days. Once at the center of a 3,000-acre plantation, the massive redbrick Georgian home is now open for tours that illustrate well the commerce of cotton in the antebellum era. *Five miles west of Washington on Highway 78; 706-678-7060.*

Before leaving Washington, stop in at **Another Thyme Cafe** for a slice of their exemplary pecan pie— sweet, and chock-full of nuts. The setting, in the lobby of an old hotel, is as charming as the pie crust is flaky. *5 East Public Square; 706-678-1672.*

Highway 44 north goes go through Tignall where the **Holly Ridge Country Inn** is set on a 100-acre farm. The inn offers 10 antique-filled rooms, all with private bath. At night the cicadas serenade you to sleep. In the morning, you wake to a cock's crow. *2221 Sandtown Road; 706-285-2594.*

*Azaleas and dogwood in bloom on the Callaway Plantation.*

*The Louis Comfort Tiffany stained glass window in the Mary Willis Library.*

■ THE "BIG LAKE" PARKS   *map page 159, F-1*

The damming of the Savannah River north of Augusta created a series of large lakes: Clarks Hill (Strom Thurmond), Russell, and Hartwell. Popular with fishermen and boaters of all types, they can be crammed with jet skis and motorboats on the weekend, but the lakes offer remote and primitive campsites, as well. Five state parks lie along the lakes: **Mistletoe** *(706-541-0321)*, **Elijah Clark Memorial** *(706-359-3458)*, **Bobby Brown** *(706-213-2046)*, **Richard B. Russell** *(706-213-2045)*, and **Hart** *(706-376-8756)*. *For camping reservations at the parks call 800-864-7275.*

■ ATHENS   *map page 177, D-1*

In the late 1970s and early '80s, two Athens bands hit it big. First came the B52s with their campy party-pop send-ups like "Rock Lobster," and later, REM with their moody jangle-rock songs like "Radio Free Europe." By the time the national press corps came calling, the B52s were spending most of their time in New York, and REM was spending all of its time on the road, touring behind albums that had rock critics and pimple-faced high-school kids alike swooning.

Invariably, the articles in *Time, Newsweek,* the *New York Times,* and the *Boston Globe* asked, "Why Athens? Why the South? How is it that the future of post-punk rock 'n' roll finds its taproot in this sleepy little college burg of 50,000 souls?"

While the national press pondered why, bands like Art 'n the Dark, Pylon, Love Tractor, Limbo District, the Method Actors, and the Barbecue Killers slogged it out night after night in cramped, sweaty bars where the rafters were concave from the weight of decades of neglect and the floors shimmied beneath the epileptic writhing of coed dervishes. Though

*The rock band REM named its album* Automatic for the People *after the slogan of Weaver D's in Athens. (See page 203.)*

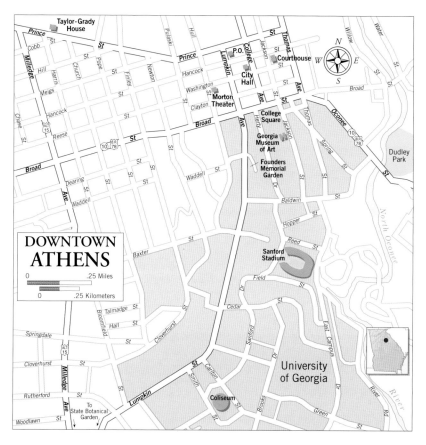

DOWNTOWN
ATHENS

0        .25 Miles

0        .25 Kilometers

University
of Georgia

at the time it was little discussed, some observers now argue that, like the Southern literary renaissance of the 1930s, the Athens music scene of the 1980s owed its origins to the self-analysis and self-expression that naturally follows a period of great turmoil. In the case of the literary renaissance, that turmoil was Reconstruction and its aftermath; for rock 'n' rollers in Athens, it was the Civil Rights Movement and the political fallout of Watergate.

And where else but the university-centered town of Athens for such a movement to coalesce?—a place where the staid School of Agriculture and the free-form School of Art held equal sway, a place where those dervishes writhing on the dance floor were but one generation removed from the farm, their parents the protectors of the Jim Crow South.

### ◆ University of Georgia

It is to the university that the town of Athens owes its birth. Founded in 1785 as the nation's first chartered state university, the University of Georgia did not open its doors for classes until 1802. North Campus, an oak-shrouded oasis at the heart of the campus, adjacent to Athens' downtown business district, maintains the intimate feel of a small college quad, despite the fact that the university now enrolls more than 30,000 students. Fueled by investment from the Georgia Lottery, the campus is awash in new buildings. *General information: 706-542-3000.*

### The Arch

Freshmen, bowing to tradition and superstition, avoid passing through the cast iron arch that frames the passage between town and gown, lest they be rendered sterile.

### Georgia Museum of Art

This modern teaching and exhibition center boasts a sizable collection of modern American painting including works by Jacob Lawrence and Georgia O'Keeffe. *706-542-4662.*

### Football

Though the university is recognized as one of the better public universities in the nation, for many of the faithful the university exists for but one reason: football. Each fall

*"Uga V," the bulldog mascot of the University of Georgia, has a camera mounted on his head.*

*Partygoers await the Magnolia Ball at the University of Georgia. (photo by Kelly Duane)*

86,000 cheering fans descend upon Athens on home-game Saturdays to watch the Bulldogs do battle "between the hedges" of Sanford Stadium. Those who visit during the off-season make their way to the glass-and-granite **Butts–Mehre Sports Museum** to relive past triumphs and view the Heisman trophies won by Frank Sinkwich and Herschel Walker.

### Founders Memorial Garden

Tucked into a little-visited corner of North Campus, the boxwood-bordered garden pays tribute to America's first garden club, established at Athens in 1881.

### State Botanical Garden of Georgia

Another tribute to Georgia's wealth of flora is located just a few miles south of town: This living laboratory was established by the university. *2450 South Milledge Avenue, North Campus; 706-542-1244.*

### The Tree That Owns Itself

Perhaps Athens' most unusual—and enduring—tribute to the natural environment is the tree whose property rights were established by Professor William Jackson when he willed to the white oak all land within eight feet of its trunk. Today the tree, ringed by a concrete retaining wall, juts out into Finley Street at the corner of Dearing.

### The Georgia Center

What the rooms at this on-campus, motel-style facility lack in charm, they more than make up for in convenience. *1197 South Lumpkin Street; 706-542-1181.*

## ◆ Seeing Athens

Athens' primary attraction might well be its street life. Downtown is a circus of cafes and coffee shops, watering holes and live music venues, record stores, and restaurants, where the modern-day inheritors of the early-1980s renaissance still throng the streets and the 40 Watt Club still hosts live music six days a week.

Any tour of Athens should include a drive down Milledge Avenue, a lush greensward of a street lined with stunning examples of antebellum architecture. Fronted by massive magnolia trees and adorned with wrought iron, many of these former mansions now do service as sorority and fraternity houses.

### Athens City Hall

Pointing north from a perch on the grounds of Athens City Hall is an infamous and ineffective Civil War curiosity, a double-barreled cannon. Designed by Athens native John Gilleland and first tested in 1863, the cannon was made to fire two chain-linked balls simultaneously. Rather than whirl out, bola-style, the chain broke, the balls sputtered left and right, and the cannon was quickly retired. *College Avenue at Hancock Street.*

### Morton Theatre

Just down the street from city hall is the Morton Theatre, built in 1890 and long-time home to performances by African-American greats like Cab Calloway. Recently restored, the warm wood auditorium now hosts a variety of community events and conferences. *195 West Washington Street; 706-613-3770.*

### Taylor-Grady House

Out on Prince Avenue, at a small remove from the downtown core, is the home where the New South booster spent his college years of 1865–1868. Grady referred to the house as "an old Southern home with its lofty pillars, and its white pigeons fluttering down through the golden air." Today it is filled with period antiques and available for tours. *634 Prince Avenue; 706-549-8688.*

### The Grit

Amid a setting of distressed brick walls festooned with funk and folk art, a cadre of tattooed waiters slings some great hash here. Try the curries and the daily vegetable plates, and for heaven's sake save room for dessert. Pray for German chocolate cake. *199 Prince Avenue; 706-543-6592.*

### Magnolia Terrace

Located in Athens' historic Cobbham neighborhood, the **Magnolia Terrace**, a 1912 Colonial-style inn is within walking distance of shops and restaurants along Prince Avenue. Well-appointed rooms and an expansive front porch with comfortable wicker furniture complete the scene. *277 Hill Street; 706-548-3860.*

*(opposite) Street scene in Athens.*

◆ BARBECUE NEAR ATHENS

**Paul's Barbecue** is a vestige of a bygone era, open Saturdays only from around nine in the morning until two, maybe three, in the afternoon. Pitmaster George Paul is justly revered for his sweet ham meat, cooked twelve or more hours over red oak and hickory embers. And the setting—a tumbledown stand hard by the highway—couldn't be more humble or welcoming. A local church group provides cakes and pies. *Highway 78, Lexington; 706-743-8254.*

■ MADISON *map page 159, D-2*

Madison, established in 1807, is not alone in claiming to have been spared by General Sherman because he considered it "too beautiful to burn"—an oft-told story. In the case of Madison, the story goes that Sen. Joshua Hill, a local Union sympathizer of sorts, persuaded one of Sherman's men, General Slocum, to spare the town. Some attribute Hill's success to the men's common bond as members of the Mason order, others to a gentlemen's agreement forged some time previously. Others say it's all a bunch of hooey. No matter, after a tour of the town, you will come to share with the good people of Madison the belief that it was indeed too lovely to torch.

Time was that Madison flourished as the seat of government in a cotton-rich county. During the antebellum boom, planters built opulent homes along the streets of this compact village. Today, more than 30 graceful period homes lie within the confines of the historic district. Most of the homes are within a few blocks of one another, set on the narrow roads just north and south of Main Street. The local welcome center supplies maps and a guided walking and driving guide. *115 East Jefferson Street; 706-342-4454 or 800-709-7406.*

◆ MADISON ATTRACTIONS AND COMFORTS

**County Courthouse**
As the seat of government for Morgan County, the city bustles with energy, yet its center is anything but typical of courthouse squares in Georgia. The courthouse itself is a Beaux-Arts beauty, built relatively late— 1905—and oddly situated not it the mid-

dle of a square of green, but catty-corner from the square itself, as if it were an afterthought rather than the focal point.

**Morgan County Cultural Center**
This towering Romanesque revival building was constructed in 1895 for the first school in the state with separate grades.

The center now hosts plays and musical concerts as well as a series of historical exhibits; the latter include the Boxwood Parlor installation, a dramatic re-creation of upper-class home life of the late 19th century. *434 South Main; 706-342-4743.*

### African-American Museum

Paying homage to the hardscrabble life of black Georgians, this simple frame home, built in 1895, is filled with mementos of black American folklife and its African roots. Works by world-renowned artist Benny Andrews and his father, George "Dot Man" Andrews, are of special note. *156 Academy Street; 706-342-9191.*

### Ye Olde Colonial Restaurant

If you can snag a table in the front room of the former Morgan County National Bank, you'll be rubbing elbows with locals, feasting on traditional Southern fare. The old vault in the back room is papered with Confederate money. *108 E. Washington; 706-342-2211.*

### Brady Inn

The heart pine floors are polished to a sheen in this late-1800s Victorian cottage. The seven rooms have private baths, and there are plenty of rocking chairs out on the front porch. A full breakfast is served. *250 North Second Street; 706-342-4400.*

### Burnett Place

Built around 1830, this Federal-style inn was restored in conjunction with the local historical preservation society. Rooms are well appointed, some with canopy beds. *317 Old Post Road; 706-342-4034.*

### Blue Willow Inn

Fifteen miles west of Madison in Social Circle is the Blue Willow Inn, serving a justifiably famous buffet, stocked with perennial Southern favorites like corn pudding, dressing and gravy, fried chicken, stewed tomatoes, good, crunchy fried green tomatoes, and ersatz oven-cooked barbecue. Popular with tourists and locals alike, this graceful home feels a bit like a small-town country club. Hoop-skirted lasses welcome you on the veranda. *294 North Cherokee Road (GA 11), Social Circle; 770-464-2131.*

## ■ ROCK EAGLE EFFIGY MOUND  *map page 159, D-2*

South of Madison along Highway 441, at the end of an ankle-wrenching flagstone path, is Rock Eagle Effigy Mound, best appreciated from a perch atop the four-story observation platform. More than 100 feet from head to tail, and with a wingspan of 120 feet, this collection of quartz rocks cuts an imposing profile among the pines and oaks of the surrounding forest. Believed to be over 2,000 years old, the mound is one of the most impressive and mysterious Native American sites in the South.

■ EATONTON   *map page 159, D-2*

Proof of the hold writer Joel Chandler Harris has on this little town is everywhere. On the square across from the beautiful redbrick courthouse sits Briar Patch Office Supply. On the courthouse lawn, a **statue of Brer Rabbit** stands in curious repose, keeping watchful eye over the comings and goings of Eatonton's residents. Harris, compiler of the *Uncle Remus Tales* and often referred to as Georgia's Aesop, was born in Eatonton in 1848.

*The first edition of* Uncle Remus *tales, published in 1881.*

Three blocks south of the courthouse is the **Uncle Remus Museum.** Housed in a collection of buildings that one observer claimed are "the world's only air-conditioned slave cabins," the museum brings Harris's African-American folktales to life through dioramas of "The Awful Tale of Mr. Wolf" and "The Wonderful Tar Baby Story," the latter of which was dramatized by the Walt Disney Company as *The Song of the South. 214 South Oak Street, in Turner Park; hours limited, call for information: 706-485-6856.*

Eatonton is the birthplace of another literary lion as well. Born in 1944, Alice Walker, author of *The Color Purple,* grew up on the outskirts of town. Though no monuments pay tribute to her achievements, a driving tour of the Pulitzer Prize–winner's old stomping grounds can be arranged through the local tourist office, and evidence of her Color Purple Foundation's work with underprivileged children can be felt throughout the community.

## ◆ MID-GEORGIA BARBECUE

Some of Middle Georgia's best barbecue joints are out in the boonies between Atlanta and Macon. *(See essay on pages 245-246 for more on Georgia barbecue.)*

### Moldin Tillman's Barbecue

In a shack set hard by the railroad tracks in Hillsboro, Tillman, a retired welder, cooks hams for as much as 24 hours, and simmers his Brunswick stew in big cast-iron wash pots. He's open on Friday and Saturday only during the months April through December, usually closing up when he runs out of meat, long before the posted hour of 9pm. Some consider this to be among the best BBQ shacks in Georgia. *Highway 11, Hillsboro; 706-468-6536.*

### Spruce's Barbecue

Housed in a drab, brown cinderblock bunker of a building, Spruce's has been in business since 1938. Cords of wood stacked by the smokehouse attest to the fact that they cook their pork the old fashioned way. Great Brunswick stew, thick with meat, and a barbecue sauce, piquant with red, black and white pepper, draw the crowds. During the summer, look for the house-made peach cream pie. *1201 Meriwether Street, Griffin; 770-412-1007.*

### Fresh Air Barbecue

It's the "mother church" of Georgia's barbecue restaurants. Opened in 1929, this Jackson Georgia institution with the sawdust-covered front porch, is justifiably famous for lean smoked pork spiked with thin, vinegary sauce. Great, finely chopped coleslaw, teeth-achingly sweet iced-tea, and okay Brunswick stew round out the menu. *On Highway 42, two miles out of Jackson in Flovilla; 770-775-3182.*

### Old Clinton Barbecue

In good smoke shack fashion, the front porch is awash in sawdust and the amenities are few. It's owned by the Coulter family who learned their barbecue tricks from the good folks at Fresh Air. Some aficionados (this author included) think they may even do it a bit better. *Highway 129, two miles south of Gray; 478-986-3225.*

## ■ MILLEDGEVILLE *map page 159, D-3*

Author Flannery O'Connor, who lived most of her life in Milledgeville, once observed that her native region was "Christ-haunted." Though a half-century of development has certainly changed Milledgeville and Middle Georgia, one can't help but posit that O'Connor would recognize what remains. On Sunday morning and Wednesday evening, churches still bustle with activity, and at almost any time of the day, local radio airwaves crackle with the sounds of a gospel choir or the rants of a country preacher.

A small room in the **Russell Library** at Georgia College and State University houses the **Flannery O'Connor Collection**. On display is her battered Royal typewriter along with family mementos and early versions of some of O'Connor's greatest works—short stories like "The Misfit" and novels like Wise Blood. A 14-minute film puts her life and work in the context of her Middle Georgia surroundings. *Corner of Montgomery and Clarke Streets; 478-445-4047.*

Though it was the capital of Georgia from 1803 to 1868, Milledgeville is a sleepy, slow-paced town at heart whose major attractions can be viewed over the course of a leisurely afternoon stroll.

## A VARIED LIFE

*H*e leaned back against the two-by-four that helped support the porch roof. "Lady," he said slowly, "there's some men that some things mean more to them than money." The old woman rocked without comment and the daughter watched the trigger that moved up and down in his neck. He told the old woman then that all most people were interested in was money, but he asked her what a man was made for. He asked her if a man was made for money, or what. He asked what she thought she was made for but she didn't answer, she only sat rocking and wondered if a one-armed man could put a new roof on her garden house. He asked a lot of questions that she didn't answer. He told her that he was twenty-eight years old and had lived a varied life. He had been a gospel singer, a foreman on the railroad, an assistant in an undertaking parlor, and he had come over the radio for three months with Uncle Roy and his Red Creek Wranglers. He said he had fought and bled in the Arm Service of his country and visited every foreign land and that everywhere he had seen people that didn't care if they did things one way or another. He said he hadn't been raised thataway.

A fat yellow moon appeared in the branches of the fig tree as if it were going to roost there with the chickens. He said that a man had to escape to the country to see the world whole and that he wished he lived in a desolate place like this where he could see the sun go down every evening like God made it to do.

"Are you married or are you single?" the old woman asked.

There was a long silence. "Lady," he asked finally, "where would you find you an innocent woman today? I wouldn't have any of this trash I could just pick up."

—Flannery O'Connor, "The Life You Save May Be Your Own," from *A Good Man is Hard to Find, and Other Stories,* 1948

**The Old Governor's Mansion**
Built in 1838, this peach-colored citadel of Georgian architecture, ringed by raggedy boxwood gardens, is open for guided tours that give a sense of upper-class life and political machinations in the antebellum era. *120 South Clarke Street; 478-445-4545.*

**Old State Capitol**
A few blocks away, at the corner of Green and Jefferson Streets is the Gothic Old State Capitol Built in 1807, this forbidding gray fortress was the seat of Georgia government for more than 60 years.

**Antebellum Inn**
Just a block from the Georgia College campus, the 1890 Greek revival Antebellum Inn features five rooms decorated with a feminine flourish. There is a large pool, and a full breakfast is served each morning. *200 North Columbia Street; 478-454-5400.*

■ MACON  *map page 159, D-3*

In 1806, the first European settlement in the Macon area was established at Fort Hawkins, on the east bank of the Ocmulgee River. Less than a mile away, the prehistoric Ocmulgee Indian Mounds loomed, a tribute to the architectural acumen of the late Mississippian culture that flourished here more than 3,000 years ago. By 1823 the town of Macon had begun to take shape on the western bank of the Ocmulgee, and as cotton brought prosperity to the Georgia interior, Macon grew steadily.

Early on, Macon served as a riverboat port, shipping cotton to the Georgia coast and on to Europe. After the Ocmulgee River became clogged with silt and detritus, railroads delivered the cotton, and Macon retained its importance in the cotton trade. During the Civil War, Macon suffered relatively little at the hands of Sherman. And yet Macon never became a bustling boomtown like Atlanta. Instead, this prosperous burg, 12 miles north of the state's geographic center, seemed to languish in the summer heat. Boosters spoke of the beauty of the city's columned mansions rather than the size of its labor force.

That all changed in 1942 with the establishment of **Warner Robins Air Force Base,** 12 or so miles down the road. During World War II and throughout the Cold War, the military installation grew. Today more than 15,000 people work at the base, making Warner Robins the state's single largest employer.

### ◆ MACON AND MUSIC

Of late, Macon has benefited from yet more governmental investment, this time from the state of Georgia. In 1996, the **Georgia Music Hall of Fame** opened, a multimedia tribute to a musical legacy that includes Macon's own Otis Redding, the Allman Brothers, and Little Richard. Arranged by period and genre, and housed in thematic sets (a faux 1960s nightclub for the R&B exhibit), the exhibits are augmented by musical accompaniment delivered via headphones hooked to CD players. In the Gospel Chapel visitors sway to the sounds of "Precious Lord Take My Hand" by gospel pioneer and Villa Ricca native Thomas Dorsey. *200 MLK Jr. Blvd.; 478-750-8555 or 888-GA-ROCKS.*

*The James Brown exhibit at the Georgia Music Hall of Fame.*

Dorsey made his name by fusing elements of blues and spiritual music. In the early 1970s, the Macon-based Allman Brothers Band made a name for itself by combining blues with rock 'n' roll to create something called Southern Rock. With songs like "Ramblin' Man" and "Statesboro Blues," they sang of a South in transition, paying tribute to the bluesmen who went before them. Today, fans of the Allman Brothers come to Carnation Ridge at Rose Hill Cemetery on Riverside Drive to visit the graves of band members Barry Oakley and Duane Allman, both of whom died in mid-1970s motorcycle accidents, or to eat at the H&H Cafe, where Mama Louise has fed generations of Macon's musical legends. At the Big House, a Tudor mansion that was once the communal home of the band, Kirk and Kirsten West serve as unofficial keepers of the **Allman Brothers archive and museum**. *2321 Vineville Avenue; 478-742-5005.*

When, in the early 1920s, millionaire entrepreneur Charles Douglas grew tired of being relegated to the balcony bench seats of the local **Grand Opera House,** he built one of the South's "first and finest" African American–owned theaters. Once host to such luminaries as Duke Ellington and Count Basie, the theater went through some years of neglect. Today, it is a vibrant venue for live performance. *651 Mulberry Street; 478-301-5460.*

◆ MACON SIGHTS

### Sidney Lanier Cottage

Sonorous sounds of a different sort are paid homage to at the boyhood home of Sidney Lanier, composer of such poems as "The Marshes of Glynn." This gabled, white frame cottage, built in 1840, is perched high on a brick street packed with beautiful homes. *935 High Street; 478-743-3851.*

### Hay House

Near the crest of Coleman Hill stands what may well be Georgia's grandest home, an Italian Renaissance revival mansion known as the Hay House. Completed in 1859, the four-level, 18,000-square-foot home was, at the time of its construction, a marvel of architectural ingenuity boasting an ingenious central heating system and an early tube-based intercom. The 45-minute tour is a spellbinding introduction to the glories of an antebellum home, with enough secret passageways to delight even the most jaded adult or overstimulated child. *934 Georgia Avenue; 478-742-8155.*

### Cannonball House

Just down the street, the diminutive Cannonball House looks like a dollhouse reproduction of a Tara stage set. The most interesting things about the house are a cannonball-pierced column and a collection of Civil War memorabilia. *856 Mulberry Street; 478-745-5982.*

### Luther Williams Field

Another downtown fixture is Luther Williams Field, former home of the Macon Peaches, now home to the Macon Braves, the Atlanta Braves' farm team. The 1920s-

*A doorway to the picture gallery in the Hay House.*

era steel-and-brick ballpark is the most intimate professional baseball field in the state. *In Central City Park; 478-745-8943.*

**Tubman African-American Museum**
Macon's African-American heritage is as well documented as that of any city in the state, thanks to the Tubman African-American Museum. Named for a onetime conductor on the Underground Railroad, Harriet Tubman, this is Georgia's largest African-American museum, featuring exhibits on African art as well as a mural of local and national notables that wends its way through the gallery space. *340 Walnut Street; 478-743-8544.*

◆ MACON CREATURE COMFORTS

Southern-style eatin' abounds in Macon. See page 203 for two of Macon's best.

**The Bear's Den**
Step up to the steam table at the best plate-lunch in town. Select from the daily specials and then carry your tray back to the tidy dining room lined with pictures of Mercer University sports teams. Though the meats are good, your first visit calls for a vegetable plate piled high with cheddar-crowned macaroni, squash casserole, dusky turnip greens, and sage-scented dressing topped with giblet gravy. *1191 Oglethorpe Street; 478-745-9909.*

**Jeneane's Cafe**
A sparkling clean downtown lunchroom with country fried steak, speckled butter beans, creamed corn, and turkey with dressing. If you show up on Thursday, top off your feast with a bowl of banana pudding. *524 Mulberry Street; 478-743-5267.*

**Midtown Grill**
Though it occupies an unimpressive, narrow maroon rectangle in a suburban shopping center, the food is some of the most consistent and tasty to be found in the city. Try the grilled pork chops or the veal-and-spinach meatloaf. A decent selection of wines is offered. *3065 Vineville Avenue; 478-745-8595.*

**Nu Way**
Famous since 1916 for the sweet heat of the chili sauce on the dogs, the parsley-flecked coleslaw, and the flaky ice in the cups of Coke, this "weenie stand" may well have been the model for its more famous rival, the Varsity, 70 miles up the road in Atlanta. Grab a seat at the counter and you're in the middle of the action. *430 Cotton Avenue; 478-743-1368.*

**Fincher's Barbecue**
It may be a local favorite, but this author just can't taste the appeal. That said, generations of Macon residents swear by the soupy sauce and revel in the knowledge that their favorite was the first barbecue to go into outer space when, in 1989, astronaut Sonny Carter took it aboard a Space Shuttle flight. *891 Gray Highway; 478-743-5866.*

**Fresh Air Barbecue**
This a branch of the original in Jackson serves the same tasty, slow-smoked 'cue. *3076 Riverside Drive; 478-477-7229.*

*Cherry blossoms bloom along a street in downtown Macon.*

**Natalia's**

Maconites call this their best restaurant and pack the cheery dining room on weekends. Here you'll find Italian-inspired dishes and triple-cut lamb chops charred to a rosy hue, and Macon's best wine list. *2720 Riverside Plaza; 478-741-1380.*

**Lodging**

Strangely, Macon has only two noteworthy places to lay your head: the **Crowne Plaza Hotel,** *108 First Street; 478-746-1461,* and the majestic, Greek revival **1842 Inn.** *353 College Street; 478-741-1842.*

♦ OCMULGEE NATIONAL MONUMENT

What is perhaps the most important site in Macon is also the oldest. Located on the eastern fringe of the city on the site of an old trading outpost, Ocmulgee National Monument is dominated by a series of earthen mounds, including the imposing Great Temple Mound, which rises some 45 feet from a base the size of 14 football fields. People first began living at this site about 10,000 years ago, but it was those who lived here between A.D. 900 and 1100 and belonged to what is known as the Late Mississippian culture, who built the temple mounds and structures such as the clay-floored "Earthlodge."

*The Great Temple Mound in Ocmulgee National Monument.*

The Mississippians were a comparatively sedentary people, inclined to farming rather than hunting and gathering. Along the river bluff they built a series of ceremonial mounds, raising them higher and higher over the years as new leaders came to power. At its height the settlement was home to more than a thousand people.

Today, the mounds the Mississippians built—basketful by basketful of dirt—are popular with hikers and amateur anthropologists alike, who travel the trails through the pastoral lands surrounding the temples, formulating their own ideas as to why it all started and how it all ended. *1207 Emery Highway; 478-752-8257.*

■ PASAQUAN *map page 159, B-4*

Just outside Buena Vista at the bend in a curve on a two-lane blacktop looms Pasaquan, a walled compound decorated with a dizzying intensity. Pasaquan was created by Eddie Owens Martin, who was born to sharecroppers here in Marion County on the Fourth of July 1908. Ostracized early on because of his sexual orientation, Martin ran away from home at the age of 14 and traveled to such exotic locales as India and Burma before settling in New York. During an extended illness in 1935, Martin had a vision of a deity whose hair reached from his head to the sky. Compelled by his vision and the voices of this deity, Martin was reborn as St. EOM of Pasaquan.

The core tenet of St. EOM's new religion was a Samsonesque belief that hair was the center of man's being; thus St. EOM bound his hair in a turban and coated it with boiled rice syrup to insure that it would reach astounding heights. In divining this new religion, he borrowed liberally from Sikh, Mayan, and Egyptian religious traditions.

Despite his affinity for the exotic, St. EOM returned home each year at harvest time to help his family bring in the crop. It was not until 1957, after both his parents passed away, that he took up full-time residence at the family farm just outside Buena Vista.

Fueled by proceeds from a flourishing fortune-telling business, St. EOM began to build the four-acre walled compound that is Pasaquan. He used the simplest of materials: Sherwin Williams house paint was his medium and concrete was his canvas. A tour of the grounds is a humbling experience.

*A brilliantly colored exterior wall at Pasaquan.*

Depictions of prototypical Pasaquayans with upswept hairdos appear throughout the work. In the land of the Pasaquan, all images carry equal weight: religious iconography shares wall space with depictions of oversize genitalia. Christianity and Buddhism coexist. Surprises are everywhere: upon closer inspection, what appeared to be a geometric abstraction is actually a hermaphroditic torso.

St. EOM continued work on his Pasaquayan homeland until his death in 1986, after which the property was given to the Marion County Historical Society. After years of deterioration, the environment has recently been stabilized thanks to the work of caretaker Gwen Martin (no relation to Eddie Owens Martin) and groups of visiting schoolchildren.

## ■ PINE MOUNTAIN AND ENVIRONS *map page 159, A-3*

At the tail end of the Piedmont Plateau, Pine Mountain rises abruptly from the surrounding plains. At some 1,500 feet in elevation, the area has long provided escape from the heat of summer, and thanks to the heated mineral springs that issue from the mountainside, it has long been a place of healing.

Among those who made their way to Pine Mountain was Franklin Delano Roosevelt, who came to the area in 1924 in search of warm water treatments for his polio-afflicted legs. With Roosevelt's help, the failing resort town of Warm Springs was recast as a polio research center and, in 1927, the Georgia Warm Springs Foundation was born. Roosevelt returned many times in the following years, developing a deep rapport with the local folk. Natives of the area, who were but children when Roosevelt visited, recall him motoring about the countryside, shouting "Hiya neighbor" in his inimitable accent.

### ◆ ROOSEVELT'S WARM SPRINGS HOME

By 1932 President Roosevelt had built a home at Warm Springs. The six-room dwelling was a simple affair, reflective of his desire for comfort and relaxation on his Southern sojourns. Today, visitors to the home, now dubbed the **Little White House,** are free to tour the grounds and wander through the home. Among the more touching items on display are the President's wheelchair, various leg braces, and a collection of canes whittled by supporters unaware of just how debilitated he was. In the living room is the portrait for which Roosevelt was posing when he died at Warm Springs on April 12, 1945. On *Highway 85, just south of the town of Warm Springs at 401 Little White House Drive; 706-655-5870.*

*Taken during FDR's 1928 trip to Warm Springs, this photo shows Roosevelt exercising his polio-damaged legs in the enclosed pool. (Underwood Photo Archives, San Francisco)*

◆ CALLAWAY GARDENS RESORT

On the other side of Pine Mountain, at about the same time that Roosevelt was re-making Warm Springs, another vision began to take hold, as textile tycoon Cason Callaway and his wife, Virginia, started buying up depleted cotton fields with the idea of transforming them into a garden of native fauna. In 1952, their private dream turned public with the opening of Callaway Gardens.

Today, Callaway Gardens Resort cuts a lush emerald swath through the red clay of Middle Georgia. Like pearls on a necklace, lakes dot the roadway that encircles the property. Though it may not live up to its billing as the "prettiest garden since Eden," Callaway Gardens delights the senses, with the rust- and orange-hued leaves of oak and elm trees in the fall and the riot of colors that comes when the world's largest collection of azaleas blooms in the spring. Indoor attractions do not disappoint, either. The Day Butterfly Center swarms with more than a thousand tropical butterflies in a crystal palace setting, while the Sibley Horticultural Center is a steamy five-acre oasis that harbors rare and exotic plants. Golf, tennis, and hotel facilities are available. *US 27 south of the town of Warm Springs; 800-282-8181.*

■ COLUMBUS *map page 159, A-4*

Chartered in 1828, Columbus began life as a frontier trading outpost. Like the cities of Macon and Augusta, Columbus owes its location to the fall line that straddles Middle Georgia, marking the dividing line between turbulent waters to the north and navigable streams to the south.

While river trade was important when Columbus was founded, it was the textile mills that became central to the city's economic life. The mills were located here because of the power generated by turbulent upstream waters. During the

*In his 1838 hand-tinted lithograph* Pont de Columbus (The Bridge at Columbus), *Francis de la Porte also depicted the city hall of Milledgeville at the top right and the bridge at Augusta in the top left. (courtesy of the Columbus Museum, Columbus)*

*The river still plays an important role in the Columbus' economy.*

MIDDLE GEORGIA

Civil War, Columbus supplied the Confederacy with more manufactured goods than any other city in the Deep South. Today, the city's Swift Textiles is still the world's largest producer of denim, yet the glory days of the textile industry are far behind. Former mills stand vacant, their somber redbrick façades a reminder of days past. Bibb City, a separate municipality once home to a massive mill and row upon row of workers' homes, is in danger of losing its state charter now that the mill has closed, leaving the city without a viable tax base.

And yet Columbus is on the rebound as the city retools, coming to life again as a financial center. Where warehouses once lined the riverfront, a graceful park borders on a revitalized shopping district, and just down the road, Fort Benning, the world's largest infantry base, pumps millions of dollars into the local economy.

◆ COLUMBUS MUSEUMS, HOMES, AND SITES

**Military Museums**

**Fort Benning** is the site of the popular **National Infantry Museum**. Dedicated to telling the story of American foot soldiers from 1750 to the present, the museum houses an eclectic collection of memorabilia ranging from a stunning display of rifles to an epaulet from Italian dictator Mussolini's uniform. *Off Highway 280 (Victory Drive) southeast of town; 706-545-2958.*

Closer to town, the **Civil War Naval Museum** pays homage to a little-known chapter of Civil War history, the pioneering Confederate deployment of submarines, naval mines, and torpedoes. *1002 Victory Drive; 706-327-9798.*

**Riverwalk**

It was Columbus' location on the Chattahoochee River that made it a manufacturing site for Confederate naval vessels, and the riverbank was also what drew industry to the city. Today, that same riverbank is home to the Riverwalk, a brick promenade at the center of 12 miles of jogging and hiking trails.

**Historic District**

Just a couple of blocks from the river, the historic district stands in testament to the wealth of the 19th century. At Tenth Street and First Avenue, the **Springer Opera House**, built in 1871 and host to such stage notables as Edwin Booth and Oscar Wilde, is a dignified brick edifice trimmed in cast iron. Also on **First Avenue** is the nation's sole double octagon house, an architectural oddity known as "The Folly."

**Ellena Amos Home**

For a glimpse of what the nouveau riche have wrought, locals recommend a trip down to the 1900 block of Wynnton Road, where you can take a gander at another folly, the **home of Ellena Amos,** widow of AFLAC Insurance Company founder John Amos. Perched atop a six-story parking garage, the red-tile-roofed Mediterranean villa faces down on the loading dock of the adjoining skyscraper.

**Rothschild-Pound House**

Built in 1870, this Victorian beauty was fully renovated in 1994 and is now Columbus's premier B&B. The eight rooms are decorated with period furniture as well as such modern amenities as coffeemakers. Afternoon cocktails and a sumptuous breakfast featuring a grits soufflé are highlights. *201 Seventh Street; 706-322-4075.*

**Bludau's Goetchius House**

This squat, New Orleans–style antebellum home is Columbus's grand old lady of dining. Here the patrons, the menu, and, most of all, the servers, are frozen in time. The setting is charming if just a tad threadbare, and the food is good, if a bit uninspired. Frog legs, duck with cherry sauce, and Veal Oscar are favorites. *405 Broadway; 706-324-4863.*

**"Ma" Rainey**

Set in humble surroundings is the last home of gospel-and-blues singer Gertrude "Ma" Rainey. Though you would never know it from the present-day appearance of this ramshackle house, Rainey was among the most popular female entertainers of the 1920s. *805 Fifth Avenue.*

## Columbus Museum
Folk art and fine art complement one another in this inviting modern facility, one of the finest cultural establishments in the Deep South. Among the highlights of the permanent collection are assemblages by Radcliffe Bailey, and Bo Bartlett's *The Homecoming,* a massive—and ghoulish—oil painting of a football player and homecoming queen posed against the backdrop of a raging bonfire. *1251 Wynnton Road; 706-649-0713.*

## Cola History
Atlanta is not the only town that lays claim to being the birthplace of Coca-Cola. Though there is some debate, locals claim it was in Columbus that pharmacist John Pemberton devised the formula for Coke. Today, the simple **Pemberton House** is open as part of a Heritage Corner Tour of five historic Columbus homes. *Seventh Street and Broadway; 706-322-0756.*

The white frame **Woodruff House,** built in 1885, was the birthplace of Coca-Cola magnate Robert Woodruff. Now an inn, 13 mini-suites are available, all with private bath and fireplace. *1414 Second Avenue; 706-320-9300.*

There is no debate as to where RC Cola was created. Long the nation's third most popular cola, RC was first concocted around 1900 in the basement of the **Hatcher Grocery** on 11th Street. Coca-Cola may be king in the rest of the country, but, judging by the billboards that dot this town, RC rules the roost in Columbus.

*A patron views Bo Bartlett's* The Homecoming *at the Columbus Museum.*

## CULINARY BASICS IN COLUMBUS

**Country's Barbecue.** They serve the best Brunswick stew in these parts, thick with smoky pork, corn, and tomatoes. Housed in a former bus station, the restaurant is a visual treat. Ribs are meaty, fries are fresh-cut, and the sauce comes in three varieties, the best of which is a thin, mustardy, vinegar-based concoction. *1329 Broadway; 706-596-8910.*

**Macon Road Barbecue.** Housed in a green cinderblock building, this barbecue joint serves chipped or chunked smoked pork along with Brunswick stew and a cheek-puckering barbecue slaw that is heavy on the vinegar. Piles of white bread are provided for sopping. *2703 Avalon Road; 706-563-0542.*

**Dinglewood Pharmacy.** Opened in 1918 as a pharmacy with a small lunch counter—today, it's the lunch counter that matters. In charge is a man everyone knows as Lieutenant. Grab a seat at the counter and listen to the local banter while savoring one of his famous "scrambled dogs," a culinary train wreck of sliced hot-dogs on a bun, topped with homemade chili, oyster crackers, and pickles. *1939 Wynnton Road; 706-322-0616.*

**Evelyn's Cafe.** A study in minimalism—and good food. Let the screen door bang behind you and settle into one of the vinyl booths for a breakfast of scrambled eggs and grits, biscuits, and strong, hot coffee. Lunchtime plate offerings are tasty, too. *2601 Hamilton Road; 706-322-9436.*

**Minnie's Uptown.** Minnie's is the country-cooking cousin of the Royal Cafe *(see below)*. Belly up to the steam table for crunchy fried chicken, perfectly lumpy mashed potatoes with gravy, and okra in many guises. The setting is country cute but spic-and-span. *104 Eighth Street; 706-322-2766.*

**Royal Cafe.** Columbus's plate-lunch palace. Factory workers and stockbrokers alike jostle for a table at this unassuming eatery, set across the street from an old foundry. Fresh rutabagas and collard greens, toothsome meatloaf, and splendid hoecakes are the best of a stellar bunch. Pay your respects to longtime proprietor Lila Star at the cash register. Serves lunch daily, breakfast on Saturdays. *600 11th Street; 706-322-9149.*

**Rose Hill Seafood.** There always seems to be a line out front of this venerable seafood house. Famous for raw oysters and fried fish, this simple eatery features the freshest seafood in town. *2621 Hamilton Road; 706-322-4410.*

*(above) Kudzu in central Georgia. Native to Asia, the vine was brought to this country to prevent soil erosion. Kudzu can grow up to 60 feet per season, and in much of the Southeast it has become a rampant weed. (below) A Georgia woman weaves a basket of the woody kudzu stem.*

MIDDLE GEORGIA

## COUNTRY COOKING AND SOUL FOOD: *IS THERE A DIFFERENCE? AND IF SO, WHAT'S THE FUSS?*

Many of the dishes that we think of as being distinctly Georgian owe their origins to European recipes and techniques - everything from hog's head cheese to desserts like chess pie. But the introduction of enslaved Africans thoroughly transformed the diet.

African Americans reinterpreted European cookery and Native American ingredients, applying African-inspired techniques and constructions. In the kitchen, African American cooks slipped in a pepper pod here, an okra pod there.

Indeed, some of the foodstuffs we now recognize as elemental to the Georgia diet owe their presence to the slave trade. Peanuts, though native to South America, arrived first in Virginia and later in Georgia, by way of slave ships on which they were valued as hardy provisions. Okra is an African plant, as is benne, also known as sesame. Ditto watermelon. Georgians of African descent cooked in deep oil as they had done in Africa. They mastered use of the sweet potato, the available tuber closest in appearance to the fibrous yams of Africa.

So if you accept the premise that Georgia cookery—whether the cookery of white or black Georgians—is, at its core, a melding of techniques and traditions, then why do folks insist upon segregating the complimentary schools of cookery into soul and country, white and black? Perhaps it has something to do with the fact that the term soul food came into popular use in the late 1960s when black power was ascendant.

### ATHENS, GEORGIA

Maybe the best thing to do is to eat your way through the question, and there's no better city in which to try than Athens. Though it's a town with many international students, most of the best eats are traditionally Southern in style or at least inspired by years of eating grits, greens, and every part of the hog but the squeal.

The **Mayflower** has been the town's country cooking standard-bearer, at least since the late, lamented Chase Street Cafe closed. If the Rotary Club doesn't meet here, it should. With its red and white-checkered tablecloths and black and white tile floor, this downtown favorite looks little changed from the day it opened in 1948. Breakfast biscuits stuffed with hand-patted sausage are favorites. *171 E Broad Street; 706-548-1692.*

**Weaver D's** won national attention when local boys REM named an album "Automatic for the People" — a tribute to the response that Weaver D's owner, Dexter Weaver, gives when somebody asks for a soulful helping of collards, a plateful of pork chops, or just about anything else at this spotlessly clean little cinderblock restaurant. Be sure and try the crusty-crowned macaroni and cheese. *1016 E Broad Street; 706-353-7797.*

**Wilson's Soul Food,** on the Hot Corner in the heart of what was once the black business district, is a trencherman's favorite, an old diner with cafeteria line service, great fried chicken, swine-scented green beans, and moist, coarse cornbread. For desert try sweet potato pie or peach cobbler. *351 N Hull Street; 706-353-7289.*

**The Five Star Day Cafe** offers a Deadhead twist on traditional Southern cooking (the collard greens are cooked with soy and garlic instead of ham hock) in a simple storefront setting. Their mozzarella-laced meatloaf is a nouveau country cooking revelation. *229 E Broad Street; 706-543-8552.*

### MACON, GEORGIA

Want to do a bit more comparison eating? Macon boasts two old line institutions worthy of consideration:

**H & H** proprietor Mama Louise Hudson used to feed soulful good cooking to local blues-rockers, the Allman Brothers Band, and she'll feed you, too. Try the fried chicken, collard greens, and sweet potato pie at this inestimable funky landmark. When you see the mushroom sign—a nod to the band's drug of choice—you will know you have arrived. *807 Forsyth Street; 912-742-9810.*

**Len Berg's,** a bastion of traditional country cooking, has been around since 1908. Try the fresh vegetables and the salmon croquettes, or in summer, a plate of cold chicken, deviled eggs, and a pimento cheese sandwich. For dessert, sample the oddly satisfying macaroon pie. If you like the food, there's a button you can push that signals a buzzer in the kitchen, telling the cooks that another happy customer has exited with a full belly. *Old Post Office Alley, off Mulberry Street; 912-742-9255.*

# SOUTH GEORGIA

## ■ HIGHLIGHTS

## ■ TRAVEL BASICS

In this agricultural heartland, much of the landscape consists of farms and orchards. You'll find fresh peaches, sweet Vidalia onions, peanuts and pecans, and acre upon acre of soybeans and sugar cane. Thomasville has a lovely Victorian historic district. Hunting is still a big draw here, as fishing is at Lake Seminole. Albany is significant for its role in civil rights history; Plains, as the home of former President and peanut farmer Jimmy Carter; and Andersonville as the site of an infamous Civil War prison camp. In the southeast lies the Okefenokee Swamp: a vast, wet world of surreal beauty.

**Getting Around:** This is no place to be in a hurry. Ease your elbow out the car window and motor down the road, taking time to delight in the graceful turn of a crop row. Though urban sprawl has engulfed Valdosta, towns like Albany and Plains are easily toured on foot. The Okefenokee Swamp is best experienced by canoe.

**Climate:** Mild winters with occasional cold outbreaks; high temperatures in the 50s and 60s F. Very hot and humid summers with frequent thunderstorms; temperatures usually in the low to mid-90s. Fall is dry and pleasant.

**Food & Lodging:** Fried mullet, swamp gravy, coleslaw, cornbread: partake of this and you'll eat well here. Somewhere south of Macon, mullet replaces catfish, and grits edge out fries as the favorite accompaniment. Barbecue changes too, with astringent sauces of mostly vinegar giving way to mustard-laced concoctions. Distinctive accommodations are hard to come by, though the turreted Windsor Hotel in Americus is a true delight, and the Melhana Resort near Thomasville will give you a taste of the golden era of plantation life. Lodging is available at many state parks, including Little Ocmulgee.

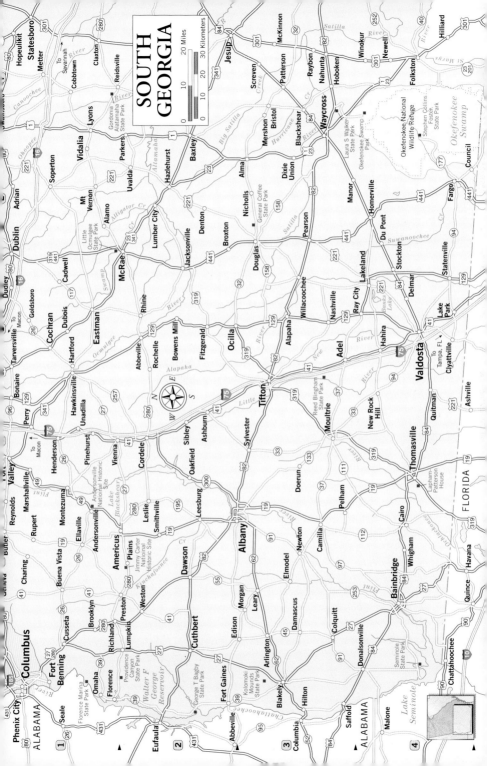

# SOUTH GEORGIA

■ OVERVIEW

Save actual, physical barriers like rivers and oceans, the boundaries of a region are often difficult to demarcate. And so it is with South Georgia. Middle Georgia is the region that more or less straddles the fall line. Northwest Georgia is the land of the Cohutta Mountains; northeast Georgia, the land of the Blue Ridge. Atlanta is, well, Atlanta. Coastal Georgia hugs the Atlantic seashore. And South Georgia, known to self-satisfied lovers of its rural expanses as "God's Country," is the land beneath the Gnat Line. Above the line, the little beasts rarely venture, but beneath a border that mirrors the fall line, they are a terror.

During the summer months, gnats—two-winged, almost microscopic, fly-like nuisances—swarm the people of the piney woods, buzzing about in ears, crawling across noses, flying unawares and unimpeded into yawning mouths. Fending them off with slaps, flicks, Tourettes-like twitches, and grunts, South Georgians curse them to high heaven. Many a local claims to have taken up cigarette smoking as a means of warding off these offensive and omnipresent airborne pests. And yet, ask a Georgian with a playful sense of her state's geography to define south Georgia, and she's likely to tell you that it's the land beneath the Gnat Line and to the west of what everyone seems to call "the Coast." Should the conversation take place in winter, when all the little creatures have died off, she might even smile when she says it.

This is perhaps the most remote region of the state, with few tourist attractions and more lovely rural vistas than any other. In the east of the region, pine trees rise high and spindly. Bare at the base, branches akimbo near the top, the pines resemble frill-topped toothpicks thrown like javelins into the soil. The farther south you travel, the sandier the soil becomes, and on the region's southeastern fringe lurks the Okefenokee Swamp, a nearly 700-square-mile waterlogged wilderness of black waters, above them towering cypress trees draped with Spanish moss. Dove-white water lilies float on the surface of the dark waters, and a menagerie of animals, among which the alligator is the most menacing and populous, inhabit the swamp. West of Okefenokee lies loamy, almost sandy terrain that in ancient times was covered by an ocean; here palmettos challenge pine trees for dominance. North and west, near Albany, pecan trees growing in red clay soil stretch row after

SOUTH
GEORGIA

*Spindly old pines contrast with fuller, young pines in this scene, which is typical of South Georgia.*

regimented row, mile after empty mile. Two-lane blacktop roads pass trailers parked in wiregrass fields and older, abandoned shotgun or dogtrot homes capped with tin roofs.

Agriculture is still big business in these parts, and around harvest time, the roads are clogged with tractors, combines in tow, headed to and from fields white with cotton, green with corn, or blanketed with peanut plants plowed up from their subterranean slumber.

No matter where you go, you can be assured that the stations you pick up on your car radio will play both kinds of music—country *and* western.

### ◆ SETTLEMENT

Compared to Middle and even northern Georgia, South Georgia was settled late by Europeans, though Spanish explorer Hernando de Soto, in his futile search for gold, marched his troops through Georgia in 1540, possibly along the Flint River.

Long the province of the Creek Indians and their forefathers, who hunted for white tail deer and farmed squash, beans, and corn, the lands of South Georgia were not given over to the slave-fueled cotton monoculture until the mid years of

*Turpentine is loaded onto a steamboat at Hawkinsville on the Ocmulgee River.*
*(Georgia Department of Archives & History)*

the 19th century, and even then some farmers subsisted by producing cane syrup and turpentine.

Though the region remains rural at heart, the cities of Albany and Valdosta thrive today as much because of industry as agriculture. Valdosta also benefits, economically at least, from its location on I-75, the primary thoroughfare hurtling beach- and Disney-bound travelers south to Florida.

## ■ UPPER FALL LINE

On the northern rim of the region, the little burg of Fort Valley is the county seat of the aptly named Peach County, and center of production for the fruit that author Melissa Fay Greene observed "is as thickly furred as a sweater, and so fluent and sweet that once you bite through the flannel, it brings tears to your eyes." During late spring and summer, numerous roadside stands offer fresh-picked peaches by the handful and bucketful. Though Georgia no longer leads the nation in peach harvest poundage, come May, the squat, stunted trees in and around Peach County hang heavy with the blush-colored fruit.

### ◆ PERRY   *map page 205, C-1*

Ten or so miles southeast of Fort Valley, across I-75, is the crossroads town of Perry, long a stop for travelers. When the Allman Brothers sang, "I was born in the backseat of a Greyhound bus, rolling down Highway 41," they sang of the old highway just east of the interstate that bisects this town of 12,000. Today the biggest attraction is the columned **New Perry Hotel,** a dowdy but charming 1925-vintage inn that faces on the Houston County courthouse. At suppertime, the hotel's **dining-room** tables groan beneath a bounty of Southern fare. Frumpy furnishings, old-fashioned servers, and reliably good Southern victuals draw diners

*Peach trees bloom in Peach County.*

off the interstate. Stick with standards like stuffed bell peppers and fried chicken. *800 Main Street; 478-987-1000.*

Or try the antebellum **Swift Street Inn**. It has four antique-filled rooms, each with private bath, and for breakfast you might be served stuffed French toast or a cheese-grits casserole. *1204 Swift Street; 478-988-9148 or 877-607-7794.*

Hand-cut fries, hand-dipped milkshakes and smoke-tinged pork with a mustard sauce are the draws at **White Diamond Grill,** a 1940s raodhouse at 497 South Highway 247 in nearby Bonaire. *478-922-8686.*

◆ NEAR PERRY  *map page 205, C-1*

Six miles south of Perry and a mile off the interstate at Highway 26, you'll find **Henderson Village**, an exquisite country resort set on 22 acres. Expect to be pampered, and to eat very well, whether it be a breakfast of country ham and eggs with Vidalia onion compote or dinner in the **Langston House,** a beautifully restored 1837 Georgian home. The dining room is a study in refined simplicity, with earth-tone walls, hardwood floors, and primitive mantles, and the menu features exquisite local game and fresh seafood as well as many French-inspired dishes, among them an excellent squab with foie gras. *125 South Langston Circle; 478-988-8696.*

Further south on Highway 41 is the town of Vienna, site of the Big Pig Jig—Georgia's "official" barbecue championship cook-off, held annually on the second weekend in October—this small Georgia town is better known among true barbecue aficionados as the home of **Mamie Bryant's BBQ Pit.** Each Thursday, J. B. Bryant puts a mess of hams on the pit to smoke and his wife, Mamie, stirs up a pot of Brunswick stew. Starting at around 10 o'clock Friday morning, a line forms out in the front yard of the small cinderblock building and by Friday afternoon—maybe Saturday morning—it's all gone. Sweet smoky 'cue and stew is all they sell. It's worth a 50-mile detour. *310 Eighth Street; 229-268-4179.*

Driving southeast from Perry, through Hawkinsville (winter home of horses on the harness racing circuit) you reach **Eastman**, onetime headquarters of the **Stuckey's** chain of stores, famed for pecan logs and other Southern confections. Farther east two miles north of the town of McRae is **Little Ocmulgee State Park.** The park boasts trails, a pool, tennis courts, and an 18-hole golf course that would be

*A road through a pecan grove near Fort Valley.*

the envy of many a country club, plus a tidy lodge and numerous cabins. *229-868-2832 or 800-864-7275.*

Spend a few hours traveling these back roads and you will soon find yourself seduced by a languor that borders on laziness. The only thing to do is relax and let your travels be an antidote to the malaise of rush.

◆ VIDALIA AND EAST   *map page 205, E&F-1*

North and east of McRae is the agricultural crossroads of Vidalia, capital of the 20-county region where the sweet onions of the same name are raised. Higher in sugar and water content than other onions, Vidalias were once available widely only in the fall; enterprising lovers of the onion were known to extend the shelf life by storing them in nylon pantyhose, hung from the ceiling with a knot separating each bulb. Now, thanks to new storage technologies, the onions some claim to be sweet enough to be eaten raw out of hand are available up to seven months after the harvest. Though Vidalia has no onion museum, intrepid travelers may seek out the historical marker on Highway 280, two miles east of town, that marks the spot where, in 1931, Moses Coleman grew one of the first commercial crops.

Though there are numerous spots in town to purchase onions, those willing to take a detour six miles down Highway 1 toward Baxley will enjoy a visit to **Herndon Farms** roadside produce stand, where, on most mornings, you can purchase vegetables fresh from the farm, with dirt still clinging to the roots and dew still blanketing the leaves—all displayed on gargantuan wooden spools set beneath the eaves of an old country store.

Head east from Vidalia along back roads that parallel I-16 and lead eventually to Savannah, and you'll reach another culinary capitol: **Claxton,** home of the much maligned Claxton Fruit Cake, a holiday fund-raising favorite made of sodden dough studded with luminescent bits of fruits and nuts.

From Claxton, a trip north on Highway 301 will be rewarded with a chance to sample the best barbecue in the region. You'll find it at **Vandy's** in the college town of **Statesboro.** The Boyd family has been in the barbecue business hereabouts since the 1920's and their mustard-kissed sauce perfectly complements the oak-smoked pork. Pitmaster Charlie Pierce has been wielding the tools of his trade—a pitchfork and a water hose—since the early 1970's. The experience shows in every bite. *22 West Vine Street; 912-764-2444.*

SOUTH
GEORGIA

# ■ ALTAMAHA RIVER BASIN

South of Claxton stretches the Altamaha River Basin, a land of remote beauty where the people are few and the pine trees many. Here timber is the primary industry, as witnessed by the pulpwood trucks that ply the roads in an eternal loop from forest to town, and the paper plants that belch sulphurous smoke high into the air. Once turpentine mills fueled the economy and Waycross, at the south end of the river basin, was a boomtown.

## ◆ WAYCROSS  *map page 205, F-3*

Today Waycross is worth a stop for barbecue before heading 10 miles south to the wilds of the Okefenokee Swamp.

**The Pig** opened its doors in 1947. Five red vinyl booths hug the wall. And a row of seven stools face the counter. Chopped or sliced pork, ribs, and chicken are

*The Okefenokee is known for its abundant flora and fauna—among them Alligator mississippiensis, the American alligator.*

*(following pages) The cypress-swamp landscapes of South Georgia include Banks Lake National Wildlife Refuge as well as the Okefenokee Swamp.*

all that emerge from the pit. This is barbecue at its best—and simplest. Icy six and one-half ounce bottles of Coke are the beverage of choice. *768 State Street; 912-283-4875.*

■ OKEFENOKEE SWAMP   *map page 219 and page 205, E&F-4*

The largest freshwater swamp in North America, the Okefenokee covers almost 700 square miles of southeast Georgia and is a landscape rich with carnivorous flora such as fly-devouring pitcher plants and equally carnivorous fauna such as the American alligator. (Technically, the Okefenokee is a peat bog, not a swamp, but few, save scientists, recognize it as such.) Once the home of the Seminole Indians, who knew this as "the land of the trembling earth," this geological oddity is at once forbidding and eerily beautiful, an otherworldly landscape more foreign at times than the lunar images beamed back to us from outer space. Most who visit traverse the swamp by water, for the peat-rich soil does indeed tremble beneath the feet, only fitfully supporting a full-grown man—and occasionally giving way.

*(above) Carnivorous pitcher plants flourish in the Okefenokee Swamp.*

*(opposite) A white water lily contrasts with the swamp's near-black water.*

SOUTH
GEORGIA

*Needles float around cypress trunks on the still, tannin-dyed waters of the Okefenokee Swamp.*

The land here was once covered by the Atlantic Ocean, which accounts for the sandy bottom of the swamp. The swamp was, in fact, a large sandbar that trapped the water as the ocean receded. The salt then evaporated, leaving a shallow lake of fresh water hospitable to plant life. As the vegetation decayed, a peat bog was born.

Though 80 percent of the area is covered by the dense cypress stands that most people associate with the Okefenokee, the geography of the swamp is actually quite diverse. The main physical features, aside from the cypress stands, are hardwood hammocks, larger islands, and watery grass fields called "prairies." The open-water areas that break up the cypress and prairie—rivers, lakes, and ponds or "gator holes"—account for only a tiny portion of the total swamp area. New hammocks and, in turn, islands are continually being formed as methane gas—released from the decaying vegetation at the swamp floor—sends peat beds shooting to the surface; new vegetation grows on these "batteries" or "blowups," finally anchoring them to the sandy bottom. Without the cyclical occurrence of wildfires, the praires and open areas would eventually be entirely filled in.

The Okefenokee is a land of surprises. From a distance, the swamp looks fetid, murky, and immeasurably deep, but a closer look reveals that the water is relatively clean and free of detritus, colored a curious tea-black by the presence of tannins—produced by the decaying vegetation and chemically the same as the tannins in wine—and shallow, with a depth typically between two and five feet. Perched at the bow of a canoe, you'll watch as the swamp glides by quietly, peacefully, beautifully—an elegant procession of water lilies framed by the black mirror of the water. Reptiles sun themselves on cypress knees beneath the boughs of trees

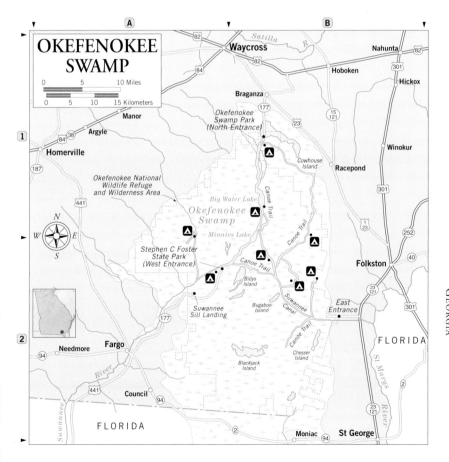

dripping with Spanish moss. Hummingbirds hover beside flowers and whooping cranes gracefully glide by. Innumerable islands dot the swamp's interior, and those exploring the swamp step out of their canoes with tentative steps, hoping the soil they step on will hold.

Within the Okefenokee are the headwaters of two rivers: the St. Mary's, which flows some 200 miles south to the Atlantic Ocean, and the Suwanee, which empties into the Gulf of Mexico. In colonial times the swamp was plumbed by trappers, and later it was invaded by lumber companies who used swamp waters to float out almost 10-million board feet of virgin cypress. Native American tribes inhabited the swamp long before European encroachment. First a mound-building society occupied the area; then came the Creeks and, finally, the Seminoles, who lived and hunted here before being forced to go west on the Trail of Tears. A handful of pioneering settlers practiced subsistence farming in the swamp starting in the 1850s, but by the 1950s, most of these people were gone.

---

## SWAMP HOLLERING

*J*ust as darkness settled in, I returned to camp. Then I heard more of that strange music which always startles me—swamp hollering. I was unversed in the unwritten rules of the matter, and I assumed my friends at the upper end of the island were having fun. Expecting to meet them on the way home, I started out toward them. Soon all of us were together again around our campfire.

Gator Joe asked me somewhat impatiently if I had heard them holler, and if so, why I hadn't answered. "When you hear anybody hollerin', you holler back," he said with undisguised sternness. Clearly he was concerned about my getting lost or being harmed. And so Joe taught me rule one about the art of hollering. Even if I had been aware of what was required, I was then—and am yet—totally incapable of producing a sound at all akin to the marvelous swamp yodeling. Of course I could have made some loud noise, but it would have been a virtual desecration in an atmosphere that had been reverberating with the exquisite music made by two masters, Gator Joe Saunders and Bryant Lee.

—Francis Harper, 1912, from *Okefenokee Album*

---

*A brilliant sunset in the swamp.*

## MAGICAL OKEFENOKEE

"We tried to destroy it....We didn't know any better." The words of Will Cox, one-time resident of the swamp, allude to the fragile and yet regenerative nature of the Okefenokee. Thanks to the work of biologist Francis Harper and his wife, Jean, who appealed directly to President Franklin D. Roosevelt, the Okefenokee National Wildlife Refuge was established in 1936; in 1974, the most remote region of the swamp was designated a national wilderness area. Visiting the Okefenokee today, one is awed by the unique and magnificent beauty of the environment—and sobered by the thought that, just a generation ago, we came close to losing such a treasure.

The Okefenokee is truly wild and remote. Traversing it is no easy feat; the navigable portion is minuscule compared to the hundreds of thousand of acres of impassable cypress stands, their canopy so dense as to cast dark shadows even by day.

The swamp supports an astonishing variety of plant life: the ubiquitous cypress draped with Spanish moss; slash and longleaf pine; black gum, red maple, bay, wax myrtle, magnolia, bamboo, holly. Meat-eaters such as the pitcher plant go far in advancing the swamp's reputation as a fierce place; but come spring, the swamp is ablaze with the delicate blooms of rare orchids and other wildflowers.

The wildlife selection is equally spectacular. Swamp mammals include the black bear, otter, armadillo, mink, six bat varieties, and the swimming marsh rabbit. The Florida puma is being reintroduced. And Okefenokee is truly a birder's paradise: more than 200 species frequent the swamp, and 75 nest here, including such rare birds as the sandhill or whooping crane, osprey, and redcocked woodpecker. But the real stars are the swamp's reptiles and amphibians, including 15,000 American alligators—which can grow to 18 feet. The swamp is also home to some 150-pound alligator snapping turtles; common snappers (which can also be quite nasty); five poisonous snake species; and a number of less menacing lizards, turtles, and snakes.

Protected from the hand of man, the swamp has healed itself. Though most of the trees are second growth, evidence of former damage is scant. Most prominent is a 12-mile stretch of the Suwanee Canal, centerpiece of an ill-fated attempt, begun in 1889, to drain the swamp for farmland. The lumber industry thought they could log the Okefenokee for hundreds of years; they nearly finished the job in 20, during which time Billys Island was a boomtown. Remnants of structures remain here and on Chesser Island.

The Chesser family belonged to a group of resourceful "swampers" who for several generations, starting in the 1850s, made their home in the Okefenokee. They grew or caught their food, raised pigs and cattle, and traded turpentine (distilled from pine resin) for the few other necessities. Their isolation and their self-sufficient life in this strange environment bred a culture all its own—including a sort of swamp "dialect," traces of which can still be heard in the surrounding area.

Naturalist Francis Harper said that the swampers, being such keen observers of their environment, had more to teach him about biology than he could ever teach them. But over the years he spent here, Harper became more and more interested in the people themselves; he filled his notebooks with their songs and stories and ideas about their world. Ironically, the establishment of the wildlife refuge is what finally drove the swampers out, as they could no longer shoot wild animals to protect their livestock.

But even an old swamper like Will Cox, while saddened by the passing of a culture, recognized the ultimate justice of the situation. After all, the Okefenokee was around long before the swampers. And as Cox put it, the Okefenokee "is God's work. Man couldn't destroy it, and now it's as beautiful as it ever was. It's the most beautiful place on earth."

—Lesley Bonnet

*Jean Harper and two of the Chessers navigate a boat on Chessers Prairie, May 1930. (University of Georgia Press)*

Today, the great majority of the swamp is a federally protected wildlife refuge. But tourism is allowed, even encouraged. For the ecologically and biologically curious, the Okefenokee may well be the state's prime attraction.

## ◆ WEATHER IN THE OKEFENOKEE SWAMP

Spring and fall are mild here, with daytime temperatures in the 70s and 80s, and nights in the 40s and 50s. Summers are very hot and humid, with highs consistently in the low to mid-90s; winter temperatures vary between 40 to 80 degrees F in the daytime and occasionally reach freezing at night. If you visit Okefenokee, and especially if you plan to canoe and hike, bring bug repellent, sunscreen, drinking water, and food; wear long pants and long-sleeved shirts.

## ◆ VISITING THE OKEFENOKEE SWAMP

There are three entrances to the Okefenokee Swamp.

**East entrance:** Most of the swamp belongs to the **Okefenokee National Wildlife Refuge and Wilderness Area.** The refuge headquarters and visitors center are located at the east entrance. *11 miles southwest of Folkston, off Highway 121/23; 912-496-7836.*

Motorboats can be rented at this entrance, and **guided night tours** of the swamp interior are available by reservation (a spooky, surreal experience wherein you glide through the pitch-black night, serenaded by unseen, cacophonous wildlife); *912-496-3331.*

**North entrance:** This is the site of the **Okefenokee Swamp Park,** with its live serpentarium shows and battered powerboats plying the swamp waters. Privately owned, this day-use facility feels a bit like an amusement park, but for those who want a peek at the swamp without taking to a canoe, it will suffice. *Ten miles south of Waycross by way of Highway 1; 912-283-0583.*

**West entrance:** Here you will find **Stephen Foster State Park,** the preferred jumping-off point for those inclined to explore the swamp by canoe—the best means of transportation for ecologically conscientious visitors and naturalist voyeurs alike. Here canoes are available for rent, as are campsites and cabins. *Twenty miles from Fargo on Highway 177; 912-637-5274 or for camping reservations call 800-864-7275.*

# ■ AGRICULTURAL HEARTLAND

## ◆ AGRIRAMA  *map page 205, C-3*

The little burg of Tifton is site of the Agrirama, a state-sponsored living history village, that, despite its location within earshot of the interstate, invokes well the spirit and feel of life in the 1890s. Along well-worn sandy paths are distributed a sawmill, feed and seed store, cotton gin, gristmill, turpentine still, and other businesses of the era, all manned by workers dressed in period costume. *229-386-3344.*

## ◆ VALDOSTA  *map page 205, D-4*

The second largest city in South Georgia, with a population of more than 50,000, Valdosta sits beside I-75 about 20 miles north of the Florida border. Though touted by boosters as the "Azalea City," Valdosta is better known to Georgians as home of the winningest high school football program in the South. With more than 20 state championship titles and six national titles, the Valdosta High Wildcats are a source of pride and entertainment for a rabid cadre of fans who fill the stadium known as "Death Valley" to capacity on fall Friday nights when the hometown boys take to the gridiron.

Valdosta proper is actually a few miles from the interstate. But along a series of corridors choked with fast-food restaurants, the city sprawls out to meet the thoroughfare. From the interstate, Valdosta looks like a neon jungle of chain motels: the Jameson Inn, *1725 Gornto Road; 229-253-0009 or 800-526-3766,* Fairfield Inn, *1311 St. Augustine Road; 229-253-9300,* and Holiday Inn, *1309 St. Augustine Road; 229-242-3881.* The latter is distinguished by **The Simmering Pot,** a country cooking restaurant favored by locals.

Visitors to Valdosta's downtown area will find the sleepy pace of an earlier era, and a few grand old homes open their doors for tours. The most majestic of the grand old homes, the **Crescent** was completed in 1898. This 23-room neoclassical mansion is fronted by a crescent-shaped portico supported by 13 Doric columns, and the interior is furnished with period antiques. Out back an octagonal schoolhouse and other outbuildings are ringed by a boxwood garden. *North Patterson Street (at Gordon); 229-244-6747.*

### ◆ HEARTLAND FISH CAMPS

Two of Georgia's best fish houses are near Valdosta.

**Ray's Mill Pond Cafe**

It's way out in the country from Valdosta—20-plus miles to be inexact—in Ray City. And the fish is better to boot. Fishnets line the walls of this low-slung restaurant perched on the edge of a 3,500-acre lake studded with Cypress knees. Order fresh fried mullet with grits or stuffed crab, served in the shell rather than in those little tin thingies. Out back, live oaks loom over a bleak but beautiful waterfront scene. *Off Highway 129, Ray City; 229-455-4075.*

**The Fish Net**

This one is closer in to town, on the edge of a cypress swamp, just where a good fish camp should be. Fried catfish is the star here, and should you wish to experience this Dixie dish at its best, have yours with a side order of grits. Avoid the phosphorescent cheese grits. *Sportsman's Cove Road, Valdosta; 912-559-5410.*

### ◆ THOMASVILLE *map page 205, C-4*

An 1887 edition of *Harper's Weekly* magazine proclaimed Thomasville, just 15 miles north of the Florida border, to be the "best winter resort in three continents." During the late Victorian era, this oak-sheltered town was one of the southernmost points accessible by rail, and a favorite retreat for wealthy Northern industrialists who built lavish hotels and converted many of the local cotton plantations to hunting preserves. Today, though the grand hotels have been replaced by chain motels, there are a number of wonderful bed-and-breakfast inns from which to choose. And the hunting preserves remain, many still owned by descendants of the same carpetbaggers who moved into the town after the Civil War, when grand manor homes and vast tracts of land could be had for a song.

Thomasville's **historic district** (centered along Madison, Broad, Crawford, and Dawson Streets) is chockablock with beautiful homes, among them the **Lapham-Patterson House,** an odd geometric folly featuring fish-scale shingles and Japanese-esque porch decorations. Built in 1884 as a winter retreat by Chicago industrialist C. W. Lapham, today the home is a state historic site open for tours. *626 N Dawson Street; 229-225-4004.*

A block north is the **Thomas County Museum.** Exhibits feature the lavish lifestyles enjoyed by Victorian-era visitors. *725 N Dawson Street; 912-226-7664.*

SOUTH
GEORGIA

A few blocks over, on Monroe Street at Crawford, sprawls the **Big Oak**. With a limb spread of more than 160 feet, the tree covers most of a downtown block, spanning the width of Monroe Street, its ancient boughs held up by a series of trusses and cables.

Thomasville's downtown streets are lined with two-story redbrick buildings, in which antique shops, art galleries, and other businesses geared for the tourist trade coexist with those patronized by locals—such as the **Billiard Academy**. Open since 1949, the four-table poolroom is complete with spittoons lining the wall for those inclined to dip and chew tobacco. Ten swivel-back stools face the bar behind which stands the proprietor, who dishes out 95¢ hotdogs—and that's all—slathered in a meaty chili topped with mustard and chopped onions. A beer sets you back $1.50. *121 South Broad Street; 229-226-9981.*

*The Lapham-Patterson House in Thomasville.*

◆ VACATION PLANTATIONS

Perhaps the grandest examples of Thomasville's golden era are the outlying plantations like Pebble Hill, now a museum, and Melhana, now marketed as "the grand plantation resort."

*Pebble Hill Plantation.*

## Pebble Hill

You'll find yourself transported back to a time when ladies rode sidesaddle and dashing, red-frocked huntsmen pursued their prey in the early morning, through the thick pine and magnolia forests, before returning to the grand manor house for an elegant hunt breakfast. Long the winter hunting preserve of the Hanna family of Cleveland, Ohio, and now open for tours. *Five miles south of Thomasville on Highway 319; 229-226-2344.*

## Melhana

Selling the good life to today's well-heeled crowd, the resort offers a taste of the opulence of plantation life in times past. The driveway is lined with majestic oaks and lustrous magnolias as it leads up to the looming mansion with its many outbuildings. Guests go horseback riding or hunting, or just bask beside the beautifully landscaped pool. *Located four miles south of Thomasville at 301 Showboat Lane; 229-226-2290 or 888-920-3030.*

SOUTH GEORGIA

◆ HUNTING

Today, hunting—of quail, deer, and other wildlife—remains a big draw in the southwest corner of Georgia. In the 1997 novel *A Man in Full,* Tom Wolfe describes a contemporary hunt scene at Turpmtime, the plantation of his protagonist Charlie Croker:

> No matter how many times you went hunting quail, you never became immune to the feeling that came over you when the dogs set the point and you approached a covey hidden somewhere in the grass. The quail's instinct in the face of danger was to hide in the tall grass and then, all at once, to explode upward in flight with incredible acceleration. Everyone used the same term for it: *explode....*

■ SUGAR CANE COUNTRY

This far south, the red clay so often associated with Middle and northern Georgia is no more. Instead, the roadways are bordered by sandy, loamy soil, and the tractors that chug slowly along on the blacktop are more likely to be traveling to the next sugar cane patch than a cotton field. Small signs tacked to telephone poles advertise "Cane Juice For Sale," and soon you are in Cairo, (pronounced KAY-ro), epicenter of the sugar-cane processing industry, birthplace of baseball legend Jackie Robinson, and home to the Cairo High Syrupmakers football team (one assumes they are slow). In the blink of an eye the town passes, and eight miles later you come upon the crossroads village of Whigham, home, on the last Saturday in January, to the annual Rattlesnake Roundup. Whigham's roundup is one of at least two such events in the state, and quite possibly the model for Harry Crews's modern-day gothic novel, *A Feast of Snakes,* wherein he recounts the importance of the annual roundup to the mythical town of Mystic, Georgia:

> The rattlesnake roundup had been going on now as long as anybody in town could remember, but until about twelve years ago it had been a local thing, a few townspeople, a few farmers. They'd have a picnic, maybe a sack race or a horse-pulling contest and then everybody would go out into the woods and see how many diamondbacks they could pull out of the ground. They would eat the snakes and drink a little corn whiskey and that would do it for another year.

◆ LAKE SEMINOLE   *map page 205, A-4*

**Bainbridge,** located near the northern tip of Lake Seminole, is as much a gathering point for fishermen as Thomasville is for hunters. Here, at one of the best bass fishing spots in the country, locals and outlanders alike try their hand at wrenching a large-mouth bass or six from the depths of the 12,000-acre lake, while those inclined to let others dip their poles in the water, head to one of the area's famous fish houses and feast on such aquatic exotica as sucker fish, shad roe, and swamp gravy.

At **Jack Wingate's Lunker Lodge** piping hot fried catfish is served in a rustic atmosphere. Set out in the boonies along Lake Seminole, this spot is popular with sportfishermen, who gather around the large tables to swap lies and scarf down hushpuppies. *Highway 97, 12 miles south of Bainbridge; 229-246-0658.*

**Andrew's Oyster Bar,** in a tumbledown shack, outfitted with four picnic tables, is the place to go for oysters—by the bushel or by the dozen. You can also get such local delights as mullet, red roe, and sucker fish, from this Step up to the window and bark out your order. *104 East Calhoun Street; 229-248-8280.*

A nice place to stay in the heart of Bainbridge is the **Gilded Cage Bed-and-Breakfast.** Built in 1855, this Victorian inn is situated in a beautiful little cottage. The location holds great appeal for fishermen as well as those who want to just soak up a bit of small-town life. *722 South West Street; 229-243-2040.*

**Seminole State Park** provides a good point of entry for a foray into the Georgia outback. Along the two-mile Goper Tortoise Trail, you will come upon wildlife skittering through the wiregrass, and in the spring and summer, wild azaleas and other bright flowering shrubs are in bloom. *Located 20 or so miles west of Bainbridge by way of Highway 253. Information: 229-861-3137. Camping reservations: 800-864-7275.*

Heading north along Highway 27, you come upon two towns in quick succession, Colquitt and Blakely—both charming, but in their present incarnations mere shadows of their once grand pasts.

◆ COLQUITT   *map page 205, A-3*

Colquitt is not on most gourmets' lists of culinary capitals, yet this pleasant little town lays claim to being the mayhaw capital of the world, a bit of hyperbole celebrated each May at the Mayhaw Festival. Little known today, mayhaws are swamp-bound trees with tart, cranberry-size fruit that locals gather in the spring to use in red-tinged jellies and other preserves.

Breakfast biscuits come with a crock of the famous mayhaw jelly at the **Tater Inn**. At dinner the chef pulls out all the stops with grilled quail in mayhaw sauce. From the inn's veranda overlooking the courthouse square, all the world seems at peace. Inside, the ceilings are high and the rooms are well-appointed. *155 South Cuthbert Street; 229-758-2888.*

Colquitt's other claim to fame is *Swamp Gravy,* a folk opera performed by a cast of locals and named for the stew-like concoction of bacon drippings, fish trimmings, and whatever else happens to be in the pantry.

For a taste of swamp gravy at its best, head back down the road to Andrew's Oyster Bar in Bainbridge *(see page 230).* For information about the folk opera—performed in April and October—call *229-758-5450.*

*The cast of the play* Swamp Gravy *hams it up outside the theater in Colquitt.*

## An Unlikely Cafe

*T*he town itself is dreary; not much is there except the cotton mill, the two-room houses where the workers live, a few peach trees, a church with two colored windows, and a miserable main street only a hundred yards long....

However, here in this very town there once was a café. And this old boarded-up house was unlike any other place for many miles around. There were tables with cloths and paper napkins, colored streamers from the electric fans, great gatherings on Saturday nights. The owner of the place was Miss Amelia Evans. But the person most responsible for the success and gaiety of the place was a hunchback called Cousin Lymon.

*It* was a good meal they had together on that night. Miss Amelia was rich and she did not grudge herself food. There was fried chicken (the breast of which the hunchback took on his own plate), mashed rootabeggers, collard greens, and hot, pale golden, sweet potatoes. Miss Amelia ate slowly and with the relish of a farm hand. She sat with both elbows on the table, bent over the plate, her knees spread wide apart and her feet braced on the rungs of the chair. As for the hunchback, he gulped down his supper as though he had not smelled food in months. During the meal one tear crept down his dingy cheek—but it was just a little leftover tear and meant nothing at all....

Having finished, Miss Amelia tilted back her chair, tightened her fist and felt the hard, supple muscles of her right arm beneath the clean, blue cloth of her shirt-sleeves—an unconscious habit with her, at the close of a meal.

—Carson McCullers, *The Ballad of the Sad Café*, 1951
The author was born in Columbus, Georgia, in 1917

■ BLAKELY  *map page 205, A-3*

Blakely sits at the epicenter of Georgia's peanut patch, and, fittingly, on the courthouse square there stands a hunk of granite with a concrete peanut perched atop, installed in 1954 and inscribed with these words:

*T*he people of Early County, the largest peanut producing center in the world, have erected this monument in tribute to the peanut which is so largely responsible for our growth and prosperity.

Deep-felt appreciation for the peanut may seem odd to city dwellers, but to people who make their livelihood from one crop, it's not odd at all. During the early years of the 20th century, when the boll weevil wreaked havoc on the cotton crop, peanuts were the savior of local farm fortunes. Today, though the economic impact of the crop has lessened somewhat, come the fall harvest, roadways are still clogged with little tractor-towed peanut wagons, trailing a cloud of dust and peanut shells. And most any social gathering calls for a big black kettle of freshly dug peanuts, boiled in the shell and well salted.

*A peanut with a presidential smile.*

## ■ KOLOMOKI INDIAN MOUNDS   *map page 205, A-3*

Six or seven miles north of Blakely are the Kolomoki Indian Mounds, a 13th-century ceremonial center for the Kolomoki tribe. Seven temple mounds are preserved here, Georgia's oldest among them. Desolate and haunting, this remote site stands in stark contrast to many of the more popular, upstate mound sites. Here all is quiet, serene even; the loudest sound you are likely to hear is the screech and clatter of black crows in the trees overhead. Mound D is the most impressive, rising more than 200 feet in height and now crowned by live oaks. Inside the museum, set incongruously in the side of one of the excavated mounds, a diorama depicts the funeral ceremony of a Kolomoki chief/priest, a bloodthirsty spectacle predicated on the strangling and cremation of his two wives. *Five miles north of Blakely, off US 27; 229-724-2150.*

■ ALBANY   *map page 205, B-2*

Albany was founded in 1836 on the banks of the Flint River, and with a population of more than 125,000, it is the largest city in the region. It is also the pecan processing center of the state. During the fall, Rube Goldberg-esque contraptions roll through the rows of the pecan orchards on the outskirts of town, grabbing the trunks of the trees in a bear hug and shaking loose the nuts from the branches. Following on the heels of these behemoths come overgrown riding vacuum cleaners of a sort, which suck up the harvest for transport back to dozens of local processing companies, who in turn transform the nuts into candies and the like. But all this takes place in the rural nether regions of the surrounding counties.

In its early days Albany was the commercial center for sharecroppers who journeyed to town each Saturday to do a little shopping and socializing. Albany still bustles with activity, especially around the Dougherty County Courthouse, where, come summer, seersucker suits are de rigueur for the local cadre of attorneys. In the fall, hunters clad in camouflage coveralls gather in the downtown cafes, hunkered down over steaming cups of coffee. Though many families have moved to the city's suburbs, the old-timers are still called by the square, like bees to a hive.

*Freedom singers and sisters Rutha and McCree Harris view the exhibits at Mount Zion Church.*

During the Civil Rights Movement, activists began a grassroots voter registration drive in Albany, hoping to capitalize on the highest concentration of potential African-American voters in the region. Fueled by support from Student Nonviolent Coordinating Committee (SNCC) members and emboldened by the arrival of Martin Luther King Jr. in November of 1961, the black citizens of Albany took to the streets—and allowed themselves to be taken to jail—in an attempt to win the right to equal representation and accommodation under the law. But by the summer of 1963, the Albany Movement was discontinued, the victim of local police chief Laurie Pritchett's use of nonviolent tactics he boasted of having learned by observing King himself.

Pritchett avoided violent confrontation by expanding the capacity of his jail cells (he negotiated space with nearly every county in a 100-mile radius) and by making efforts to see that prisoners were treated in a relatively humane fashion. The chief even gave a course in nonviolence to some of his officers. Pritchett's strategy worked. By the summer of 1963, the Albany Movement was disbanded. "[We thought] we could fill up the jails," SNCC worker Bill Hansen explained. "We ran out of people before he ran out of jails."

Mount Zion Church, at the corner of Whitney and South Jefferson Streets, was the site of many of the mass meetings during the movement. The church is home to the **Albany Civil Rights Museum.** Glass-cased displays share the space with a stage where local gospel choirs gather on occasion to sing freedom songs made popular in the 1960s by locals like Bernice Johnson Reagon, founder of the modern-day a cappella quartet Sweet Honey in the Rock. *Albany Civil Rights Museum: 326 Whitney Avenue; 229-432-1698.*

A few blocks away, at the corner of Highland and South Jackson Streets, is a fountain built in tribute to the movement. Marble tablets surrounding the fountain are engraved with quotes from people involved in the movement. The most affecting quote is from Martin Luther King Jr.: "When Negroes in Albany decided to straighten their backs up, whenever men and women straighten their backs up, they are going somewhere, because a man can't ride your back unless it is bent."

Contributions of African peoples are also honored at the **Albany Museum of Art,** with the South's largest collection of sub-Saharan art, a gift of former U.S. Ambassador and Albany native, Stella Davis. *311 Meadowlark Drive; 229-439-8400.*

Music fans and chauvinistic Georgians alike might take pleasure in knowing that Albany was once the home of Ray Charles, composer of the state song, "Georgia on My Mind."

SOUTH
GEORGIA

## ◆ ALBANY COMFORTS

**Carter's Grill**

Open since 1968, this local institution is famed for its soul food. Served cafeteria-style are butter beans and field peas, pigs' feet and neckbones, all deftly seasoned, all priced at a pittance. At breakfast, salmon croquettes and grits draw a crowd. *321 West Highland Avenue; 229-432-2098.*

**Aunt Fannie's Checkered Apron**

Bright orange slabs of rutabaga, dusky turnip greens swimming in a porcine pot-likker, and crusty fried chicken are offered at this cream-colored cinder-block restaurant on a side street in a somewhat derelict neighborhood. At lunch, suits and laborers alike fill the 20-odd tables. Breakfast and lunch. *826 Byron Road; 229-888-8416.*

**Chef Gwen's Bistro**

The interior, festooned with palm trees, is a riot of color. The Caribbean offerings—ox-tails and various jerked meats and curried vegetables—are no less vibrant at this quaint and funky hideaway. *303 West Highland Avenue; 229-888-0401.*

## ■ AMERICUS  *map page 205, B-1*

Forty miles north of Albany by way of Highway 19 (and 30 miles west of I-75) is Americus, founded in 1832 on the site of a Creek Indian granary. By the 1890s, Americus, like Thomasville and other towns near the end of the southbound rail lines, was a booming wintertime resort. Today the only vestige of that era is the turreted, redbrick **Windsor Hotel.**

Built in 1892, the hotel has been restored to its former glory: an opulent marvel, with fanciful brick and terra cotta work. The three-story lobby, outfitted in gleaming golden oak, is alone worth the visit. Rooms are spacious. The suites (two are in a tower) are a worthwhile indulgence. *125 West Lamar Street; 229-924-1555.*

## ◆ HABITAT FOR HUMANITY

West Lamar Street in Americus is the headquarters of Habitat for Humanity, an ecumenical Christian ministry that serves by building low-cost, owner-occupied housing with volunteer labor. Started in 1976 by Linda and Millard Fuller, the organization owes its philosophical origins to another ecumenical experiment started years earlier at **Koinonia Farm,** just south of Americus.

Koinonia means "fellowship" in Greek, and at the time of its founding in 1942 by Clarence Jordan, the farm was an experiment in utopian, agricultural ideals. In the early 1970s, Millard Fuller, after a crisis in his marriage, abandoned a successful law career, sold his house, gave most of his possessions to charity, and moved to

*The Windsor Hotel in Americus.*

Koinonia. He lived and worked there until 1976, when he founded Habitat for Humanity.

Today Habitat occupies a good portion of the office space in downtown Americus and can boast of having partnered with more than 65,000 families to build simple, decent homes in every state in the nation and more than 50 other countries. Visitors may tour the organization's headquarters, where the atrium balconies are fashioned from picket fencing and Millard Fuller's Presidential Medal of Honor is on display. There is also a village of the different prototype houses from around the world. *322 West Lamar Street; 229-924-6935.*

Among the advocates of Habitat for Humanity are former President Jimmy Carter and his wife Rosalyn, who were both raised just up the road in Plains and who on occasion pick up hammer and nail to work with other volunteers at a house raising. "I've learned more about the needy than I ever did as governor or President," said the 39th President. "The sacrifice I thought I would be making turned out to be one of the greatest blessings of my life. I don't know of anything I've ever seen that more vividly demonstrates love in action than Habitat for Humanity."

SOUTH
GEORGIA

*Cotton field and farm near Americus.*

◆ AMERICUS AMERICANA CUISINE

### Big Jake's Barbecue

"I got in a little trouble and took a six-year break from cooking," says the proprietor. Be glad he's back. Ribs are the specialty here, served from Big Jake's front yard. Look for the monstrous cookers that sit hard by the road. The day starts with late lunch and goes late into the night. *Lee Street, across the tracks; no phone.*

### Monroe's Hot Dogs and Billiards

In a separate, smoke-filled back room, a band of wizened regulars shoots pool from morning to night. In front, Monroe's dishes dogs piled high with chili and capped with coleslaw to office and construction workers alike. The slogan: "Best dogs ever bitten by man." *318 West Lamar Street; 229-924-4106.*

■ PLAINS  *map page 205, B-2*

Eight miles west of Americus, Plains is the antithesis of the older county seats of the region. Where those are dominated by a courthouse—grand, looming, and often the largest building in town—Plains resembles a frontier town of the West.

SOUTH GEORGIA

In this settlement of less than 750 people, all commerce and life is centered around the rail tracks that bisect the hamlet, and the largest building in sight is a corrugated-metal peanut warehouse. Life here is slow, sublimely so. And a dog sleeping in the middle of the street is a real possibility, not a hackneyed stereotype, so check your rear-view mirror before you back out of that parking space.

But in 1975, this little town came alive when favorite son Jimmy Carter declared his candidacy for President. Carter first entered politics in 1961 and was elected governor of Georgia in 1971, announcing during his inauguration speech, "I say to you quite frankly that the time for racial discrimination is over." When Carter began his presidential campaign after just four years as Georgia's governor, many asked, "Jimmy Who?" Yet thanks to strong grassroots support and tireless campaigning, Carter won the Democratic Party nomination. In the wake of the mendacious mess that was Watergate, Carter promised that he would not lie to the American public, and they believed him. In 1977 he was sworn in as the 39th President.

*Downtown Plains, home of former President Jimmy Carter.*

◆ JIMMY CARTER SIGHTS

Today, the old green-and-white clapboard depot that used to be Carter Campaign Headquarters is open for touring. On display are campaign ephemera like a poster for a July 19, 1976, cattle auction held in Woodbury, Georgia, emblazoned with the slogan, "Got a beef with Bureaucracy? Grind it. Help send Jimmy Carter to Washington."

Also on view are displays that detail Carter Administration accomplishments, from the signing of SALT II treaty with the Soviet Union to limit nuclear proliferation, to the signing of a peace treaty by Egyptian President Anwar Sadat and Israeli Prime Minister Menachem Begin to end hostilities in the Middle East.

Across the tracks are arrayed a series of businesses, some of which sell geegaws. Others, like the Carter Worm Farm Office, are vestiges of past business activity. In the window of cousin Hugh Carter's antique shop, a handwritten sign is posted when the Carters are in town. It reads: "President Jimmy Carter will teach the Sunday school lesson at **Maranatha Baptist Church** this Sunday at 10:00 A.M. You are invited." The church, located just north of town on Highway 45, is a simple brick affair, well suited to this former peanut farmer. On the same road, a bit closer to town, is the graceful redbrick Plains High School, where both President Carter and his wife Rosalynn attended school. Now a part of the 70-acre **Jimmy Carter National Historic Site,** the school has been converted to a museum dedicated to Carter's education and life. *West of Americus on Highway 280; 229-824-4104.*

Visitors in search of Carter kitsch will want to stop off at late brother Billy's gas station (now closed) on Church Street, or take a gander at the giant, smiling goober just north of town near Maranatha Baptist Church.

◆ STAYING IN PLAINS

Well situated in downtown, just across from the old railroad depot, is a pink-and-cream Victorian lady called **Plains Bed-and-Breakfast.** Though a bit worn at the edges, the four-room inn is quite comfortable—and quite reasonable, and a hot breakfast is served daily. *100 West Church Street; 912-824-7252.*

In nearby Preston is **Mom's Kitchen** where the biscuits are justifiably famous. Baked by the family matriarch, Evelyn Hollis (Mom's mom), they taste best hot from the oven and burbling with butter. But there are other treats to be had at this simple brick-fronted cafe: crisp fried chicken and sandy-brown fried catfish, baked sweet potatoes and wonderful sweet iced tea. *At Highways 41 and 280, Preston; 229-828-7285.*

■ ANDERSONVILLE NATIONAL HISTORIC SITE *map page 205, B-1*

North and east of Plains on Highway 49 is the town of Andersonville, site of Camp Sumter, a Confederate prison camp notorious for its inhumane treatment of Union troops. Established in 1864, near the end of the Civil War, the camp housed more than 45,000 troops. Of these, more than 13,000 perished, the victims of dysentery, severe malnutrition, and a range of other maladies. So little food was allowed the prisoners that Confederates were accused of purposely starving the inmates, but officers responded that the Confederate government was virtually broke by 1864, and that they had no funds to buy food.

On July 8, 1864, Sgt. David Kennedy, of the 9th Ohio Calvary, recorded these observations in his diary:

> *Wuld* that I was an artist & had the material to paint this camp & all its troops or the tongue of some eloquent Statesman and had the privleage of expressing my mind to our hon. rulers at Washington. I should gloery to describe this hell on Earth where it takes 7 of its occupiants to make a Shadow.

On November 10, 1865, Confederate captain Henry Wirtz, the officer in charge of the stockade, was hanged, the only Confederate to be executed for war crimes after the close of the Civil War. Today many Confederate heritage groups believe—as did many Southerners at the time of his hanging—that Wirtz was a scapegoat. They claim that Wirtz, a Swiss-born physician who had lived in Louisiana prior to the start to the war, was blamed for the atrocities committed under his watch, atrocities that were perhaps abetted by his superiors. Accordingly, in the center of the little village of Andersonville, there stands a marble obelisk, erected not to the Confederate dead of the county or the state, but to Wirtz, in the hope that its presence might help to "rescue his name from the stigma attached to it by embittered prejudice...."

Today, the site of the former prison camp is operated by the National Park Service, and the grounds are open for touring. Also on-site is the **National Prisoner of War Museum,** a bunker-like redbrick fortress housing multimedia displays that poignantly portray the horrors of POW life. As you step into the first exhibition gallery, a spotlight sweeps across the wall, sirens wail, and the staccato crackle of machine gun fire caroms off the ceiling. A tour of the facilities is unsettling, even disturbing. As you hear the voices of soldiers recounting their time in prison, the walls seem to close in around you, and the words give you pause. "War was supposed to be clean...all crisp and decisive," says one Vietnam POW. "Instead I felt like some helpless cornered prey." And though the focus is on POWs from all American wars, there are a significant number of artifacts from Camp Sumter on display, including the original lock, key, and hinge from the south gate of the camp—eerie reminders of what once stood here among the pines. *Highway 49, 10 miles north of Americus; 229-924-0343.*

■ LUMPKIN  *map page 205, A-2*

History of a more palatable sort is in the offering west of Andersonville, at the delightful antebellum village of Lumpkin. On the square here you will find the oldest operating hardware store in Georgia—the Singer Company—which first opened its doors in 1838. Just down the street is Hatchett's Drug Store Museum, shrine to the old-fashioned soda fountain, where cherry and vanilla cokes, not to mention banana splits, are served with aplomb.

On the edge of town, a half mile south down Martin Luther King Drive, is **Westville** ("where it's always 1850"), a living history museum where potters, soap makers, and other craftspeople practice their craft. Unlike the Agrirama in Tifton, Westville is far removed from any signs of modern-day life. An afternoon spent wandering the dirt pathways that lead from house to house, from mill to millinery store, is time well spent. And if you're lucky, you will pass by the old Marrett farmhouse just as the cook is pulling a batch of biscuits from the fire. *Off US 27; 229-838-6310.*

*(opposite top) Over 13,000 Union soldier prisoners died at Camp Sumter in Andersonville. (Lithograph by John Walker, Library of Congress)*

*(opposite below) Rows of headstones in Andersonville National Cemetery.*

### ■ PROVIDENCE CANYON

On Georgia's western extreme, just a scant few miles from the Alabama border, is a geological curiosity: Providence Canyon, which looks like it belongs in Arizona rather than within a couple of hour's drive of Atlanta. Known to many as Georgia's "little Grand Canyon," it was named for the church that had to be moved when the clay soil continued to erode. But this so-called canyon is, in all actuality, a Brobdingnagian gully. Due to poor farming practices, the gully first began to appear in the 1800s, and it now reaches depths of over 150 feet. At sunset or sunrise, when the sun's rays slant across the walls of the canyon, a kaleidoscope of colors plays across the hoodoo-like rock formations. *Highway 39 C, seven miles west of Lumpkin; 229-838-6202 or 800-864-7275 for camping information.*

*Providence Canyon began as a gully in the 19th century. Today it is a full-fledged canyon, reaching depths of 150 feet in some places.*

## Barbecue in Georgia

Barbecue, as savored in the Georgia, is usually pork shoulder, rib, or butt meat that has been smoked over a hardwood-stoked pit for hours, sometimes days at a time, before being doused with sauce and served alongside a variety of side dishes like potato salad, coleslaw, and baked beans, .and Brunswick stew, a huntsman's stew once chock full of squirrels and other such furry creatures and now is more likely a gallimaufry of chicken—maybe a bit of pork—along with corn tomatoes and maybe even butterbeans.

Contrary to the contentions of our neighbors to the north, barbecue is a noun, not a verb. Barbecue is the end result of a time-intensive marriage of smoke, meat, sweat, and sauce. When Norm from New Jersey rolls his flimsy grill out onto the patch of pavement he calls his backyard and throws a few patties of ground beef on to cook, he may well call that barbecue. Down in Georgia, we know it by another name—heresy.

Regional sociologist John Shelton Reed once posited that, "Southern barbecue is the closest thing we have in the U.S. to Europe's wines or cheese; drive a hundred miles and the barbecue changes."

The man knows his 'cue. Spend any time driving the blacktop back roads of the South and you will soon discover that, in parts of northwestern Alabama, they douse their pork in a white sauce of mostly mayonnaise and vinegar. In eastern Arkansas, baloney is smoked by the stick before being sliced, slathered with a ketchup-based sauce, and sandwiched between two slices of cottony white bread. Around Memphis, Tennessee folks love their barbecue spaghetti, a side dish comprised of limp noodles, sauce and a bit of chopped pork. In Opelika, Alabama natives think nothing of eating tepid barbecue atop iceberg lettuce, smothered with a vinegary sauce. And in Oxford, Mississippi, you can even sink your spoon into a barbecue sundae, a concoction of alternating layers of meat, coleslaw and beans, topped with a dollop of tomato-based sauce.

Georgians tend to comparatively hidebound when it comes to 'cue. But that is not to say that we are absent intraregional variation. There are no hard and fast rules, but a cultural geographer with a barbecue bent might map the state by sauce type, moving from north to south, from the sweet and viscous sauces of the mountains, through the thin vinegary belt of central Georgia, on to the sweet heat of southern Georgia, and, finally, the mustard-kissed stuff they slather on along the coast. And if he did, he would be well advised to seek out some of the following smoke shacks:

## NORTHWEST AND NORTHEAST GEORGIA BARBECUE

Northern Georgia suffers from a blight of touristy places that roast a hunk of hog flesh in the over, pour on some bottled sauce, and call it 'cue. Eater beware! That said, the following spots are worth a 50-mile detour: **Two Brother's Barbecue** in Ball Ground *(see page 68)*, **Colonel Poole's Barbecue** in Ellijay *(see page 71)*, and **The Pink Pig** in Cherry Log *(see page 72)*.

In **Atlanta**, sauce styles are likely to run the gamut. And you might just encounter a modern fillip or two: **Harold's Barbecue** *(see page 133)*, and **Twelve Oaks Barbecue**,*(see page 151)*.

## CENTRAL GEORGIA BARBECUE

Here, in what may well be the buckle of the state's barbecue belt, roadside joints proffer pork that has been smoldered hour upon hour over a hardwood fire, before being pulled from the bone and napped with a thin sauce tasting of peppers, vinegar, and just the slightest hint of tomato. The following easily warrent a detour: **Paul's Barbecue** in Lexington *(see page 182)*, **Moldin Tillman's Barbecue** in Hillsboro *(see page 185)*, **Spruce's Barbecue** in Griffin *(see page 185)*, **Fresh Air Barbecue** in Flovilla *(see page 185)*, and **Old Clinton Barbecue** in Gray *(see page 185)*.

## SOUTHERN AND COASTAL GEORGIA BARBECUE

Driving south from Middle Georgia into the piney woods of southern Georgia, you will notice slight changes in restaurant menus. Somewhere south of Macon, sauce changes, with astringent sauces of mostly vinegar and tomato giving way to concoctions with a bit of mustard added, and maybe an extra shot of ketchup for good measure. Try **Vandy's** in Statesboro *(see page 212)*.

Waycross even has its own distinctive sub-style, with many joints serving buns of chopped pork, bound by bit of mustard sauce and then drizzled with a vinegar sauce, before being squashed flat and then warmed on a flattop griddle or in a two-sided toaster. In Waycross you'll find **The Pig** *(see pages 213, 216)*.

Vienna is the site of the **Big Pig Jig**—Georgia's "official" barbecue championship cook-off, held annually on the second weekend in October—this small Georgia town is better known among true barbecue aficionados as the home of **Mamie Bryant's** barbecue shack *(see page 211)*.

And then by the time you hit **Savannah,** the taste of mustard predominates. Look for **Wall's Barbecue** *(see page 263)*, and **Johnny Harris** *(see page 274)*.

SOUTH GEORGIA

*A plate of 'cue at Colonel Poole's in Ellijay.—just before the fork hits.*

# SAVANNAH
## & THE GEORGIA COAST

■ HIGHLIGHTS *page*

■ TRAVEL BASICS

Savannah is a city splendid enough to seduce even the most jaded traveler. Verdant, almost tropical in its lushness, it is a place of great natural beauty. And for those who come in search of architectural jewels, Savannah does not disappoint, with its regal redbrick townhouses and Gothic-spired cathedrals. South of the city stretches a coastline more remote than might be imagined, what with controlled-access enclaves like Cumberland and Sapelo Islands. Down around Jekyll and St. Simon's Islands, white-sand beaches call. As you make your way closer to the sea, dull gray sand gives way to sparkling white, pine trees to palmettos, and soon the beach beckons, calm and peaceful. Thanks to the miles of coastline, the Georgia beaches are rarely overcrowded. There's always a spot to throw down a blanket, soak up some sun, maybe meander a mile or two down to where the pier juts out into the lolling surf. At night, there's usually a ramshackle fish house just down the road, where the beer is ice cold and the fresh boiled shrimp are delicious.

Between South Carolina and northern Florida, the Atlantic coastline arcs pronouncedly inward. In all of this area, known as the Georgia Bight, the tidal fluctuation is extreme. In Georgia, tides vary up to 10 feet between high and low tide—which accounts for the wide salt marshes found all along the coast. High tide brings seawater as much as 40 miles up the coastal rivers, creating extensive brackish estuaries. These distinctive habitat types make Georgia's coast an amazing place to view wildlife, especially birds.

SAVANNAH &
THE COAST

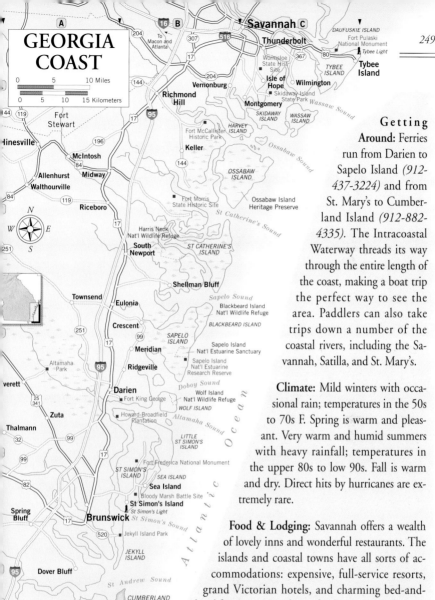

# GEORGIA COAST

| 0 | 5 | 10 Miles |
| 0 | 5 | 10 | 15 Kilometers |

**Getting Around:** Ferries run from Darien to Sapelo Island *(912-437-3224)* and from St. Mary's to Cumberland Island *(912-882-4335)*. The Intracoastal Waterway threads its way through the entire length of the coast, making a boat trip the perfect way to see the area. Paddlers can also take trips down a number of the coastal rivers, including the Savannah, Satilla, and St. Mary's.

**Climate:** Mild winters with occasional rain; temperatures in the 50s to 70s F. Spring is warm and pleasant. Very warm and humid summers with heavy rainfall; temperatures in the upper 80s to low 90s. Fall is warm and dry. Direct hits by hurricanes are extremely rare.

**Food & Lodging:** Savannah offers a wealth of lovely inns and wonderful restaurants. The islands and coastal towns have all sorts of accommodations: expensive, full-service resorts, grand Victorian hotels, and charming bed-and-breakfast inns. Upscale sea-food restaurants abound, but so do fish houses and crab shacks serving tasty, less fancy fare. Brunswick offers a number of chain motels that lack charm but are inexpensive. And Jekyll Island has 200 spots at an ideally situated, oak-shaded campground. *Jekyll Island Campground: 912-635-3021.*

# ■ OVERVIEW

Savannah is a city of many charms and many contradictions. Azaleas and camellias, dogwoods and crepe myrtle trees flourish in the semitropical swelter of a Savannah spring afternoon. Moss-draped oaks lend a shadowy, almost brooding quality to a bright winter morning. Regal redbrick buildings stand in haughty repose, proud testament to the city's past.

Like New Orleans, Savannah is a house-proud city, a city seemingly drunk on architecture. Unlike New Orleans, this is not a city prone to public displays of hedonism. Here, for the most part, drinking and debauchery are private affairs, taking place far from prying eyes. Walking the streets of Savannah, you get the feeling that something very devilish is going on behind the doors of those lovely townhouses.

And yet, it is the serenity of the city, indeed the gentility, that will seduce you. There is order and beauty to be found here, a sense of man and nature as complementary forces. Nowhere is this gentility more evident than in the vest-pocket parks that dot the city, enclaves of green not so much contained by redbrick

*(above) Vest-pocket parks add charm and serenity to Savannah's historic districts.*

*(opposite) The* First Lady *is one of the old-fashioned riverboats that plies the Savannah River.*

borders as protected by them. These squares, part of founder James Oglethorpe's original plan for the city, are the jewels in Savannah's architectural crown.

South of Savannah lies a marshy coastline where golden-tipped marsh grass waves in the salty breeze and Spanish moss drips from the boughs of live oak trees. Rivers curve through these marshlands, creating a series of low-lying islands, each with its own charm—from Sapelo Island with its dense tropical overgrowth and crumbling ruins, to luxurious resort enclaves like Sea Island.

## ■ HISTORY

In 1566, a battle-tested Spanish conquistador named Pedro Menendez de Aviles came ashore on St. Catherine's Island, south of Savannah. His intention was to set up missions and presidios off the southeastern coast of North America, to encourage Spanish settlement and protect Spain's most important trade route from the French and British.

*In this painting by William Verelst, James Oglethorpe presents Yamacraw chief Tomochichi to the trustees of the colony of Georgia in London in 1734. (Henry Francis DuPont Winterthur Museum, Delaware)*

At St. Catherine's, Mendendez met with an Indian chief, Guale, whose name the Spaniards thereafter gave to the entire area. Menendez left behind a garrison of 30 men, and soon Spanish Jesuit missionaries were landing on the sea islands.

The native Creeks, farmers who lived in small villages along the coast, initially showed interest in what the missionaries had to teach, but after a few years they grew hostile and drove the Jesuits out. Franciscan missionaries followed the Jesuits, but the Spanish influence remained negligible.

When James Oglethorpe and a group of 114 British settlers arrived off the coast of Georgia on a February morning in 1733, they were welcomed by Tomochichi, chief of the the Yamacraws, a member tribe of the Lower Creek Confederacy. With Tomochichi's guidance Oglethorpe selected a spot on a 40-foot bluff over-looking the Savannah River some 17 miles from the Atlantic coast. "The last and fullest consideration of the Healthfulness of the place was that an Indian nation, who knew the Nature of the Country, chose it for their Habitation," Oglethorpe later reported to the colony's sponsors in England.

Oglethorpe's early description of Savannah's setting still rings true. He wrote in a 1733 letter to the trustees:

> The river has formed a half moon, around the side of which the banks are about forty feet high, and on the top a flat which they call a bluff.... Upon the river-side, in the center of the plain, I have laid out the town, opposite to which is an island of very rich pasturage. The river is pretty wide, the water fresh, and from the quay of the town you can see its whole course to the sea.

Oglethorpe had the most profound effect of any one person on the city of Savannah, and his original plan for the city, which artfully fits its setting, endures to this day. With its fine avenues and public squares, the plan focused the life of the new city on its common green spaces, making for an urban environment of physical beauty and pleasing interaction.

Oglethorpe left Georgia in July of 1743, never to return, but the year before he left he fought a final battle with the Spanish, defeating them at the Battle of Bloody Marsh on St. Simon's Island and driving them from Georgia.

In the ensuing years, the utopian community Oglethorpe had envisioned—free from the ill effects of slavery or land speculation—succumbed to economic and political pressures. Early attempts to raise wine grapes and silkworms failed, and

*Rice cultivation on the Ogeechee River near Savannah, after a wood engraving by A. R. Ward for* Harper's Weekly. *(Library of Congress)*

Georgian whites looked enviously toward South Carolina, where crops of rice and indigo, tilled by slaves, were bringing large profits.

By the time of the Revolutionary War, slavery was legal in Georgia and the port city of Savannah was thriving. But the town's location at the tail end of the colonial territory left it susceptible to attack, and in December of 1778, the city was captured by the British; it would remain in the hands of the redcoats until after the close of the war in 1782.

The years between the Revolutionary War and the Civil War would prove to be Savannah's heyday as cotton and the slave trade brought untold wealth to the port city. As Savannah prospered, the city's residents began constructing many of the elegant homes that now grace the town squares. By 1820, Savannah was among the 20 largest cities in the United States.

During the Civil War, Union blockades cut off Savannah from trade, but the city did not suffer the physical damage that many Georgia towns did. Gracious Savannah remained above the fray, enduring Yankee occupation as if it were a prolonged visitation from a particularly uncouth uncle, rather than a hostile invasion.

It would be a grand oversight to say that nothing of import has transpired in the near century and a half since the close of the Civil War. During World War II, the city's shipyards built boats by the score. And during the Civil Rights Movement, black citizens of Savannah, through a series of boycotts, won a series of decisive battles in the struggle for equal accommodation under the law. The real story, though, is not what has changed but what has endured.

## ■ SAVANNAH  *map page 258*

The original plan for Savannah called for 24 squares, spaced at regular intervals throughout the business and residential districts of the city. Twenty-one of those squares remain, due to preservation efforts spearheaded by the Historic Savannah Foundation. Faced in the 1950s with the prospect of losing many of the squares and not a few of the grand old buildings at the city center to "urban renewal," a dedicated band of urban guerrillas in petticoats worked to engineer a solution, soliciting federal grants and twisting the arms of local loan officers in an effort to revitalize row upon row of antebellum homes.

*An early morning haze lingers above Orleans Square in the city's historic district.*

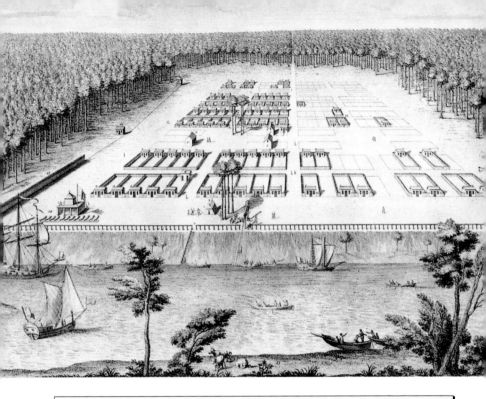

*This engraving by P. Fourdrinier, after a drawing by Peter Gordon, shows Savannah as it stood on March 29, 1734. Bull Street runs north to south through the center of the plan, which shows five of Savannah's original 24 squares. (Library of Congress)*

## SAVANNAH'S ANCIENT PLAN

*T*he plan of Savannah was based on a sketch in *Villas of the Ancients* by Robert Castell, who died in one of the English debtor prisons that Georgia was founded to relieve. From this sketch Oglethorpe, founder of the city, and Colonel William Bull, an engineer of South Carolina, designed the Colonial city on a plan which has persisted.

For all their contrasting details there is a certain unity in the older Georgian Colonial, Classical Revival, Greek Revival, and Victorian houses, which are built on a level with the sidewalk and often joined in rows. Usually they have three or four stories, including a raised basement, and stairs ascending to a high stoop. Some were constructed of crude brick brought from Europe as ballast in early sailing vessels, others show in their soft colors that they were built of the celebrated Savannah grey brick from the old kiln of the Hermitage, etc.

*ᘓᕼᕽᕽᗯᕼᘓ*

*A*long Bull Street, which forms the central axis of the city, are five squares that in the original plan were designed as centers of defense against Spanish and Indian invasion. Now two centuries old, these small parks embody Savannah's characteristic, semitropical and hence lush growth, subdued to the precise lines of a formal beauty. Italian cypresses, tall cabbage palmettoes, blossoming bays, and English yews are among the trees that increase the depth of a natural growth of oaks....Flower beds are bright in season with flame and other azaleas, with glossy green-leaved and white wax-blossomed gardenias, and with both single-colored and variegated camellias. Paths through the grassy plots are lined with benches that offer an invitation to rest and contemplation, and in many of the parks monuments to past heroes create a sense of the continuous ebb and flow of life.

—George G. Leckie, *Georgia: A Guide to its Towns and Countryside*, 1940

*An 1855 view of Savannah by J. W. Hill, looking north on Bull Street, Savannah's central thoroughfare, from Monterey Square. In the foreground stands the Pulaski Monument, and at the far end of Bull Street is the Cotton Exchange. (Collection of the Mariners Museum)*

Savannah's architecture spans both distance and time, as early vernacular architecture gives way to Greek revival and then Victorian. At the southern end of the historic district, at DeRenne Avenue, the 20th century arrives with monotonous commercial buildings. An aged local perhaps put it best when she said, "Darling, anything south of DeRenne might as well be Jacksonville, Florida."

| | | | |
|---|---|---|---|
| Calhoun Square 23 | Ellis Square 2 | Madison Square 18 | Telfair Square 8 |
| Chatham Square 21 | Franklin Square 1 | Monterey Square 22 | Troup Square 20 |
| Chippewa Square 15 | Green Square 12 | Oglethorpe Square 10 | Warren Square 5 |
| Columbia Square 11 | Johnson Square 3 | Orleans Square 14 | Washington Square 6 |
| Crawford Square 16 | Lafayette Square 19 | Pulaski Square 17 | Whitefield Square 24 |
| Elbert Square 13 | Liberty Square 7 | Reynolds Square 4 | Wright Square 9 |

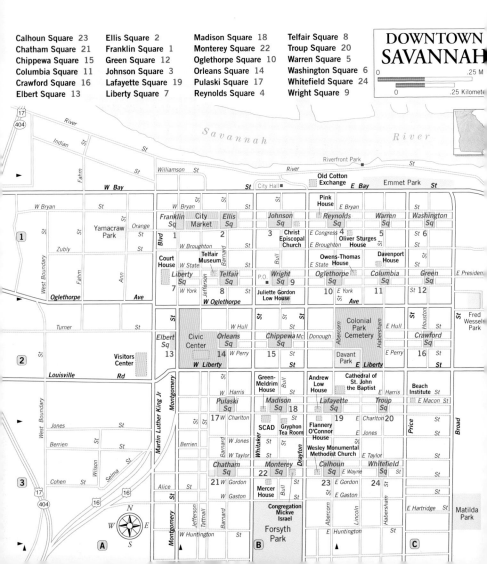

DOWNTOWN SAVANNAH

The three-square-mile historic district stretches south from River Street to the southern tip of Forsyth Park. Plan to spend an afternoon ambling from square to square enjoying verdant parks, inhaling the scent of magnolia, and admiring regal redbrick homes and stately public buildings.

*The old Cotton Exchange is perched on Yamacraw Bluff.*

◆ **BAY AND RIVER STREETS** *map page 258, A, B & C-1*

At 100 East Bay Street, near the intersection with Drayton, stands the old **Cotton Exchange**, a Romanesque beauty perched on Yamacraw Bluff. Once the hub of activity for the cotton warehouses that line River Street below, this 1886 building with a fanciful terra cotta front now stands in noble repose beside the Bourbon Street–like circus that unfolds at the riverside. Stretching east and west from the Exchange is a series of brick buildings, once the offices of the cotton factors who made their millions trading long-staple Sea Island cotton, and now home to antique dealers and attorneys.

River Street, a cobblestone lane that runs the width of the historic district, affords an unparalleled view of the Savannah River. The other side of River Street is lined with rough ballast-and-brick buildings, where barkers hawk quart-sized draft beers and any manner of T-shirts. And if your visit happens to coincide with the celebration of St. Patrick's Day (Savannah's celebration is second in size only to New York City's), then you can bet that the beer will be dyed an Irish green.

The River Street area offers lodging in a big **Hyatt Regency,** *2 West Bay Street; 912-238-1234,* or in places with more charm like the **East Bay Inn,** *225 East Bay Street; 912-238-1225,* and the **Mulberry Inn** in a former livery stable, *601 East Bay Street; 912-238-1200.* A favorite with the St. Patrick's Day crowd is the **River Street Inn** with its graceful appointments and canopied beds, and ten rooms with balconies overlooking River Street. *115 East River Street; 912-232-4650.*

SAVANNAH & THE COAST

*Cobblestoned River Street runs the width of Savannah's historic district.*

But River Street is an anomaly, a ticky-tacky blight upon what is truly one of the most serenely beautiful cities in the South, indeed in the whole of the United States. Even in the dead of winter, the city resembles an oasis of green, profuse with giant oaks and the lustrous sheen of azalea and camellia bushes, while during the spring and summer the city flushes with vivid color as crepe myrtles, dogwoods, magnolias, and wisteria vines burst forth in a kaleidoscope of blossoms.

◆ CITY MARKET  *map page 258, B-1*

City Market is a pedestrian-only warren of narrow streets set between Franklin Square and Ellis Square. It is lined with some of Savannah's toniest shops and best restaurants.

### Lady and Sons

The menu here contrasts such dainty dishes as asparagus sandwiches against substantial southern-style meals served buffet style. Don't pass up the fat, crusty hoecakes and thick, cheesy biscuits, or the iced tea spiked with mint leaves. The restaurant is a favorite of ladies-who-lunch and tourists. *311 West Congress Street; 912-233-2600.*

Savannah Market, *by Harry Leslie Hoffman, 1915. (Private collection)*

**Sapphire Grill**
This chic temple of haute cuisine is the place to go for inventive cooking in a setting that feels more SoHo than Savannah. Offerings might include: a fricassee of local white shrimp, country ham and roasted leeks with a lobster scallion fritter, yellow pepper oil, and fried thyme, and Colorado free range Sapphire Grill lamb lollipops. Fortunately, the chef is as skilled as the menu writer is florid. *110 West Julian Street; 912-443-9962.*

◆ SAVANNAH, SQUARE BY SQUARE

**Johnson Square** *map page 258, B-1*
Astride Bull Street between Bryan and Congress is Johnson Square, the first square laid out by Oglethorpe. Named for Robert Johnson, the governor of South Carolina at the time of Georgia's founding, the square is anchored on the east by **Christ Episcopal Church**, the first congregation organized in the colony. The present structure, the fourth at this site, is a study in simplicity, fronted by staid Corinthian columns and noticeably absent of any joyfully bright stained glass windows. It was on this site that John Wesley held the first Sunday school class in North America. Wesley, who came to America as a missionary for the Church of England, proved to be an unpopular and antagonistic sort. He would later leave Georgia after being indicted for interfering in the secular affairs of the colony. Back in England, he rekindled his religious fervor and founded Methodism.

In the center of the square is a monument to Revolutionary War hero Gen. Nathanael Greene, and it is here that you will find his grave.

**Reynolds Square** *map page 258, B-1*
Just a couple of blocks east of City Market, astride Abercorn Street, is Reynolds Square.

On the northeast corner you will find the **Old Pink House** restaurant. The rose-colored stucco building with Palladian windows is one of the few structures to survive the great fire of 1796, when more than 200 homes were destroyed. Today, the restaurant features nine dining rooms, including the cozy and dark tavern downstairs. Fresh seafood and expertly prepared meats are house specialties. The restaurant is considered one of Savannah's best. *23 Abercorn Street; 912-232-4262.*

Across the square at 27 Abercorn is the **Oliver Sturges House,** an 1818 brick home distinguished by playful dolphin-shaped downspouts that decorate the side of the house.

❖

Farther east are **Warren** and **Washington Squares,** added to Oglethorpe's original 24 in 1790.

**Columbia Square** *map page 258, C-1*
Just south, astride Habersham Street between State and York, is **Columbia Square,** added in 1799.

On the northwest corner you will find the **Isaiah Davenport House Museum,** a Federal-style brick building with wrought iron touches. It was the imminent destruction, in 1955, of the then derelict Davenport home that many credit as the catalyst for Savannah's historic preservation movement. *324 East State Street; 912-236-8097.*

**Green Square**   *map page 258, C-1*
On a narrow alley off Green Square you'll find **Wall's Barbecue**. This shack serves good, cheap deviled crabs, red rice, and smoked ribs slathered with a mustard sauce. There are only a few tables available so most everyone gets their food to go. *515 East York Lane; 912- 232-9754.*

**Oglethorpe Square**   *map page 258, C-1*
On Oglethorpe Square at Abercorn Street is one of three extant homes designed by noted English architect William Jay: the **Owens-Thomas House**, a Regency-style home of unparalleled opulence, built in 1817 and filled with period furnishings. The National Trust for Historic Preservation calls this "Savannah's most sophisticated house, then and now." Today it is operated as a museum by the Telfair Academy of Arts and Sciences. *124 Abercorn Street, 912-233-9743.*

*Springtime in Telfair Square*

**Telfair Square**   *map page 258, B-1*
Also of English Regency style and designed by Jay is the **Telfair Museum of Art,** the oldest art museum in the South, featuring a collection strong in the decorative arts— just what you might expect in house-proud Savannah. *121 Barnard Street; 912-232-1177.*

**Wright Square**   *map page 258, B-1*
Wright Square was named for Sir James Wright, the last royal governor of Georgia. But the real reason to visit this green space is to pay homage to Chief Tomochichi. The chief, aided by Mary Musgrove, an interpreter of mixed European and Native ancestry, signed the formal treaty that allowed Oglethorpe's colonists to peacefully settle among the indigenous tribes. In 1734, Tomochichi traveled with Oglethorpe to England, where he was received by King George II at Kensington and by the Archbishop of Canterbury at Lambeth Palace.

A short stroll south along Bull Street brings you to the **Juliette Gordon Low Birthplace**, an imposing white masonry home completed in 1821, where Girl Scouts founder Low spent her childhood years. In addition to serving as a house museum outfitted in grand Victorian style, the home displays family mementos including a childhood portrait of a precocious-looking Low. *142 Bull Street; 912-233-4501.*

**Chippewa Square**   *map page 258, B-2*
Farther south along Bull Street, at Perry, is Chippewa Square, site of a monumental

*The family parlor in Juliette Gordon Low's birthplace.*

*The drawing room of the Owens-Thomas House.*

statue of colony founder James Edward Oglethorpe. Attired in the full-dress regalia of a British general, his sword unsheathed, Oglethorpe is shown with his eyes fixed southward toward Florida—long the bastion of the Spanish Empire, England's rival for control of the southeastern seaboard.

And a couple of blocks east, on Abercorn Street, is Colonial Park Cemetery, final resting place of many of the town fathers. The cemetery is an outdoor sculpture garden of sorts, thick with beautiful testaments to the dearly departed. Though Bonaventure Cemetery east of town has won praise for its marsh-side beauty and notoriety for its prominence in John Berendt's *Midnight in the Garden of Good and Evil*, Colonial Park casts an equally powerful and timeless spell.

Stretching from west to east between Harris and Charlton Streets are Pulaski, Madison, Lafayette, and Troup Squares; of these, Madison and Lafayette are most interesting.

### Madison Square   *map page 258, B-2*

The northwest corner of the square is occupied by the **Green-Meldrim House**, a brick Gothic structure that served as Union general Sherman's headquarters during the Civil War. This unusual building is flanked by flagstone piazzas and festooned with ironwork. Here the general and his officers met with local blacks, working to devise the ill-fated "40 acres and a mule" plan intended to guarantee freed slaves a means of support. And it was from here that Sherman sent his now famous telegram to President Lincoln announcing the capture of

Savannah and offering the city as a Christmas present to his commander-in-chief.

Today the building serves as the parish house for neighboring St. John's Episcopal Church, and is open for tours. *One Macon Street; 912-233-3845.*

Catty-corner from the parish house is the old **Savannah Volunteer Guards Armory**, a redbrick Romanesque building that now houses the headquarters for the **Savannah College of Art and Design**—known to locals and students alike as SCAD. Founded in 1979, the college is the single largest landholder in the historic district. Its 3,500-plus students pursue bachelor and master of fine arts degrees in topics such as art history, architectural history, graphic design, photography, video, and historic preservation. Students of the latter discipline use Savannah itself as a laboratory. On display at the administration building are student art and design projects ranging from the surreal (computer-generated landscapes) to the absurd (packaging proposals for cartons of flea killer).

Across Bull Street is the **Gryphon Tea Room**. Once the home of Solomon's drugstore, this ornate building was refurbished by the Savannah College of Art and Design, and now functions as a quirkily charming tea room, serving salads, sandwiches, and soups along with an encyclopedic selection of hot teas. Take a gander at the carved mahogany gryphon clock that gives the place its name. *337 Bull Street; 912-238-2481.*

Heading down Bull Street to shady, West Jones you'll find the venerable **Mrs. Wilkes' Dining Room** where locals line up each weekday at 11 A.M. for fried chicken, snap beans, black-eyed peas, and candied yams. The line snakes to the street from the basement entrance of this former boarding house. *107 West Jones Street; 912-232-5997.*

**Lafayette Square**  *map page 258, C-2*
Lafayette Square, east of Madison, is the site of the **Andrew Low House**, a burnished pink, stuccoed mansion built in 1848. It was here that Juliette Gordon Low first called to order a meeting of the Girl Scouts, in March of 1912. The building is now open as a house museum. *329 Abercorn Street; 912-233-6854.*

On the opposite corner is the twin-spired **Cathedral of St. John the Baptist,** the oldest Catholic church in Georgia and scene of the mass celebrated each St. Patrick's Day morning before a parade that wends its way through the historic district.

Across the way is the **Flannery O'Connor Childhood Home.** The author lived at the simple four-story townhouse from her birth in 1925 until 1938, and attended the local Catholic grade school. *(See pages 185-186 for more details on her career.)* Today, precious few mementos of her time here remain. *207 East Charlton Street; 912-233-6014.*

❖

Just about any one of Savannah's city squares is a fine place to wile away an hour or so, soaking up the dappled sunlight that plays through the trees on a late fall afternoon, or seeking the cool spots beneath the towering boughs of an ancient oak on a stultifyingly hot summer day. But perhaps the most pleasant of the squares—the two that boast the finest blend of natural beauty and architectural splendor—are Monterey and Calhoun, sandwiched between Taylor and Gordon Streets just a few blocks north of Forsyth Park.

**Monterey Square**  *map page 258, B-3*
Monterey Square commemorates the 1846 capture of Monterey, Mexico, by U.S. forces, and is graced by a statue of Polish-born Revolutionary War hero Casimir Pulaski. On the southeastern corner is **Congregation Mickve Israel**, founded in 1733, the oldest congregation now practicing Reform Judaism in the United States. In a 1790 letter to the congregation, President George Washington expressed his wishes that "the same wonder-working Deity, who long since delivering the Hebrews from their Egyptian oppressors...still continues to water them with the dews of Heaven and to make the inhabitants of every denomination participate in the temporal and spiritual blessings of that people whose God is Jehovah."

On the southwestern corner, is **Mercer House,** a private residence once home to the ancestors of composer Johnny Mercer, winner of four Oscars for such songs as "Moon River" and "On the Atch- inson, Topeka, and Santa Fe." The redbrick Italianate house with wisteria-draped, wrought iron balconies has won more notoriety of late as the former home of antique dealer Jim Williams, protagonist of John Berendt's *Midnight in the Garden of Good and Evil,* known to locals as simply "The Book."

SAVANNAH &
THE COAST

## SAVANNAH CHARACTERS

*Best-selling novel* Midnight in the Garden of Good and Evil *by John Berendt tells the story of Jim Williams, a socialite antique dealer accused of killing local tough Danny Hansford. Though, at its heart, John Berendt's 1994 nonfiction work is a murder mystery, the enduring appeal of the book is in its portrait of Savannah's hedonistic aristocrats and flamboyant ne'er do wells.*

"Savannah's a peculiar place, but if you just listen to your Cousin Joe you'll get along fine. You need to know about a few basic rules though.

"Rule number one: *Always stick around for one more drink.* That's when things happen. That's when you find out everything you want to know."

"I think I can live with that one," I said.

"Rule number two: *Never go south of Gaston Street.* A true Savannahian is a NOG. NOG means 'north of Gaston.' We stay in the old part of town...."

☙ ❧

Savannahians drove fast. They also liked to carry their cocktails with them when they drove. According to the National Institute of Alcoholism and Alcohol Abuse, more than 8 percent of Savannah's adults were "known alcoholics," which may have accounted for the disturbing tendency of motorists to run up over the curb and collide with trees. The trunks of all but one of the twenty-seven oaks that lined the edge of Forsyth Park on Whitaker Street, for instance, had deep scars at fender level. One tree had been hit so many times it had a sizable hollow scooped out of its trunk. The hollow was filled with pea-size crystals of windshield glass that glittered like a bowl of diamonds. The palm trees in the center of Victory Drive had the same sort of scars, and so did the oaks on Abercorn.

*The center of the novel is wealthy, ambitious Jim Williams.*

Williams was gaining stature in Savannah, to the irritation of certain blue bloods. "How does it feel to be *nouveau riche?*" he was asked on one occasion. "It's the *riche* that counts," Williams answered. Having said that, he bought Mercer House.

Mercer House had been empty for more than ten years. It stood at the west end of Monterey Square, the most elegant of Savannah's many tree-shaded squares. It was an Italianate mansion of red brick with tall, arched windows set off by ornate ironwork balconies. It sat back from the street, aloof behind its apron of lawn and its cast-iron fence, not so much looking out on the square as presiding over it…[I]n 1970, he gave a black-tie Christmas party and invited the cream of Savannah society. On the night of his party, every window of Mercer House was ablaze with candlelight; every room had sparkling chandeliers. Clusters of onlookers stood outside watching the smart arrivals and staring in amazement at the beautiful house that had been dark for so long. A pianist played cocktail music on the grand piano downstairs; an organist played classical pieces in the ball-room above. Butlers in white jackets circulated with silver trays. Ladies in long gowns moved up and down the spiral stairs in rivers of satin and silk chiffon. Old Savannah was dazzled.

—John Berendt, *Midnight in the Garden of Good and Evil,* 1994

*Mercer House, in Savannah's historic district.*

*A spring morning mist envelopes Forsyth Park.*

**Calhoun Square**  *map page 258, B-3*
Calhoun Square, four blocks east of Monterey, was named for South Carolina statesman John Calhoun and is the site of soaring, Gothic-spired **Wesley Monumental Methodist Church**. The church was built in tribute to the brothers John and Charles Wesley, who came to Georgia with Oglethorpe as missionaries for the Church of England and later returned to England to establish the Methodist Church.

Until recently, the corner cafe called **Clary's** was a drugstore with a lunch counter. Now, folks stop in for burgers or Caesar salads, though many opt for just a malted milkshake. Breakfast is especially good. *404 Abercorn Street; 912-233-0402.*

**Forsyth Park**  *map page 258, B-3*
On the southern fringe of the historic district, where antebellum architecture gives way to Victorian and then early bungalow-style, is this 26-acre green space park, laid out in 1851. The landmark cast-iron fountain near the center of the park is similar to one that graces the Place de la Concorde in Paris. To the south is the towering marble **Monument to the Confederate Dead**, inscribed with the words, "Come from the Four Winds, O Breath, And breathe upon these slain that they may live."

## SAVANNAH'S HISTORIC INNS

A night in one of Savannah's better historic inns can be appreciated as a sort of extended stay at a living history museum. You get the sense that you were on a guided tour, and someone locked the door before you exited.

At the **Ballastone,** snifters of brandy are proffered in the evening, and a full breakfast with fresh-baked breads is served in the morning. 18 rooms are offered for let at this mansion built in 1838, many of which are furnished with four-poster rice beds. *14 East Oglethorpe Avenue; 912-236-1484.*

The **Eliza Thompson Inn** is an 1847 Federal style mansion. There are 25 recently renovated guestrooms, all with private bath. They offer a complimentary full breakfast, and intrepid travelers hoof it up the street to the venerable Mrs Wilkes' Boarding House for lunch. *5 West Jones Street; 912-236-3620 or 800-348-9378.*

*The parlor at Eliza Thompson Inn*

The proprietors of **Foley House** boast that they have what every tourist is looking for: a tangible link to the movie *Gone With the Wind.* In this case, it's a brass lamp used as a prop. Apart from the lamp, the look and feel here is late Victorian; gilt and chintz predominate. The location, a redbrick row house facing on Chippewa Square, couldn't be better. Full breakfast, afternoon tea and sweets. *14 W. Hull Street; 912-232-6622 or 800-647-3708.*

The **Gastonian** is actually two antebellum mansions joined by an aboveground walkway. It's among the most popular of Savannah inns. Each of the 17 rooms has a working fireplace and Persian rugs cover the hardwood floors. The veranda is wide and welcoming. And there is even a sun deck with a hot tub, one of the few in town. *220 East Gaston Street; 912-232-2869 or 800-322-6603.*

The **Hamilton-Turner Inn** was, until recently, a true house museum. This striking Victorian-Gothic inn sits facing majestic Lafayette Square. In the parlor, an Empire era sofa, acquired from the Mercer estate, faces an ornate white marble fireplace. In the guestrooms, understated opulence prevails, and hardwood floors shine. The carriage house, also available for rent, is a virtual home, complete with 2 bedrooms, living room, dining room, and two and one-half baths. A full, southern-style breakfast is served. *330 Abercorn Street; 912-233-1833 or 888-448-8849.*

**Magnolia Place Inn,** overlooking verdant Forsyth Park, is a grand Victorian mansion built in 1878. In the main house there are 12 guestrooms, many featuring fireplaces and jacuzzi tubs. Enjoy afternoon cocktails in the parlor, and pralines and cordials in the privacy of your room before bed. In the morning, breakfast is served on the veranda if you please, or, for late risers, delivered to your room on a silver tray. *503 Whitaker Street; 912-236-7674 or 800-238-7674.*

**Planter's Inn** was originally opened in 1912 as the Wesley Hotel. This seven-story 56-room property has all the conveniences of a major hotel, albeit in a setting that is much more intimate. Rooms have four-poster beds and are furnished with antiques and quality reproductions. Continental breakfast is served in the morning, and a complimentary glass of wine is offered in the afternoon. *29 Abercorn Street; 912-232-5678.*

*The parlor at the historic Ballastone Inn.*

◆ OUTSIDE THE HISTORIC DISTRICT

### Savannah History Center

Housed in the old passenger shed of the Central of Georgia Railway, the museum displays a broad collection of artifacts: everything from old fanners used to separate the rice kernels from the chaff during harvest, to a plaster reproduction of the sculpture whose picture graces the original cover of *Midnight in the Garden of Good and Evil*—a diminutive gray figure nicknamed the Bird Girl. (The original Bird Girl sculpture has been moved from its graveplot at Bonaventure Cemetery and is now on display at the Telfair Museum of Art *(see page 264). History Center: 303 MLK Jr. Boulevard near the Liberty Street intersection; 912-238-1779.*

### Ralph Mark Gilbert Civil Rights Museum

A few blocks south is the new Ralph Mark Gilbert Civil Rights Museum, named for the long-serving pastor of Savannah's First African Baptist Church who was a leader of the NAACP during the early years of the Civil Rights Movement. The museum features a reconstructed lunch counter from Levy's department store, scene of boycotts protesting the store's refusal to serve food to blacks. Also on display is a timeline of black achievement in Savannah and the South, punctuated by film footage of civil rights workers and their activities in Savannah. *460 MLK Jr. Boulevard; 912-231-8900.*

### Beach Institute

Black achievement of another sort is honored at the Beach Institute. Established by the American Missionary Association in 1865 as a school for freed slaves, the institute now operates a museum. Among the museum's holdings of African-American art is a remarkable collection of hand-carved wooden busts of former Presidents, fashioned by the self-taught, folk sculptor Ulysses Davis. After losing his job in the Savannah railroad office, Davis built a barbershop behind his home, cutting hair by day and carving wood by night. As carved by Davis, Abraham Lincoln has Negroid features and Dick Nixon looks trickier than ever. *502 East Harris Street; 912-234-8000.*

### King Tisdale Cottage

Around the corner in this 1896 frame cottage with gingerbread woodwork is a collection from the Beach Institute that documents the vernacular architecture and cultural achievements of Savannah's long-established African-American community. *514 East Huntington Street; 912-234-8000.*

### Johnny Harris

Savannah's oldest restaurant opened in 1924. In the front dining room, a circular, domed affair with booths on the perimeter, big bands once played and Savannah swells danced the night away. These days Johnny Harris is a restaurant that coasts along on a reputation won long ago, serving everything from prime rib to crabmeat au gratin. That said, the smoked pork and lamb aren't bad, especially when napped with a bit of the mustardy barbecue sauce. *1651 East Victory Drive; 912-354-7810.*

*The barbershop of late folk-artist Ulysses Davis became a dense artistic environment filled with elaborate sculptures and highly detailed wood reliefs. (photo courtesy Richard Sommers)*

## ■ SOUTH AND EAST OF SAVANNAH *map page 249, C-1*

### ◆ WORMSLOE

An oak-lined avenue leads from Skidaway Road to Wormsloe, the tabby ruins of a plantation constructed by English physician Noble Jones, who came to Georgia in 1733 with Oglethorpe. Wormsloe was named in honor of the silkworm, which the colony's trustees wished their settlers to raise on mulberry trees (eventually leading to the manufacture silk to grace English royalty). Though the ruins conjure up a picture of colonial life, the real attraction is the canopy of more than 400 oaks that span the narrow lane, punctuated by shafts of light that only occasionally pierce the heavy foliage. Also on-site is a museum where you can learn about the early, hopeful days of the colony. *7601 Skidaway Road; 912-353-3023.*

◆ ISLE OF HOPE  *map page 249, C-1*

Tucked into a bend on the Skidaway River just north of Wormsloe, the Isle of Hope is perhaps the most picturesque community in coastal Georgia. A collection of two- and three-story frame homes—all of them gleaming white—faces the tidal marshlands, bogs of water-saddled grasses that sway in the salty breeze. Take a drive along these narrow serpentine lanes and you will soon be confoundedly, hopelessly, and pleasantly lost.

◆ THUNDERBOLT  *map page 249, C-1*

A few miles north of the Isle of Hope is Highway 80, also known as Victory Drive, which leads the way east to the sea. Just before you reach the Wilmington River, take the last left turn into the little fishing community of Thunderbolt, and soon you are snaking along a narrow road that leads its way marshward to **Bonaventure Cemetery.** Fans of *Midnight in the Garden of Good and Evil* know this as the place where author John Berendt was first introduced to the peculiarities of Savannah society, by way of a martini-fueled lecture at the gravesite of the poet Conrad Aiken. Site of a colonial plantation that has long since burned, the cemetery is as famed for the natural surroundings as it is for the spectacular statuary. Berendt described it as looking like a "live-oak forest of a primeval dimension."

Thunderbolt has two venerable seafood shacks with steamed oysters served by the bucket. **Desposito's Seafood** is a neat-as-a-pin, tin-roofed relic that looks like it's been there forever. Yesterday's newspaper serves as today's placemat. *187 Macceo Drive; 912-897-9963.* **Teeple's Restaurant and Market** might have less charm than Desposito's, but it has no less quality. Toss the shells in the hole in the center of the table and cast off your cares. *2917 River Drive; 912-354-1157.*

East of Highway 80, marshlands looking much like placid plains of grass stretch almost to the horizon. Above, seagulls bank and circle, their cries filling air heady with the rich and rank smell of pluff mud. With the crossing of each bridge, you come upon another small spit of land—Isle of Armstrong, Oatland Island, Talahi Island, and, finally, just before land's end at Tybee Island, the turnoff for Fort Pulaski.

*Spanish moss serves as a moody background for this statue in Bonaventure Cemetery.*

◆ FORT PULASKI  *map page 249, C-1*

Completed in 1847 and fortified with more than 25 million bricks, Pulaski was supposedly indestructible. "You might as well bombard the Rocky Mountains," boasted a general with the Corps of Engineers. One of the fort's engineers was young Robert E. Lee, stationed here soon after his graduation from West Point.

The fort, which faces the sea, was captured by Confederate troops early in the Civil War and protected blockade runners from attack by the Union navy. Thus it became one of the priorities of the Federals. In 1861, they secretly hauled 36 cannon over mud flats to Tybee Island and concealed them in 11 batteries.

The fort fell to Union bombardment in April 1862, the casualty of new bullet-shaped artillery shells fired from more than a mile away. This success ushered in a new era in fort construction strategy. Today, the formidable pentagonal redbrick fort, surrounded by a seven-foot-deep moat, is maintained by the National Park Service and is open for tours. *Off Highway 80, 16 miles east of Savannah on US 80. 912-786-5787.*

*The northwest wall of Fort Pulaski National Monument at sunset.*

◆ TYBEE ISLAND  *map page 249, C-1*

Long known as "Savannah's Beach," Tybee Island is a shabbily genteel seaside community, blessed with two long, wide beaches, a low people-to-pelican ratio, and a central business district that exudes a tawdry Coney Island-esque charm. Though the landmark DeSoto Hotel was recently torn down in favor of a condominium development, residents have rallied to enact a moratorium on new multiple-unit construction, thus ensuring that the community does not go the way of South Carolina's Hilton Head Island.

Most of the activity centers on Butler Avenue, on the island's eastern edge, where a pier juts out into the surf. On the pier is a pavilion, originally built in 1891 and reconstructed in 1996. During the 1940s the pavilion was the scene of big-band dances; today it's home to purveyors of cotton candy and corndogs. Here you will find ample parking for beach excursions, and, during the summer high season, a carnival-like atmosphere.

The best meal on the island for the money might be at the **Breakfast Club.** This warren of interconnected rooms is welcoming—and immensely popular. Breakfast is the best bet, featuring such inventive fare as chorizo and eggs, shrimp and grits, and the Grill Cleaner's Special: a kitchen-sink conglomeration of sausage, cheese, eggs, and whatever else the grill cook rummages up. *1500 Butler Avenue; 912-786-5984.*

**Williams Seafood,** on the banks of the Bull River, is a Savannah-Tybee institution, serving simple seafood dishes in a utilitarian dining room. Open since 1936, the restaurant may have become just too darn popular over the years, but they still pack 'em in. *8010 Highway 80; 912-897-2219.*

Tybee's upscale favorite is **George's,** set in a comfortable bungalow and serving the likes of pulled pork over caramelized apples with red cabbage and Vidalia onions in a mustard sauce, or sautéed black grouper over a ragout of lima beans with tasso and cremini mushrooms. *1105 East Highway 80; 912-786-9730.*

Just a half-block from the ocean is the **17th Street Inn,** a sturdy little two-story building, fronted by screened porches, that looks like the overgrown beach house that it is. Rooms are furnished simply, with old-fashioned iron beds and antique bureaus. *12 17th Street; 912-786-0607.*

North of "the strip" along Pulaski and Taylor Streets is a second beach scene more popular with locals than with tourists. This comparatively remote enclave is dominated by the looming Tybee Lighthouse and crumbling Fort Screven, the latter a Spanish American War-era fort, now deserted by the military but maintained in part as a museum. When the lighthouse was originally constructed in 1736, it was the highest in America. A portion of the present structure dates from 1773. A long, 178-step climb ascends from deck to beacon. The refurbished, circa-1900, Victorian cottage just below the lighthouse is the **Fort Screven Inn.** *24 Van Horn Street; 912-786-9255.*

Just off the beach at Fort Screven you'll find the **North Beach Grill,** a tropical shack that serves jerk chicken, curried lobster, and other Caribbean dishes, and a good measure of Southern specialties to boot. It's funky, fun, and a bit removed from the scene, so tourists are few. *41-A Enddin Drive; 912-786-9003.*

Just beyond the fort, the surf beckons, a lazy, rolling blanket of foam that laps the shore. In the fall and winter, this section of the island borders on desolate, and Tybee Islanders revel in their isolation, before preparing once again for the summer tourists, relatively few though they may be.

## ■ SOUTH BY WAY OF THE COASTAL HIGHWAY

Cars and trucks barrel south along I-95, a ribbon of hot white concrete that can take them from Savannah to Jacksonville, Florida, in less than two hours. Highway 17, the old Coastal Highway, is less hectic, wending its way south past chancy flea markets, ramshackle barbecue joints, and abandoned roadhouses.

About ten miles south of Savannah on Highway 17, just north of Richmond Hill, is the **Bamboo Farm and Coastal Gardens,** operated by the University of Georgia College of Agriculture. Once the site of plant introduction experiments, the farm is now home to the largest grove of bamboo in the States, with some stalks towering more than 75 feet. It's a surreal site, worthy of a detour. *2 Canebreak Road; 912-921-5460.*

### ◆ RICHMOND HILL *map page 249, B-1*

Just down the road is the town of Richmond Hill, conceived in the 1920s as a winter home by industrialist Henry Ford. Built on the site of the former

Richmond Plantation, Richmond Hill was once a "company town" where locals lived off the Ford family largess, inhabiting Ford-built homes and, of course, driving Ford-built Model Ts. Today, Savannah is sprawling southward and Richmond Hill is slowly being transformed into a bedroom community for its neighbor to the north, but the small **Richmond Hill Historical Museum** pays tribute to the bygone days. *11460 Ford Avenue; 912-756-3697.*

### ◆ FORT MCALLISTER *map page 249, B-1*

Just south of Richmond Hill on Highway 144 is Fort McAllister, site of the last line of resistance the Confederate forces were able to muster in the face of General Sherman's march on Savannah in 1864. In 1863 alone, the fort withstood seven attacks by Union gunboats hurling hundreds of rounds of ammunition shoreward. No matter the intensity of the bombardment, the fort held. Finally, Sherman's ground troops stormed the garrison and in so doing definitively closed down trade through the port of Savannah, cutting off the Confederacy from a major supply route and ensuring waterborne support for Union troops stationed there.

Today there is a museum on-site, replete with artifacts from the Confederate blockade-runner boat, *Nashville,* which sank in the Ogeechee River during a battle with the Union ironclad *Montauk.*

Many visitors who come here picnic on the bluff high above the river—bringing along a few dozen boiled river shrimp for an afternoon snack.

### ◆ MIDWAY *map page 249, A-2*

Settled by Calvinists of English and Scottish extraction in 1754, Midway—on Highway 17 just above Riceboro—was once home to two of Georgia's three signers of the Declaration of Independence, Lyman Hall and Button Gwinett. Today, little remains of this once-thriving community, save the white-framed, three-story Midway Congregational Church (built in 1792 to replace an earlier structure burned by the British in 1778) and a colonial-era cemetery with moss-covered tombstones pitching this way and that. The **Midway Museum**, built in a style reminiscent of nearby plantations, is outfitted with properly austere period furnishings. *912-884-5837.*

SAVANNAH &
THE COAST

◆ OSSABAW ISLAND   *map page 249, B & C-2*

Parallel to the coastline, a string of virtually inaccessible islands stretches south from Savannah.

Ossabaw Island, a state-owned wilderness preserve, is rife with feral hogs, descendants of Spanish pigs brought to the New World over 400 years ago. The Ossabaw pigs are distinct, due to their long years of isolation on the island, and thus, are a valuable resource for scientific study. The island also has a rich human heritage with more than 200 archaeological sites and artifacts dating back 4000 years.

Those interested in learning more about the island should contact the Ossabaw Island Foundation; *145 Bull Street, Savannah, GA 31401; 912-233-5104* .

*Sand dunes and beach grasses characterize the pristine beaches of Ossabaw Island.*

*(opposite) A feral hog crosses a road lined with live oak on Ossabaw Island.*

◆ St. Catherine's Island   *map page 249, B-2*

Just south of Ossabow is St. Catherine's Island, once the center of the Spanish missions built in 16th-century Georgia and later one of several Sea Islands where freed slaves attempted to establish a republic of their own. Following General Sherman's vision that every man was entitled to 40 acres and a mule, the freed slaves attempted to distribute land and to set up an independent kingdom.

The Noble Foundation and the New York Zoological Society, act as stewards of St. Catherine's; the island is closed to visitors.

Thanks to recent digs on St. Catherine's and adjacent islands, archaeologists are learning more about the native people who once thrived on these barrier islands. One of the first travelers to notice evidence of these people was botanist William Bartram, who wrote in 1773:

> *I* observed among the shells of the conical mounds, fragments of earthen vessels, and of other utensils, the manufacture of the ancients; about the center of one of them, the rim of an earthen pot appeared among the shells and earth, which I carefully removed, and drew it out, almost whole; this pot was curiously wrought all over the outside, representing basket work, and was undoubtedly esteemed a very ingenious performance, by the people, at the age of its construction.

◆ Blackbeard and Sapelo Islands   *map page 249, B-3*

Farther south still are Blackbeard and Sapelo Islands, the former a national wildlife refuge that was once the stomping grounds of pirate Edward Teach, better known as Blackbeard. As the story goes, Teach occasionally used the island as both a hideout and a base of operations from which he carried on a campaign of thievery against English and colonial American merchant ships in the early 1700s. Blackbeard's more permanent lair was at Ocracoke Island, off the North Carolina coast, but while in Georgia waters he settled into an abandoned Spanish mission. Legend has it that Teach beheaded his 16th wife and six members of his crew at this spot, burying them in a shroud of gold doubloons.

Sapelo, perhaps the most easily accessible and well known of the islands, is home to a sizeable community of Geechees, people descended from the slaves who first worked the island plantations. The Geechee have, thanks to their comparative isolation, maintained a lifestyle that is remarkably African. Their religion, similar

## AFRICAN TRADITIONS

*I*solated on the vast rice plantations of the coast, with their white masters in residence only a short part of the year, the coastal Negroes evolved a unique language—haunting, poetic, and to most whites, almost totally incomprehensible....

The majestic blue heron who sweeps and dives across the emerald marshes at Sapelo is called "poor Joe—Padzo is the name of a similar heron in Africa. The tortoise is called a cooter; near Timbuktu, it is called a kuta. And the small wild horses that roam the coastal islands are known as takis, the West African name for horse. You'll hear them speak of "toting" cotton, a word that derives from tota, in Congo "to pick up." and the Foulah numbers to ten are still in use.

The old plantation books from Kelvin Grove on St. Simon's abound with names still common on the coast—Bina (Tuesday), Cuffy (Friday), Quanimina (Wednesday). The custom of naming children for the day of their birth derives from the Eve tribes of Dahomey and Tago, who borrowed the custom from the Twai people.

⤚❦⤙

*G*hosts abound, as in West Africa, where every man can expect to meet his "duppy" at least once in his lifetime. And in the little settlements like Sandfly, some still talk of being ridden by witches at night, an ancient belief of the Vais.

According to the Vais legend, when a witch comes in the door he takes off his skin and lays it aside in the house, rides the victim through the night and returns him to his bed in the morning.

⤚❦⤙

*I*n Savannah, the Geechee Negroes, who take their name from their birthplace near the Ogeechee River, follow the old Vais custom of sprinkling salt and pepper in the corners of the room, a practice which is supposed to prevent the witch from putting on her skin.

—Betsy Fancher, *The Lost Legacy of Georgia's Golden Isles*, 1970

*This walking stick by William Rogers (circa 1938) shows that African-influenced carving traditions lasted in the South long after Emancipation. Considered by many to be coastal Georgia's master carver, Rogers also worked as a farmer, carpenter, state legislator, and preacher. (collection of Mr. and Mrs. Harvey Granger, Jr.)*

to that of South Carolina's Gullah people, is a melding of West African animism and Christianity, while their dialect preserves many African words.

An excellent introduction to the island's funky, laid-back lifestyle can be arranged by calling Nancy Banks, an island resident who leads tours and runs a lodge called **The Weekender** for overnight guests. In her capable hands, you will tour the sugar mill ruins at Long Tabby and pass by the old R. J. Reynolds mansion near Nannygoat Beach before stopping off at B.J.'s Confectionery, the de facto community center for the village of Hog Hammock. The Weekender is a no-frills operation in a funky, almost forlorn setting. The rooms and cabins are a bit expensive for the level of comfort, but, then again, this unvarnished type of hide-out is getting harder and harder to find on the coast. *Nancy Banks: 912-485-2277.*

Little evidence remains of the Creek people who once lived here, save a couple of Indian mounds and a ring of oyster shells that may have been used for ceremonial purposes. The Spanish mission built here 400 years ago (by Jesuits hoping to save Creek souls) long ago succumbed to the elements. One of those early missionaries was Pedro Menendez, the scholarly Jesuit of San Jose Mission who authored the first book ever written in America—a little grammar in the Yammassee tongue for the Indian children on the island.

Tangled vine tendrils envelope the ruins of **Le Chatelet** plantation, now referred to by the locals, in a beautiful bit of elision, as Chocolate. Le Chatelet was built by a Marquis de Montalet (by one account an exiled French royalist, by another a Santo Domingo planter kicked out in the 1806 slave rebellion). Montalet carefully trained his black chef in the ways of French cooking and awarded him the cordon bleu when he succeeded in mastering puree of artichoke and poulard in olive oil with sweet cream. The marquis hoped to find truffles growing in the New World, believing they could make men merry and women tender, and civilize barbaric America. To this end he often led a truffle-sniffing pig beneath the moss-draped oaks of Sapelo Island.

Travelers exploring these islands should keep their eyes peeled for notices of performances by the Sea Island Singers, a troupe of Geechee songsters whose polyphonic chanting and clapping has been enjoyed by audiences as far away as Carnegie Hall and as close by as the **Sea Island Festival**, held in August of each year on nearby St. Simon's Island.

For the schedule of ferries to the island call *912-437-3224.* Bus tours of the interior are available through the **McIntosh County Welcome Center in Darien.** *912-437-6684.*

■ DARIEN AND ENVIRONS  *map page 249, A-3*

On the mainland, Highway 17 snakes ever southward past boggy fields where blond reeds of rice wave in the morning breeze. Soon you are entering Darien, a coastal settlement established in 1736 by Scots Highlanders under the aegis of Oglethorpe himself. During the antebellum years, Darien rose to prominence as a port from which rice and cotton were shipped. Later, lumber replaced rice as the primary export, as huge mills sprang up on the riverbanks to saw trees into board lumber that was then floated downstream. During the late 20th century it has been the shrimping industry that has supported the citizens of Darien and surrounding communities. Today the banks of the Altamaha River are lined with scruffy shrimp boats, their nets cast high while in port. Fittingly, in the nearby fishing villages of Crescent and Shellman Bluff are three of the state's best fish houses, vestiges of a time when the shrimp you ate that evening had spent the previous night not in an importer's deep freezer but in a nearby river

*Shrimp boats moored for the night on the Darien waterfront.*

## ◆ NEARBY FISH CAMPS

### Archie's Restaurant

Open more than 60 years, this concrete bunker eatery turns out locally prized fried shrimp. The catfish they fry is river-caught, not pond-raised and anemic. Their motto: "Seafood served in this restaurant slept in the river last night." *Highway 17 in Darien; 912-437-4363.*

### Buccaneer Club

Once a private club (you still have to ring a buzzer to gain entry), this funky outpost has a pleasing patina of age. The fried shrimp, served in heaping mounds, is the best on the coast. Good cocktails to boot: stop here for a drink and peruse the menu, a delightful doggerel-filled tome. Of the Crabs Galore, the menu says, "If you think we ain't got crabs (HA HA), just listen at this combination!" *Located off Shellman Bluff Road, Crescent. Call for directions; 912-832-5171.*

### Hunter's Cafe and the Mud Bar

This fish camp looks the part: screened door, hardwood floors, ramshackle but well maintained, reached by a narrow sandy lane. The menu is simple as can be: raw oysters; rich, milky crab stew; and fried seafood (oysters, shrimp, scallops, flounder). This is the real deal, unpretentious and good. *Located off Shellman Bluff Road, Shellman Bluff. Call for directions; 912-832-5771.*

### Speed's Kitchen

That this place is a jumble of three barely disguised trailers shouldn't dissuade you from visiting this fish camp. Great crabmeat au gratin and buttery oyster stew. The food may be a bit better than Hunter's *(see above)*, but there's no beer to be had—if that matters. *Located off Shellman Bluff Road, Shellman Bluff. Call for directions; 912-832-4763.*

On Vernon Square in Darien proper you'll find the **Open Gates Bed-and-Breakfast.** The owner's boat is at your disposal for day trips into the marsh or down the Altamaha River. The 1876 home, which belonged to a timber baron, is one of the best lodging bargains on the coast. There's a large pool out back and the house faces on lovely Vernon Square. *912-437-6985.*

Five miles south of Darien on Highway 17 is **Hofwyl-Broadfield Plantation,** a remarkably intact antebellum rice plantation, where you can wander the levees that controlled the water flow and watch a film on the task system of labor that defined life on a rice plantation prior to the Civil War. *Information: 912-264-7333.*

# FISH CAMPS OF SOUTHERN AND COASTAL GEORGIA

Fish camps and fry houses, like barbecue stands and rib shacks, are fast vanishing Georgia icons— victims of a new brand of customer who prefers to eat his catfish and crabs and shrimp in a vacuous, but convenient strip mall setting rather than out in the piney woods at the end of a sandy lane. And let's not forget the restaurant owners who care more the nightly cash register receipts than whether the coleslaw is creamy, the hushpuppies crunchy.

Many of the best, like the venerable Pritchett's, once the pride of Columbus, closed a while back. And yet, there are survivors, places where the sweet, white catfish shatters beneath your teeth, and the beer is so cold it makes your molars ache, where fish are fried in cast iron skillets the way God intended them to be.

Problem is, such places rarely advertise. There's no need. The gravel parking lot is packed every weekend. So how does the visitor to southern and coastal Georgia determine whether they have found the real thing? To weed out imposters, we have devised a grading system.

**Fish Camp Authenticity Test**

| | |
|---|---|
| Open over 25 years | 5 points |
| Building is of a style that might best be termed Vernacular Funk | 3 points |
| Part of building juts out over a body of water | 3 points |
| Whole as well as filleted fish available | 5 points |
| Fish fried to order (no buffet line) | 5 points |
| Serves no steaks or other distracting items | 3 points |
| Cold beer or sweet tea are the primary beverages | 5 points |
| Hushpuppies studded with onions and peppers | 3 points |
| Grits available as a side dish | 2 points |
| Fries are hand-cut | 2 points |
| Homemade tartar sauce | 2 points |
| Seating is in old church pews or bench seats removed from pickup trucks | 2 points |
| **Total points of a possible 40** | _____ |

You can't go wrong at any of the following:

# FANNY KEMBLE'S INCENDIARY JOURNAL

It was on Butler Island, just across the bridge from Darien, that Frances Anne (Fanny) Kemble, wife of rice planter Pierce Butler, wrote her *Journal of a Residence on a Georgian Plantation in 1838-1839*. English by birth and a talented Shakespearean actress, she became famous for her portrayal of Juliet at Coventry Garden in 1829, and in 1832 she began touring the United States. One critic wrote of her performance at Park Theater in New York: "Fanny Kemble was to New York something of a divine manifestation…"

In June of 1834 Fanny married Philadelphian Pierce Butler, a member of an eminent American family and owner of two Sea Island plantations tilled by 700 slaves. When the couple and their two small daughters visited in the winter of 1838, little escaped Fanny's interest, even the particulars of rice cultivation at Hopeton Plantation.

Fanny recorded in her journal the sorrowful lives of her husband's slaves. Upon her return to Pennsylvania, she made a copy of it and expressed her desire to have it published. Her husband forbade it, and infuriated by his wife's abolitionist sentiments, he divorced her in the Pennsylvania courts and was granted custody of their children. Fanny returned to Europe, where she continued to act but lived in an emotional limbo, waiting for the day her daughters would gain their majority and she could see them again.

In 1859, 400 of the slaves on Butler's Georgia estate were sold to pay debts. A *New York Tribune* article on the sale included this description of a scene involving two slaves, Dorcas and Jeffrey:

> *I* see Dorcas in the long room, sitting motionless as a statue…and I see Jeffrey, who goes to his new master, pulls off his hat and says, 'I'se very much obliged, mas'r, to you for trying to help me [by buying my wife]…thank you—but—it's—berry—hard'—and here the poor fellow breaks down entirely and walks away covering his face with his battered hat, and sobbing like a child. He is soon surrounded by a group of his colored friends, who with an instinctive delicacy…stand quiet…about him.

Fanny went on to publish her journal in 1863, and it became an abolitionist rallying cry in England and the United States in years leading up to the Civil War.

It's interesting to note that many African farmers from the rice-growing regions of Angola and Gambia were sold as slaves into the Sea Islands and were actively sought out by planters for their skills; in July of 1785 a *Charleston Gazette* advertisement announced the arrival of a "choice cargo of windward and gold coast negroes, who have been accustomed to the planting of rice."

## ■ GOLDEN ISLES

Unlike Sapelo and St. Catherine's—islands which can only be reached by ferry— the Golden Isles of St. Simon's, Sea Island, and Jekyll Island can be reached by highway and bridge. Filled with resorts and restaurants, these islands are destinations in themselves.

### ◆ BRUNSWICK  *map page 249, A-4*

Jumping-off point for any island adventure is the seaport of Brunswick, a town where the ships in dock tower over the city, their stacks looming higher than any building in the business district. Yet the natural beauty of the area is stunning. Even on the main thoroughfares, the sea and marsh are ever present. Just north of town, in the median that bisects Highway 17, is the oak under which Sidney Lanier, composer of the poem "The Marshes of Glynn," sat and "looked out over a world of marsh that borders a world of sea."

Cross the causeway that leads east from Brunswick, and within moments you are on St. Simon's Island, a lush, almost edenic oasis of green ringed by white beaches.

### ◆ ST. SIMON'S ISLAND  *map page 249, B-4*

#### Fort Frederica
St. Simon's was settled early by the British; the site was staked out in 1734 by Oglethorpe himself. By 1740 Fort Frederica was a thriving military town, and when Oglethorpe repelled the Spanish advance on Georgia at the Battle of Bloody Marsh in 1742, it was from Frederica that he commanded his troops. But by 1755, with the Spanish no longer a threat, the fort was in shambles. Today, all that remains are a few tabby ruins, now maintained by the National Park Service. *912-638-3639.*

#### Christ Episcopal Church
Nearby is Christ Episcopal Church, to which Charles Wesley came as a missionary for the Church of England in 1736. The church on the site today dates from 1884. In the neighboring cemetery, seemingly ancient gravestones lean to and fro beneath live oaks dripping tendrils of Spanish moss.

## Epworth by the Sea

Farther south, on the site of the former Hamilton Plantation, is Epworth by the Sea, a retreat operated by the Methodist Church and constructed in part as a tribute to the denomination's founders, brothers John Wesley and the aforementioned Charles. Charles was recruited by Oglethorpe to work with the island's Native American tribes—a task that he quickly abandoned in favor of working with the settlers. His older brother John was assigned duty in Savannah. "I went to America to convert the Indians," he later wrote, "but, Oh! Who shall convert me?" Today, the church operates a conference center and motel (that rents out rooms to nonbelievers too—at some of the most reasonable rates on the island). There is also a museum on premises which documents the Wesley brothers' disillusionment, return to England, and spiritual rebirth, which resulted in the founding of Methodism. *100 Arthur J. Moore Drive; 912-638-8688.*

## Lighthouse Museum

At the southern tip of the island is the commercial district, home to the 1872 lighthouse and a collection of low-key restaurants, bars, and shops. Those curious about the island's history should seek out the museum housed in a bleached-brick Victorian home in the shadow of the lighthouse. *101 12th Street; 912-638-4666.*

## Bloody Marsh Battle Site

For more history, traipse out Demere Road to the Bloody Marsh Battle Site, a now quiet patch of wetlands where in 1742 the British repelled a Spanish advance in a battle so vicious that onlookers said the marsh ran red with blood. Little remains to remind us of the fray, save a marker inscribed with the words of Oglethorpe: "We are resolved not to suffer defeat. We will rather die like Leonidas and his Spartans, if we can but protect Georgia and Carolina and the rest of the Americas from desolation."

## King and Prince Resort

On the eastern edge of the island are the best beaches—flat expanses of hard-packed gray sand touched by a soft, almost placid surf. Here you will find the King and Prince Resort, as well as public beach access. Opened as a private club in 1935, the King and Prince is a little less opulent than some other coast resorts. It's got a lovely indoor pool and a beach with white-gray sand stretching for what seems miles. *201 Arnold Road; 912-638-3631 or 800-342-0212.*

## Crab Trap

Throw your crab shells through the hole in the middle of the table at this purposefully funky seaside dive. Tabby floors and retired outboard motors are the essential design elements. Stick to the simplest seafood and you will eat well. Their motto: "Where the elite eat in their bare feet." *1209 Ocean Boulevard; 912-638-3552.*

◆ SMALLER ISLANDS  *map page 249, B-4*

Two islands nuzzle the St. Simon's coastline: Little St. Simon's and Sea Island.

Little St. Simon's is a private island, maintained as a rustic resort where the emphasis is on isolation and enjoyment of natural beauty. Old rice levees and shell middens can be found here and there, and there are seven miles of beach to enjoy. **The Lodge on Little St. Simon's** is family-owned and eco-sensitive. It offers cabins and rooms in a setting that will remind you of summer camp. Birding expeditions and nature walks can be arranged. Three home-cooked meals are served each day. And should your group want the ultimate in privacy, the entire island is available to let—at a price. For daytrips or overnight stays, call the lodge. *912-638-7472.*

*The Lodge on Little St. Simon's*

*A courtyard fountain at the Cloister*

◆ BLUEBLOOD
RESORTS ON SEA
ISLAND AND JEKYLL
ISLAND

*map page 249, B-4&5*

A narrow bridge crosses from St. Simon's to **Sea Island**, site of the super-deluxe resort known as the **Cloister**. A seaside enclave of manicured lawns, well-trimmed palms, and Mediterranean-style villas, this resort is without peer on the Georgia coast. It has long been the haunt of the rich, bluebloods, and poseurs who enjoy five miles of beaches, 1,000 acres of woodlands, and world-class golfing. Rates include three meals a day. Jackets are required for the evening meal, and big bands often serenade. *100 Hudson Place; 912-638-3611.*

For a look at how these bluebloods once lived, travel south via a seven-mile causeway to **Jekyll Island**. During the early years of the 20th century, Jekyll was the private playground of families with names like Rockefeller, Pulitzer, Astor, and Vanderbilt. Similar in style to the northeastern resort town of Newport, Rhode Island, Jekyll was home to a collection of what were termed, quaintly, "cottages."

These shingled mansions, most of which were built between 1890 and 1925, now form the basis for an open-air museum of sorts, with their former clubhouse—an asymmetrical, turreted Queen Anne mansion—restored to its former elegance and serving as a resort called the **Jekyll Island Club Hotel**. Housed in the former stable is a museum whose exhibits tell the story of the island's heady past.

Today, though croquet courts and indoor tennis courts still abound, Jekyll is among the most democratic of resorts on the coast, for the island is now under state control, with businesses operated under a private-public partnership. The resort now welcomes one and all, and even those with ordinary red blood can enjoy the magnificent view of the water from the resort's **Grand Dining Room** where graceful columns grace the large space decorated in pink and white. The ambience may be valued more than the haute Southern cuisine. *371 Riverview Drive; 912-635-2600 or 800-535-9547.*

*Grand dining room at the Jekyll Island Club Hotel*

More modest lodging options are also available on Jekyll Island. Try the sprawling **Jekyll Inn,** where most rooms have their own private decks. There's a large pool out back with a thatched-hut bar serving fruity drinks. *975 North Beachview Drive; 912-635-2531.*

There are also a number of chain motels, most of which are recently refurbished, nondescript relics of the '60s. Among the choices are the **Clarion Buccaneer,** *85 South Beachview Drive; 912-635-2261,* the **Comfort Inn,** *711 North Beachview Drive; 912-635-2000,* and the **Ramada Inn Oceanfront,** *150 South Beachview Drive; 912-635-2111.*

◆ HISTORY AND WILDLIFE ON JEKYLL ISLAND *map page 249, B-5*

The earliest people known to live on Jekyll Island were the Muskogean people of the Creek nation. Writes Betsy Fancher in *The Lost Legacy of Georgia's Golden Isles:*

> *A*grarians, their year revolved around the the feast of the First Fire. It opened with the Green Corn Festival in the square of the village Ospo, where trials were held for the year's offenses and culminated with the ritual of the black drink, in a huge bonfire in which the residue of the old year, from old clothes to garbage was burned in a great conflagration with ceremonial dances. But the Muskogeans could be cruel—prisoners were tortured until dead in the town square and scalps were taken and used in orgiastic victory dances....

At a bend in the road along Riverview Drive, the ruins of the island's early plantations stand in eerie repose. Stop here for a peek at the construction methods once used on the barrier islands, techniques that employed a material known as "tabby," a cement-like mixture composed of sand, lime, oyster shells, and water. Linguists believe that the word tabby is of African origin and was originally defined as a wall made of earth and masonry.

At the northern end of the island, along a small creek at a place called Ebo Landing, the slave ship *Wanderer* brought a group of Africans in 1858, half a century after the international slave trade had been banned in the United States. The owners of the ship, the notorious Captain W. C. Corrie of New York, and his partner, Charles A. L. Samar of Savannah, planned to hide slaves on Jekyll until they could be sold. Before federal authorities got wind of the ship's mission, all but 100 of the 300 *Wanderer* slaves who landed on Jekyll had been sold in South Carolina.

*In this photograph from the 1850s, slaves sit in front of houses made of tabby—a combination of oyster shells, sand, lime, and water. (collection of the New-York Historical Society)*

At the southern tip of the island is South End Beach, a premier spot for viewing wildlife including brown pelicans, which nest here, and bottle-nosed dolphins. Between Jekyll Island and Cumberland Island is the wide, marshy mouth of the Satilla River, which canoeists can paddle down for 149 scenic miles starting at Waycross, north of Okefenokee

■ ST. MARY'S   *map page 249, A-6*

Back on the mainland is the little village of St. Mary's, point of departure for the ferry and a charming and storied settlement in its own right. Settled by the British in 1787 on a site long favored by Native American tribes, St. Mary's survives today as a fishing village and as a bedroom community for the nearby King's Bay Naval Submarine Base.

St. Mary's makes a good place to stay for those planning daytrips to Cumberland Island.

From the **Spencer House Bed and Breakfast Inn,** it's only a short walk to the Cumberland Island ferry dock. The rambling pink home, built in 1872, has 14 rooms, some with four-poster beds and a clawfoot tubs. A full breakfast is served each morning, and the inn-keepers will be happy to pack a picnic lunch if you're headed to the island. *200 Osborne Street; 912-882-1872.*

*A swamp estuary near Darien.*

Most days at the **Riverview Hotel,** you'll find Beggar, the family pooch, lounging on the couch in the black-and-white tiled hallway. The rooms upstairs are calico-cute but nice, befitting what feels like an old railroad hotel. A balcony, also on the second level, is outfitted with rockers and affords a grand view of the river. The 1916 structure was first a bank, and then the telephone company. *105 Osborne Street; 912-882-3242.*

**Seagle's Restaurant,** on the ground floor of the Riverside Hotel, offers to treat you to your first order of rock shrimp dip. Take them up on the offer, and then move on to sample the boiled shrimp. Keep it simple and you'll eat well. Lunch and dinner. *105 Osborne Street; 912-882- 4187.*

When in season, the rock shrimp are a favorite in the region, and at **Lang's Marina Restaurant** they are fresher than fresh because the proprietor operates a fleet of fishing boats that bring the shrimp, or whatever is in season, right up to the dock. This little box of a building facing on the river also dishes out various seafood platters and steaks for lunch and dinner. *307 West St. Mary's Street; 912-882-4432.*

The **Greek Mediterrranean Grill** is housed in a building whose tabby exterior is painted a vibrant maroon. The interior is splashed with murals of Greek life. Grilled Octopus, spanakopita, and shrimp scampi are favorites. And the owner is a generous and affable host. *122 Osborne Street; 912-576-2000.*

■ CUMBERLAND ISLAND  *map page 249, A-6*

South of Jekyll is Cumberland Island, Georgia's largest barrier island. Over the years, numerous attempts have been made to wrest Cumberland Island from the wild. Behind palmetto thickets lurk mansion ruins and rusted car chassis, testaments to a time when the island was little different from St. Simon's or Jekyll. From 1881 until the mid-20th century, Cumberland was a millionaire's retreat, the property of the Carnegie family. One their former mansions, Plum Orchard, now stands vacant, while another, **Greyfield,** serves as an elegant and exclusive inn where one dresses for dinner in the evening yet never feels the arctic chill of an air-conditioner, for the steady breeze of ceiling fans stirs the air

The **Greyfield Inn** occupies a white clapboard and stone mansion, built in 1901 for the daughter of industrialist Thomas Carnegie. It has been an inn since the 1960s. Simple elegance abounds at what many consider to be the nicest, most unique property on the Georgia coast. It's accessible by boat only. Rates include all meals. *904-261-6408.*

The real attractions are to be found on the island's remote fringes, where feral horses roam and bobcats stalk their prey. Thanks to the National Park Service which now oversees a good portion of the island, only 300 visitors are allowed to make the 45-minute ferry ride from St. Mary's each day, ensuring that the miles of beach remain, for the most part, unpopulated. You can literally spend a day wandering the woods or combing the shoreline without seeing another soul. And should you wish to spend the night, campsites are plentiful. *National Park Service; 912-882-4335.*

*The road to Sea Camp Beach on Cumberland Island.*

*The sun rises behind the twisted form of a live oak on Jekyll Island.*

## WEATHER IN GEORGIA TOWNS

| WEATHER STATION | AVG. TEMPERATURES (° F) | | | | RECORDS | | PRECIPITATION (IN) | | | | ANNUAL | |
|---|---|---|---|---|---|---|---|---|---|---|---|---|
| | JAN | APR | JUL | OCT | H | L | JAN | APR | JUL | OCT | R | S |
| Albany | 62/38 | 78/53 | 91/71 | 78/55 | 106 | -2 | 4.2 | 4.0 | 6.1 | 2.3 | 49 | 0 |
| Athens | 50/31 | 72/50 | 89/69 | 72/51 | 108 | -3 | 4.5 | 4.2 | 5.0 | 3.3 | 50 | 2 |
| Atlanta | 50/32 | 73/50 | 88/70 | 72/51 | 105 | -9 | 4.7 | 4.3 | 5.1 | 2.8 | 50 | 2 |
| Augusta | 58/33 | 78/50 | 91/70 | 78/50 | 108 | -1 | 3.8 | 3.3 | 4.4 | 2.6 | 43 | 1 |
| Clayton | 47/28 | 70/41 | 85/61 | 71/42 | 102 | -12 | 6.1 | 6.0 | 6.6 | 4.6 | 70 | 10 |
| Columbus | 58/36 | 78/51 | 90/70 | 78/55 | 104 | -2 | 4.2 | 4.4 | 5.7 | 2.0 | 50 | 1 |
| Macon | 54/35 | 75/50 | 91/71 | 75/53 | 105 | -4 | 3.8 | 3.7 | 5.0 | 2.5 | 44 | 1 |
| Rome | 49/30 | 72/43 | 87/66 | 72/46 | 107 | -7 | 5.1 | 4.7 | 5.0 | 3.2 | 54 | 5 |
| Savannah | 60/39 | 79/55 | 90/72 | 79/58 | 105 | 3 | 3.3 | 3.1 | 6.8 | 2.5 | 49 | 0 |
| Valdosta | 65/43 | 80/55 | 91/72 | 80/56 | 105 | 12 | 3.5 | 3.6 | 6.3 | 2.1 | 49 | 0 |

## METRIC CONVERSIONS

To convert feet (ft) to meters (m), multiply feet by .305. To convert meters to feet, multiply meters by 3.28.

| | |
|---|---|
| 1 ft = .30 m | 1 m = 3.3 ft |
| 2 ft = .61 m | 2 m = 6.6 ft |
| 3 ft = .91 m | 3 m = 9.8 ft |
| 4 ft = 1.2 m | 4 m =13.1 ft |
| 5 ft = 1.5 m | 5 m =16.4 ft |

To convert miles (mi) to kilometers (km), multiply miles by .62. To convert kilometers to miles, multiply kilometers by 1.61.

| | |
|---|---|
| 1 mi = 1.6 km | 1 km = .62 mi |
| 2 mi = 3.2 km | 2 km = 1.2 mi |
| 3 mi = 4.8 km | 3 km = 1.9 mi |
| 4 mi = 6.4 km | 4 km = 2.5 mi |
| 5 mi = 8.1 km | 5 km = 3.1 mi |

To convert pounds (lb) to kilograms (kg), multiply pounds by .46. To convert kilograms to pounds, multiply pounds by 2.2.

| | |
|---|---|
| 1 lb = .45 kg | 1 kg = 2.2 lbs |
| 2 lbs = .91 kg | 2 kg = 4.4 lbs |
| 3 lbs = 1.4 kg | 3 kg = 6.6 lbs |
| 4 lbs = 1.8 kg | 4 kg = 8.8 lbs |

To convert degrees Fahrenheit (°F) to Celsius (°C), subtract 32 from degrees F and multiply by .56. To convert degrees C to degrees F, multiply degrees C by 1.8 and add 32.

| | |
|---|---|
| 0°F = -17.8°C | 60°F = 15.5°C |
| 10°F = -12.2°C | 70°F = 21.1°C |
| 32°F = 0°C | 80°F = 26.7°C |
| 40°F = +4.4°C | 90°F = 32.2°C |
| 50°F = +10.0°C | 98.6°F = 37.0°C |

# I N D E X

# COMPASS AMERICAN GUIDES

**Critics, booksellers, and travelers all agree: you're lost without a Compass.**

"This splendid series provides exactly the sort of historical and cultural detail about North American destinations that curious-minded travelers need."
—*Washington Post*

"This is a series that constantly stuns us; our whole past book reviewer experience says no guide with photos this good should have writing this good. But it does."
—*New York Daily News*

"Of the many guidebooks on the market, few are as visually stimulating, as thoroughly researched, or as lively written as the Compass American Guides series."
—*Chicago Tribune*

"Good to read ahead of time, then take along so you don't miss anything."
—*San Diego Magazine*

## NEW FROM COMPASS:

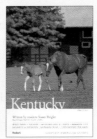

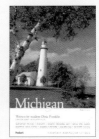

Georgia
$19.95 ($29.95 Can)
0-679-00245-6

Gulf South
$21.00 ($32.00 Can)
0-679-00533-1

Kentucky
$21.00 ($32.00 Can)
0-679-00537-4

Michigan
$21.00 ($32.00 Can)
0-679-00534-X

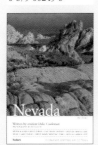

Nevada
$21.00 ($32.00 Can)
0-679-00535-8

Pennsylvania
$19.95 ($29.95 Can)
0-679-00182-4

Southern New England
$19.95 ($29.95 Can)
0-679-00184-0

Vermont
$19.95 ($27.95 Can)
0-679-00183-2

*Compass American Guides are available in general and travel bookstores, or may be ordered directly by calling (800) 733-3000. Please provide title and ISBN when ordering.*

**Alaska** (3rd edition)
$21.00 ($32.00 Can)
0-679-00838-1

**Arizona** (5th edition)
$19.95 ($29.95 Can)
0-679-00432-7

**Boston** (3rd edition)
$21.00 ($32.00 Can)
0-676-90132-8

**Chicago** (3rd edition)
$21.00 ($32.00 Can)
0-679-00841-1

**Coastal CA** (2nd ed)
$21.00 ($32.00 Can)
0-679-00439-4

**Colorado** (5th edition)
$19.95 ($29.95 Can)
0-679-00435-1

**Florida** (1st edition)
$19.95 ($27.95 Can)
0-679-03392-0

**Hawaii** (5th edition)
$21.00 ($32.00 Can)
0-679-00839-X

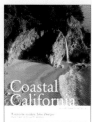
**Idaho** (2nd edition)
$21.00 ($32.00 Can)
0-679-00231-6

**Las Vegas** (6th edition)
$19.95 ($29.95 Can)
0-679-00370-3

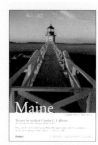
**Maine** (3rd edition)
$19.95 ($29.95 Can)
0-679-00436-X

**Manhattan** (3rd ed)
$19.95 ($29.95 Can)
0-679-00228-6

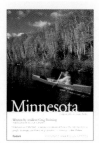
**Minnesota** (2nd ed)
$19.95 ($29.95 Can)
0-679-00437-8

**Montana** (4th edition)
$19.95 ($29.95 Can)
0-679-00281-2

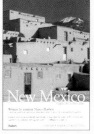
**New Mexico** (4th ed)
$21.00 ($32.00 Can)
0-679-00438-6

**New Orleans** (4th ed)
$21.00 ($32.00 Can)
0-679-00647-8